ENGAGE!

**Setting the Course for Independent Secondary Schools
In the 21st Century**

Carolyn Kost

Engage! Setting the Course for Independent Secondary Schools In the 21st Century

East West Educational Consulting
370 Golfview Rd, Suite 801
North Palm Beach, FL 33408

www.eastwesteducationalconsulting.com

ISBN-13: 978-1511459082
ISBN-10: 1511459085
CreateSpace Publishing
North Charleston, South Carolina

"If there is any period one would desire to be born in, — is it not the age of Revolution; when the old and the new stand side by side and admit of being compared; when the energies of all…are searched by fear and by hope; when the historic glories of the old can be compensated by the rich possibilities of the new era? This time, like all times, is a very good one, if we but know what to do with it."

Ralph Waldo Emerson in "The American Scholar"

"New opinions are always suspected, and usually opposed, without any other reason but because they are not already common."

John Locke

Audentes Fortuna Iuvat. Fortune favors the bold.

ENGAGE!
Setting the Course for Independent Secondary Schools In the 21st Century

Conclusion

Appendix

Introduction

Challenges and Opportunities for Independent Schools

"To boldly go where no one has gone before."

When the Captain of the USS Enterprise in Star Trek proclaimed to the helm officer, "Engage!" it was the signal that a new adventure was afoot "to boldly go where no one has gone before." That is the situation in which we find ourselves at the dawn of the 21st century. It's a whole new world and we must impart fresh and new knowledge to students in innovative ways. Alas, this is a fraught mission for many independent schools. Unlike public schools, which federal, state and local agencies periodically compel to adapt to new initiatives, standards, curricula, standardized tests, independent schools take comfort in staying the course.

In fact, in the American imagination, private education has enjoyed a singular place precisely as a bastion of tradition for well over a century. Ask most Americans to describe a private school and they will likely describe the crested blazer-sporting offspring of the moneyed caste forging their bonds to one another while being groomed to attend top tier universities by inspiring, illustrious, occasionally nonconformist, teachers within the ivy covered walls of a place with brimming coffers. However well this romantic image may have served in the past when the *ancien regime* steadfastly maintained the custom of independent schooling and the *nouveau riche* aspired to access that network, it disintegrates in an era characterized by sweeping changes in the domestic and global economy, societal expectations for education, and the ingenious applications of technology. Independent schools must be positioned as intrepid explorers on the forefront of innovation and excellence, instead of merely conservators of tradition.

Those of us in independent schools know that our sector is certainly not homogeneous. Our schools are centuries old and quite new. Our students range from privileged to marginalized. They hail from the United States and abroad, and they engage in a variety of ventures upon graduation. We are secular or religious but we all share part of the same mission: to shape the intellect with a broad base of general knowledge and the skills to think critically, to inculcate certain values, and to provide opportunities to forge meaningful relationships and grow and mature within a caring community. We believe that what we do is well worth paying for.

But are we doing what we do so extraordinarily well that it presents a conspicuous and indisputable comparative advantage over public options that warrants the price tag? Evidently, we are not. Private school enrollment has declined by nearly 16%, almost one million students, from 2001 to 2012, while public school enrollment has continued to rise and charter school enrollment has quintupled.[1] The rate of homeschooling has increased 75% from 1999 to 2011.[2]

In the same period, private school tuition has doubled[3] at four times the rate of inflation, yet many schools struggle to meet their budgetary goals. Those of us in boarding schools tend to treat the enrollment of international students like a spigot increasing or decreasing the flow depending upon domestic (full-pay) enrollment. The smallest schools have experienced the greatest monolithic surges in Chinese-speaking enrollment, which is helpful to no one as schools comprised of international populations over 30% find their appeal diminished with both domestic and Asian students, especially when one language block dominates, as is increasingly the case.[4]

Contrary to popular assumptions, the downward trend in enrollment is not due to recession of 2007-08, as its documented origin is earlier, but it was likely

---

[1] In 2001-2, public school enrollment was recorded between 47M and 48M; private school enrollment at 5.3M. In 2011, public: 49M; private 4.5M.
Public school data NCES Table 44;
Private school data for 2001-02
http://nces.ed.gov/surveys/pss/TableDisplay.asp?TablePath=tables/table_23.asp
Data for 2011-12 http://nces.ed.gov/surveys/pss/tables/table_2011_04.asp
Charter school data NCES Table 117

[2] The homeschool population doubled from 850K in 1999 to 1.78M in 2011. http://nces.ed.gov/pubs2009/2009030.pdf The change in the homeschooling rate (from 1.7% in 1999 to 2.2% in 2003 to 2.9% in 2007) represents a 74% relative increase over the 8-year period and a 36% relative increase since 2003.

[3] Table 61, 2002 Tables and 205.50 2013 tables Digest of Ed Stats. National Center for Education Statistics
[4] The number of Chinese students at U.S. private high schools soared more than 100-fold to 6,725 in 2010-11 from 65 in 2005- 06, according to the U.S. Department of Homeland Security. China has displaced South Korea as the top source of international students at boarding schools, with the smallest schools having the biggest increases in Chinese enrollment, said Peter Upham, executive director of the Association of Boarding Schools, quoted in Golden, Daniel. "Chinese Lose Promise for $52,000 as U.S. Schools Exploit Need." *Bloomberg Business Week*. 19 Oct. 2011. Web. 20 Dec. 2014.

exacerbated by it.[5] Founders League and others of generous endowments are apt to continue to thrive, but many other schools with colonial-era pedigrees are just as challenged as others, thus past performance is no guarantee of future success.

Moreover, demographic data indicates that the number of children is shrinking across the nation in counties with the highest income and best-educated populations.[6] Thus, not only independent K-12 schools but private colleges are in tenuous straits. According to Moody's Investment Services, which has downgraded many universities' ratings, enrollment declines exceeding 10% are not uncommon and the number of closures and mergers will certainly grow. The recently announced demise of Sweet Briar College (despite an endowment exceeding $80M) is not an isolated case. Harvard Business School professor Clayton Christensen has famously predicted the closure of half the colleges in the country within two decades.[7] It is alarmingly clear that this trajectory in private education is not sustainable and we in independent schools need to consider how we plan to secure our future and flourish in the next decades.

In the past several years, I have reviewed the programs and curricula of hundreds of independent schools, and have spoken with stakeholders from over one hundred. The vast majority of these schools were in financial straits ranging from slightly troubling to dire, with alarming deficits, deferred maintenance and steadily declining enrollment. Administrators and trustees demonstrated an astonishing lack of awareness of market realities, particularly the threats to the schools' market share presented by the proliferation of area charter schools and the inventive programs that the neighboring public, independent and faith-based schools were offering. Not surprisingly, the trustees, administrators and faculty with whom I spoke presented fixed mindsets about the way to "do school" and persisted in practices reflecting an obsolete reality in which information was difficult to access, students would go on to a single traditional career-for-life, and AP courses were the curricula of the elite. Too often and for too long, we in independent schools have leaned too heavily upon our rich heritage, employing what has been, rather than innovating, looking ahead and engaging what could be.

---

[5] http://www.census.gov/hhes/school/files/ewert_private_school_enrollment.pdf
[6] Selingo, Jeffrey. *Shaping the Class: How College Enrollment Leaders View the State of Admissions and their Profession.* The Chronicle of Higher Education, 2014. p 1.
[7] McDonald, Michael. "Small U.S. Colleges Battle Death Spiral as Enrollment Drops." *Bloomberg.com.* 14 Apr. 2014. Web. 20 Dec. 2014.
See also Denneen, Jeff and Tom Dretler. *The Financially Sustainable University.* Bain & Company. 2012. The accompanying website was updated in 2014:
www.thesustainableuniversity.com

On the other hand, there are creative people in schools and colleges that fully embrace what it means to be independent, free from the traditional conventions, free to experiment, to offer engaging programs, to energize staff, and to wisely steward resources. They understand that to truly prepare students for success in the 21st century, independent school staff must develop and implement ways to foster autonomy, initiative, and self-direction, as well as the skills of analytical thinking, collaboration, and communication. We must help our students to learn to learn, be resilient and creatively adapt to frequent and seismic shifts due to disruptive technologies.

In writing this book, I intend to highlight some of these successes, provoke discussion, call into question the ways we in independent schools have been running our organizations and propose a variety of changes to the curriculum, ways to fortify the community, and methods to establish a culture of collaboration and innovation.

For many years I have had one foot in secondary education, where I have taught and served as an administrator, and another in higher education, where I also taught and where I continue to spend a great deal of time and focus much of my attention as a college admissions counselor for secondary students. It is perplexing how little communication there is between the two sectors despite their interdependency. Fallacious assumptions abound in secondary schools about "what colleges want" and "what students need to be successful in college." (Clearly something is wrong when 20% of college students need remediation—and private school students are by no means exempt from that).[8] Independent schools would do well to learn from the inspiring and creative ways that some colleges and universities are implementing radical change more quickly than any other time in history.

By and large, we identify as college preparatory institutions, but what will that mean in the coming years? The age is nigh of the Open Loop University,[9] which students enter at any age and re-enter throughout their lives as needed to acquire new knowledge and skills and put these in conversation with their life

---

[8] http://nces.ed.gov/pubs2013/2013013.pdf Remediation is not limited to public school students. Howell (2011) "The average proportion of CSU students from public high schools in California who are math proficient exceeds the average proportion from private high schools in all seven years of the sample." Howell, Jessica S. "What Influences Students' Need for Remediation in College?: Evidence from California." *The Journal of Higher Education* 82.3 (2011): 292-318.

[9] http://www.stanford2025.com/open-loop-university/

experience, and the University of Everywhere,[10] open to anyone in the world with an Internet connection at a reasonable price, with instruction highly individualized through the use of artificial intelligence. Portfolios of work will replace transcripts. What will that mean for our identity and purpose?

It is my contention that private colleges and universities serve as a harbinger for independent schools. We face many of the same challenges and opportunities. Private colleges and universities have far more extensive resources for institutional research than independent schools, but we can and must access and apply the data that they gather, analyze, and extrapolate, the trends they forecast, and the astute strategies used by the colleges that are flourishing. They are responding to and anticipating disruptive innovation, spurred by the same sense of urgency I am attempting to instill here. To do otherwise, to forge on using the same methods, or to alter our programs in insignificant ways (though they may *feel* significant to traditionalists), will not serve our students or our institutions in the coming years.

Chapter 1 traces the shift in society's expectations for what the *objectives of education* should be and reveals the rather dismal outcomes of tertiary education. It urges assessment with greater acuity of the quality of what we offer to determine if what we promise and presume is actually what we deliver.

Chapter 2, Part I, surveys the *curricular landscape*, which is dominated by the College Board's Advanced Placement courses, with the International Baccalaureate in a distant second place and the Advanced International Certificate of Education (Cambridge). Since these are offered by public schools as well as independent schools, they serve to concede the lack of comparative advantage, at least in terms of academic program. We must capitalize on our strengths and differentiate our schools, particularly in terms of evidence-based best practices in education. One of the most significant of these is certainly the formative and narrative assessment of students' learning, which should enable students to master material and improve within a feedback loop. Part II presents best practices for summative narrative comments.

Chapter 3 presents the ways that *disruptive innovation* through technology is changing education and the opportunities it offers to expand options, increase engagement, and customize education for our students. We must be flexible in terms of format, scheduling, and space. Most of all, we must foster autonomy in our students, for among the most important 21st century skills are the ability to

---

[10] Carey, Kevin. *The End of College*. Riverhead, 2015.

manage oneself, determine what one needs to know and how to go about learning it.

Chapter 4, Part I, elaborates an alternative paradigm, one that fully harnesses technology and understands that students can now access more information in one minute than a scholar could in a lifetime just a few decades ago. Information is plentiful; our students need to know how to make meaning from it and apply it. Independent school stakeholders are advised to carefully consider their resources and develop *signature programs* that do not duplicate what neighboring schools offer and that are not easily replicable. Part II provides an in-depth example of how project-based learning can work and how it can forge fruitful partnerships.

Chapter 5 scrutinizes the curriculum as it exists in most schools and calls into question *why we teach what we teach* and proposes certain revisions, additions and deletions that reflect the needs of the age and those on the horizon.

Chapter 6 affirms school staff as *professionals* committed to reflecting on and improving their practice. The impetus for innovation should be the desire to find a better way, not change for the sake of novelty. Staff should be committed to continuous growth, action research, and a spirit of experimentation. It is imperative to hire staff for their ability to be cross-functional team players who engage students in purposeful relevant work and help them construct meaning.

Chapter 7, Part I, discusses the importance of *community* as well as how to assess it and how to foster cohesion. Staff and students must perceive their work as "meaningful, purposeful, sensible, and significant" on an individual and synergistic level. The ways that staff and students interact with the community beyond school walls have tremendous potential for shaping how students perceive their roles in and responsibilities toward their future communities. Part II describes a dynamic way to introduce students to activism and social justice to affect lasting systemic change.

Chapter 8 advocates the adoption of selected best practices from *business management*, including rewarding productivity (not merely longevity), cost-benefit analysis coupled with granular accounting, strategic human resources, competitive intelligence, and the diversification of funding streams. It is further advised that staff be assisted to understand the big picture of the school in the effort to break down some of the barriers between administration and other staff and encourage their full participation in the organization. Managing change wisely is crucial. Systems theory can help to unpack and defuse the chronic anxiety endemic to secondary schools (and many other organizations) that gives rise to dysfunction and resists the changes necessary to securing our communities' future.

It bears repeating that this book is intended to provoke discussion and reflection, but most importantly, action. The disruption occurring in all sectors of education presents a spectacular opportunity to independent school stakeholders intrepid enough to embark on a thrilling new adventure (and a colossal threat to those who are not). I sincerely hope that this book serves to inspire independent school stakeholders

- to appreciate the urgent impetus for change
- to envision and implement creative and effective principles, practices, and programs
- to demonstrate unequivocally that independent schools are the best choice for innovative, challenging, individualized, and evidence-based best-practices education
- to cultivate cohesive and caring communities that foster ethical conduct and civic responsibility
- to wisely steward our schools' resources of all kinds in trustworthy transparent ways that secure the future.

While valuing the past, we must re-examine the present while we set our course for the future. Engage!

One Success Story

Imagine having a blank slate to develop a school.

What would students experience as they go through their day? *What* would students learn? *How* would they learn? Would they be at desks? Would they be outside? How would technology be deployed? How would the school be staffed and structured? What would the teachers do to engage students? How would they work together? How would decisions be made? How would the school contribute to the larger community? How would the parents be involved in the school? How would the roles of the leaders and trustees be constituted?

These were not merely abstract musings for me, but serious considerations. I had the great privilege of serving as the founding academic director of a new independent high school. The composition of all policies and structures relating to academics and student life was to be based on research in learning, adolescent development, and educational practices attuned to the twenty-first century.

We hired superlative faculty and staff members from around the world to engage the students in challenging hands-on activities with real-world relevance. Students and staff were urged to regard the community as an extension of the classroom by actively pursuing experiential learning and service opportunities and collaborations with talented entrepreneurs, artists, and other professionals, and with organizations ranging from universities to clinics and laboratories.

The results of energizing and inspiring educators and providing them with more tools to enrich their toolboxes were considerable in just the first two years *without any seniors and with a student body that earned mostly average scores in standardized testing prior to admission*:

- 60 9th graders wrote novels for National Novel Writing Month
- Two 10th graders secured patents
- 10th grader presented her paper on local community well research at a national professional conference *as an adult*
- 10th grader's statistical analysis of ground balls winning lacrosse games was utilized by top Division 1 College programs, from Johns Hopkins to UVA
- 9th grader won Third in Category at the Intel International Science and Engineering Fair for her work on pharmaceuticals in the local groundwater
- 12 students reached State level for National History Day
- School team won State level, Spanish *Conferencia*
- 6 students earned Superior [highest] ratings at the Florida Bandmasters Competition
- School teams reached National level in Forensics and Computer Science
- School ranked 15th in State in Math League *(again, with no seniors and fewer than 50 juniors)*
- Significant sustained community service projects, including biweekly environmental science service learning, weekly mutual language exchange with farm workers' children and weekly activities with the developmentally disabled

Many education experts visited the school, including acclaimed author and Innovation Education Fellow at Harvard Tony Wagner and they have found it to be an extraordinary place. Interest in the school was phenomenal, mostly due to word of mouth from our passionate students and parent base regarding the curriculum focused on rigor, creativity, collaboration, and communication, high community standards, and quality of teaching. Personally invested in following through on all promises that we made, I often surveyed the students, parents, and staff for their suggestions and their degree of satisfaction with the school. I am proud to report that 90% of respondents reported being "Highly" to "Completely Satisfied."

From its opening in September, 2011, to 2013, the school grew from 125 students to 500, with an acceptance rate of 25% and yield exceeding 80% for September, 2013, with an extensive waiting list for 2013, *despite the presence of two public high schools within seven miles that are consistently ranked in the top 75 high schools in the country by U.S. News & World Report, The Washington Post, and Newsweek,* as well as several highly respected and established independent and faith-based schools. I was a passionate and tireless advocate for the school, toured prospective K-8 feeder schools, and met with various constituencies throughout the area.

My vision for the school was in large part inspired by the work I had done previously as a Library Director. In that capacity, I helped innumerable students with projects, from selecting a workable topic of interest to them through final presentation. I had witnessed what students were capable of when they had autonomy and control over their field of inquiry, when they were inspired, and, especially, when they recognized that their work had potential for having an impact on their world. I had been further inspired by chaperoning student presenters at the Intel International Science and Engineering Fair. This is an experience that every educator should have because it reveals and raises expectations of what teenagers are capable of accomplishing when suitably engaged and networked with the right peers and mentors. It was clear that these students were experiencing deep learning and transformation that transcended anything that the typical curricula such as Advanced Placement, International Baccalaureate or Advanced International Certificate of Education could possibly provide yet, unfortunately, tend to supersede. Part of my purpose in writing this book is to add to the conversation about how to create schools that inspire students and staff to develop life-changing learning experiences and ambitious goals of their own.

Chapter 1

How Did We Get Here?
Changing the Portrait of an Educated Person

It has always seemed to me one of the great advantages of the course of study generally pursued in our English schools, that it draws our minds so continually to dwell upon the past. Every day we are engaged in studying the languages, the history, and the thoughts of men who lived nearly or more than two thousand years ago.
—Thomas Arnold (1795-1842)

Entrusted with turning out polished, cultured, *educated* graduates, independent schools in the first half of the 20th century offered programs of study that responded to the prevailing notions of their day predicated upon privileged White Anglo-Saxon Protestant experience as the cultural norm and aspirational goal. They promoted granular and so very Eurocentric ideas about what an educated person should be able to do at a minimum: distinguish a Van Gogh from a Miró, Beethoven from Chopin, describe the most commonly accepted explanations of the origins of revolutions and the rise and fall of empires from pharaonic Egypt to Rome, toss about Latin phrases like *post hoc, ergo propter hoc*, understand the basic laws of physics (but, curiously, not the systems of the body or environmental ecosystems), be fluent in at least one other [usually *European*] language, refer to and quote fragments of canonical literature relevant to a conversation or situation. In short, the independent school has historically intended to transmit cultural capital.

The expectation is that students would emerge "all of one pattern," ("a Choate boy" or "a Foxcroft girl"), apprehend uncritically specific pieces of knowledge, and conform to orthodoxy. With the exception of those influenced by Dewey and other progressive educators, students were *not* encouraged to submit theories to "unlimited verification and revision" and then synthesize, extrapolate, and integrate them with or alter previous established assumptions.[11]

Where does the curriculum of independent schools stand vis-à-vis these formerly prevailing norms at the dawn of the 21st century and how did they arrive

---

[11] Paul, Richard, and Linda Elder. *Critical Thinking: Tools for Taking Charge of Your Professional and Personal Life*. Upper Saddle River, NJ: Financial Times/Prentice Hall, 2002, quoting Sumners Folkways, p 630.

at this point? Naturally, the path followed varies with the school, but as a whole, depending upon one's perspective, schools have not traveled very far afield at all, a point of pride for many, and the paths are surprisingly convergent. It is revelatory to examine the original purpose and how it has shifted with time.

Cultural Capital

Perhaps above all, the independent school has historically intended to transmit the standards of knowledge and behavior that Pierre Bourdieu describes as cultural capital, the social exchange that serves as the means by which individuals are located within a society and which they may utilize, albeit unconsciously, to pursue "gain and advantage."[12]

> "Specifically, cultural capital exists in three forms (Bourdieu, 1986). First, cultural capital is embodied in styles and manners and in modes of bearing, interaction, and expression. It is also embodied in cultural preferences and affinities, in apparently intuitive responses to valued distinctions and institutional expectations, and in ease and facility with valued ways of knowing and reasoning and with valued schemes of appreciation and understanding. Finally, it is embodied in the command of valued cultural knowledge."[13]

Cultural capital is not an explicit set of rules. Its opaque and arbitrary nature actually fortifies its ability to legitimate the social order. Through the "invisible curriculum," of cultural norms, schools transmit the manners, affinities, and forms of expression that comprise cultural capital. Naturally, elite students transmit the elite versions of these, a particularly appealing feature of independent schools to members of those elites and those who aspire to access that network.

Shamus Khan's ethnographic study of his alma mater, St. Paul's School (NH), reveals the dimensions at work.[14] He affirms that "privilege means being at ease," a kind of pervasive indifference, "no matter what the context." This echoes earlier accounts attesting to a "pseudo-aristocratic insouciance" characterizing

---

[12] Olneck, Michael. "Can Multicultural Education Change What Counts as Cultural Capital?" *American Educational Research Journal.* 37.2 (2000): 317-48.Web. 20 Jun. 2014., p. 319.
[13] Ibid.

[14] Khan, Shamus Rahman. *Privilege: The Making of an Adolescent Elite at St. Paul's School.* Princeton, NJ: Princeton UP, 2011

"collegiate style" at least since the mid 19th century.[15] Khan observes that students from less socio-economically privileged backgrounds and females find this far more difficult to achieve than elite males. (This recalls Uri Treisman's famed Berkeley study of the culturally conditioned propensities of Asian American students to study in groups and African-American students to study alone, which accounted for their respective success and lack thereof).[16] They often work harder and more assiduously than the elite students and this indicates their inferior status. Through subtle cues, successful students cultivate an overarching openness, as well as the techniques to "game the system" and "get by."

Khan writes that "[e]lites have incorporated some of the cultural attributes and tastes of those that they had previously excluded. Yet this new practice—omnivorous consumption—is…their own mark of distinction." Other research has confirmed this omnivorousness among elites, finding that while they do consume more highbrow culture, they also consume more middlebrow and popular culture.[17] "What St. Paul's is teaching," Khan concludes, "is a style of *learning* that quickly becomes a style of *living*, with an emphasis on ways of relating and making connections rather than with a deep engagement with ideas and texts." According to Khan, the sense of ease and the omnivorous attitude toward culture are precisely the means by which privilege is maintained and inequality obscured. He muses in his conclusion that "…cultural hierarchies are not simply imposed from above by exclusive practices but maintained from below….by non-elites who do not engage in practices marked as culturally elite."[18]

Ancestral pedigree and financial resources are perceived to be less important than experience, which creates the appearance of egalitarianism and success as proceeding solely from earned merit. Khan remarks that, in terms of the curriculum, omnivorousness means that what matters is "not what but how you know;" and how well students are able to draw connections among seemingly disparate things. Students compare Beowulf to Jaws as products of virtually congruent cultural value. Thus, the final facet of cultural capital, "command of valued cultural knowledge" is demonstrated in a way that is quite different from the past.

---

[15] Spoehr, Luther. "Review of Shamus Rahman Khan's." *History News Network* 26 Aug. 2011. Web. 19 Dec. 2014.

[16] Tresiman, Uri. "Studying Students Studying Calculus: A Look at the Lives of Minority Mathematics Students in College." *College Mathematics Journal* 3.5 (1992): 362-72. Nov. 1992. Web. 14 Nov. 2014.

[17] Chan, Tak Wing. *Understanding Cultural Omnivores: Social and Political Attitudes.* Department of Sociology University of Oxford, 17 Oct. 2013. Web. 30 June 2014. p.1.

[18] Be assured that Khan does not blame the non-elites for their non-participation.

Moreover, as Thomas Leitch indicates in *Wikipedia U: Knowledge Authority, and Liberal Education in the Digital Age* (2014), the combination of this democratization of information and the sharing economy leads to threats to scholarly authority, which is on decidedly shaky ground, based as it is on numbers of citations conditioned by "stochastic factors, intellectual fads, social networks, and other processes that have been studied by sociologists of science"[19] and subject as it is to invalidation based on new information. Epistemological authority is up for grabs and that is an enormous shift in the paradigm.

Such is our postmodern world. Briefly, and without hooking arms with Derrida and Foucault and tumbling down the rabbit hole, the modernist fragmentation and deracination of conventions led to postmodernism and its notions of deconstruction, its declarations of reality as socially constructed, its dissolution of the high culture/low culture dichotomy so that there is only culture without hierarchical distinctions. "But what happens when there is no linguistic norm? When culture consists in endless diversity and heterogeneity? When there is no 'master code?'"[20] One consequence is that the power once held by select arbiters of culture has dissipated and the determination of quality lies in the receiver's perception of the message (i.e. the cultural product). Thus, Jaws and Beowulf stand on level footing as equally worthy subjects of study. Postmodernism affirms that Dante's *Inferno* equals *Charlie and the Chocolate Factory* equals *The Matrix* equals *Harry Potter*, without much weight assigned to historical impact and influence on culture.

Multiculturalism

> *I embrace the common, I explore and sit at the feet of the familiar, the low. Give me insight into today, and you may have the antique and future worlds....We have listened too long to the courtly muses of Europe.*—Ralph Waldo Emerson, *The American Scholar*

In the first decades of the 20th century, "well over one-third of all Americans were of British ancestry, 80 percent were Protestant."[21] The Western Canon and an overall Eurocentric, if not specifically Anglocentric, worldview held sway for good

---

[19] Brown, Clifford T. "Measuring the Value of Literary Research." Letter to the Editor. *The Chronicle of Higher Education.* 1 Jan. 2012. Web. 21 Feb. 2015.

[20] Connelly, Sean. "Postmodernism and Consumer Society (HUM415)." *Analepsis.* 19 Oct. 2011. Web. 19 June 2014.

[21] Unz, Ron. "The Myth of American Meritocracy: Endnotes." *The American Conservative.* 28 Nov. 2012. Web. 19 Jun. 2014.

reason: it was representative of the cultural ideals of the populace. Currently, 5.5% of the US population reports English ancestry (16% identifies as Hispanic) and 76% affiliates with some form of Christianity, with 1% of those Episcopalian and 25% Catholic.[22] Despite the best efforts of Allan Bloom, E.D. Hirsch, and William Bennett to promote a Eurocentric cultural core literacy in the 1980s, to continue to ascribe primacy to British cultural ideas is indefensible.

Certainly the 1960s and 70s were a time of great upheaval in independent schools and society at large. The Civil Rights Movement and its codified results such as Brown v. Board of Education (1954), The Civil Rights Act (1964), and Title IX (1972) occasioned a dramatic shift in public schools by overturning the principle of "separate but equal" schooling and affirming the need for multicultural education and gender equality. These summoned educators to recognize that institutionalized oppression excluded the experience and history of many groups that have contributed immensely to not just the United States but to civilization as a whole, and galvanized them "to ensure educational equity for members of diverse racial, ethnic, cultural, and socioeconomic groups, and to facilitate their participation as critical and reflective citizens in an inclusive national civic culture."[23] As a result, public schools implemented (with varying degrees of commitment and success) pedagogical and curricular changes to reflect the new goal of affirmation and inclusion rather than assimilation of minority groups. In some, particularly those in urban areas, independent schools benefited tremendously from the upheaval, as enrollment in private schools doubled from .7M to 1.4M from 1961 to 1971, although enrollment in Catholic schools decreased from 5.3M to 4M.[24] Some of this growth came from the burgeoning segregation academies as well as established schools. In Mississippi alone, enrollment in private schools "rose by 170% between 1968 and 1970."[25] This is not a proud chapter in the history of independent schools to say the least.

To be sure, some independent schools have a long tradition of social justice, inclusivity and multiculturalism, but most stand at different places on the spectrum

---

[22] http://factfinder2.census.gov/faces/tableservices/jsf/pages/productview.xhtml?src=CF
http://www.census.gov/compendia/statab/cats/population/religion.html Accessed 23 Jun. 2014.

[23] Banks, James A., and John Ambrosio. "Multicultural Education." *Education Encyclopedia.* StateUniversity.com, n.d. Web. 19 Dec. 2014.

[24] Long, James Edgar and Eugenia F. Toma. "The Determinants of Private School Attendance: 1970 - 1980." The review of economics and statistics 70.2 (1988): 351-7.
and Clotfelter, Charles T. "School desegregation, tipping, and private school enrollment." *Journal of Human Resources* (1976): 28-50.

[25] Clotfelter, p. 29.

of structural responses to inequality and diversity with respect to enrollment and financial aid, composition of faculty, pedagogy, and curriculum. It is unfortunate but instructive to note that, as of 2009, only 4% of NAIS member schools had completed the Assessment of Inclusivity and Multiculturalism, which intends primarily to assist schools to assess the current climate of diversity and multicultural initiatives.[26] The primary focus in this section is to examine the consequences of this societal shift on the curriculum of independent schools.

In keeping with the principle of elite omnivorousness, the curricula of the schools that *Worth Magazine* famously identified as the top "feeder schools" for Harvard, Yale and Princeton are characterized by a multicultural and pluralistic worldview, offering courses such as 20th Century Japanese Literature, Modern India, and Introduction to Islamic Civilization. In contrast, struggling schools often have curricula stuck somewhere between the 1950s and the 1970s and stubbornly adhere to antiquated and chauvinistic notions of European dominance. Following our earlier postmodern formula equating *Beowolf* with *Jaws*, multiculturalism's iteration would be: Shakespeare equals Toni Morrison equals Simin Behbahani equals Gabriela Mistral.

If there is no "high culture" liberal arts canonical knowledge to impart, it follows then that the actual academic content of the curriculum becomes arbitrary. Cultural capital is then principally transmitted by the invisible curriculum, which assumes primacy. Along with the rise of the consumer model for education, it also explains the decline of the liberal arts. I contend that enrollment in independent schools is declining in part due to the demise of the commodities of which they have traditionally been purveyors: liberal arts and by extension the cultural knowledge and norms that embody social capital. It is certainly true that in previous periods of economic contraction, interest in the liberal arts declines. Even if this is a temporary oscillation, it is likely to be a protracted one, even taking into account only the seismic shifts in the economy on both domestic and global scales and the commodification of education (and considerations of its cost and return on investment). Defenders of the liberal arts invidiously champion their cause by proclaiming the ability of their fields to teach critical thinking and communication skills, as though that were not also a primary objective of virtually all educational enterprises, however technical.

---

[26] http://www.slideshare.net/hamlard/nais-state-of-diversity-practice-public-summary and http://www.nais.org/Articles/Pages/Assessment-of-Inclusivity-and-Multiculturalism-(AIM)-Goals.aspx

Whither Liberal Arts?

Let the liberal arts colleges be the canary in the coal mine for the independent school market. Many of them devote extensive resources to institutional and market research and access savvy consultants for strategic planning and visioning. We must take note when liberal arts colleges, even venerable ones like Smith, with healthy endowments and credit ratings, admit to looking to the future with growing unease and uncertainty as they question whether the current model of "small classes, relatively rigid schedules, limited course and major offerings, and intense academic rigor, is going to continue to appeal to students."[27] The exorbitant cost of higher education has lead the public to regard it as largely a "commercial exercise" and to question the value proposition. Those who major in humanities have lower starting salaries and "earnings are still substantially depressed 10 years after graduation."[28] Independent schools must sit up and take notice of the dramatic shrinking of the market experienced by their counterparts on the tertiary level.

> As recently as the mid-1950s, liberal arts colleges constituted around 40 percent of the total number of institutions of higher education, and they enrolled about 25 percent of all undergraduates. By the early 1970s they had come to account for only about a quarter of all institutions and enrolled no more than eight percent of all students. Between 1967 and 1990 some 167 private four-year colleges disappeared, either by closure or by merger. And to such losses one should add that only four percent of all American graduates get their degrees from residential liberal arts colleges.[29]

As an update to that grim news, "the number of liberal arts colleges nationwide has dropped from 212 in 1990 to only 130 today."[30]

---

[27]Kiley, Kevin. "Starting to Worry." *Inside Higher Ed*. 10 Oct. 2011. Web. 10 Nov. 2014.

[28] Von Wächter, Till. "Young Workers: In a Wage Rut for Years." *The New York Times*. 25 May 2011. Web. 14 Nov. 2014. See http://www.payscale.com/college-salary-report-2014/majors-that-pay-you-back

[29] http://www.acls.org/uploadedfiles/publications/op/59_liberal_arts_colleges.pdf Even at Harvard University, Yale University, and the University of Chicago, only half of the bachelor's degrees are in liberal arts (natural sciences, social sciences, and humanities).

[30] "Jilting Liberal Arts Can Hurt the US, to a Degree." *The Fiscal Times*. 9 Jan. 2013. Web. 19 Dec. 2014.

A brief review of the history of the liberal arts reveals the origins and influences on the mission, values, and tensions. In *Ave Atque Vale*, Donald Kagan writes that the purpose of education has historically been fourfold: to nourish the life of the mind, to inculcate virtue, to prepare for a profession, and to realize one's obligation to society.[31] The Greeks and Romans trained students for civic leadership. The medieval European university trained students for professions in medicine, theology or law. Education was essential to set apart the "gentle from the simple." Kagan writes, "Education was meant to shape character and manners much more than intellect." The Renaissance courtier was expected to be a "well-rounded man who united in his person a knowledge of language, literature, and history with athletic, military, and musical skills, all framed by good manners and good moral character."

In the 18th century, however, "Since university education was no longer merely for churchmen and clerks, gentlemen of the landed gentry and wealthy bourgeoisie began to attend," which led to less to the cultivation of lofty virtues than to a degree of dissipation and carousing that would not be out of place in the contemporary scene.[32] This emphasis on "sociability above the solitude of hard work" dominated in England and was exported to the New World. The function of schools as a place to form friendships, described by one schoolmaster as "the means of advancing a man's fortunes in this world" certainly has not receded, as revealed by a range of research addressing related topics from stagnant social mobility (Gregory Clark, *The Son Also Rises: Surnames and the History of Social Mobility*, 2014), to self-perpetuating elites who game meritocratic practices (Chris Hayes *Twilight of the Elites*, 2012*)*, as well as the role of colleges in assortative mating and the growing income inequality in the US.[33]

In the 19th century, the introduction of examinations (practiced in China for centuries) enhanced the status of universities. The socio-political tumult of the day called for leaders who could draw upon a broad foundation of knowledge and apply it wisely to the issues of their day. The earlier belief that there was a fixed body of knowledge that was capable of being mastered was quashed permanently with the rise of the German model with its openness to exploring

---

[31] As a Classicist, Kagan has a limited Eurocentric view, but we are striving to understand the cultural influences on the liberal arts, which in the US are overwhelmingly European. Kagan, Donald. "Ave Atque Vale." *The New Criterion*. June 2013. Web. 19 Dec. 2014.

[32] Horowtiz, Helen Lefkowitz. "Liberal Arts Colleges in American Higher Education: Challenges and Opportunities." American Council of Learned Societies. Occasional Paper No. 59 (2005).

[33] Morin, Rich. "New Academic Study Links Rising Income Inequality to 'Assortative Mating'." *Pew Research Center RSS*. 29 Jan. 2014. Web. 18 Dec. 2014.

9

new questions and old in new ways, with a bold willingness to challenge accepted opinion unhampered by traditions from the past. Originality and discovery became the prime values. The idea of the university as a museum, a repository of learning, gave way to the notion that it should be dynamic, a place where knowledge was discovered and generated.[34]

The ascendancy of science also devalued a broad and general education and gave rise to increasingly narrow study and specialization as there were ever more questions to explore and knowledge to master. "Preparation for and advancement in a career became the chief concern of both. The distinction between a liberal and a professional education became ever more vague."[35]

For minorities and women, who had previously been denied access, a liberal arts education provided a way to a fuller life and a pathway to the professions. Even among these groups, there was tension between "rarified" liberal arts and reified vocational training. W.E.B. DuBois promoted the notion of "The Talented Tenth" of one in ten Black men becoming educated in the liberal arts, leading others to a better life and elevating the race, while Booker T. Washington criticized the elitism of this notion and encouraged vocational training as the practical means toward progress.[36] The two camps continue in their dynamic tension, but professional training certainly has the upper hand at this point in time.

Perhaps we hew to an idealized notion of the liberal arts college as a place where students gather at an impressionable age to gain, as the famed 1828 Yale Report defending the college's purpose put it, "the discipline and the furniture of the mind: expanding its powers, and storing it with knowledge," where students engage with texts that challenge traditional "values and prejudices," broaden their minds, and help them to form their own opinions and ways of crafting meaningful lives, aware of their duties to society. There is a constellation of fallacies here. Today, students arrive with an ideology that Kagan describes as relativist, nihilist, and characterized by "a kind of individualism that is really isolation from community." Universities are themselves characterized by a hodgepodge of courses and the absence of an agreed upon collection of valued works that merit examination, a unifying pedagogy or "method of training the mind," and a useful means of verifying mastery. Kagan's solution entails re-implementing a canon and

---

[34] Kagan, op cit.
[35] Ibid.
[36] Horowitz, op.cit. 19.

directing attention to the study of history in the effort to instill in students a sense of civic responsibility, but this ingenuously misses the point. There is and can no longer be a "distillation of culture in a curriculum."[37]

Comfort and Challenge

That fact renders all curricular decisions debatable. Independent schools are no strangers to parental opposition to curricular choices, but they are likely to take a new turn. In the past several years in higher education, students' vocal and adamant protests for "trigger warnings," cautionary notices that some work to be examined in class might cause emotional distress or offense, are provoking conciliatory responses, including this one in a draft guide to faculty from Oberlin that asked professors to include such warnings in their syllabus:

> Triggers are…anything that might cause trauma. Be aware of racism, classism, sexism, heterosexism, cissexism [against transgendered], ableism, and other issues of privilege and oppression. Realize that all forms of violence are traumatic, and that your students have lives before and outside your classroom, experiences you may or may not expect or understand. [38]

On the supporting side, Eric Hoover in *The Chronicle of Higher Education.* presents the attitude expressed by one student at Rutgers as emblematic,

> "These are students trying to change the course of their own education, as in saying what they would like in the classroom, what they're comfortable with in the classroom." In other words, they're consumers, making buying decisions. [39]

For the opposition, in an article appearing in *The Atlantic*, Karen Swallow Prior, a professor at Liberty University, described the issue as an unfortunate outgrowth of the political correctness of the 1980s and 90s:

> While political correctness seeks to cultivate sensitivity outwardly on behalf of those historically marginalized and oppressed groups,

---

[37] Ibid.

[38] Medina, Jennifer. "Warning: The Literary Canon Could Make Students Squirm." *The New York Times*. The New York Times, 17 May 2014. Web. 09 Mar. 2015.

[39] Hoover, Eric. "The Comfortable Kid." *The Chronicle of Higher Education*. 28 July 2014. Web. 07 Mar. 2015.

11

empathetic correctness focuses inwardly toward the protection of individual sensitivities. Now, instead of challenging the status quo by demanding texts that question the comfort of the Western canon, students are demanding the status quo by refusing to read texts that challenge their own personal comfort.[40]

How will we in independent schools respond? Boarding school staff often feel a bit more at liberty since they tend not to have the Velcro-parent supervision present in day schools, but the issue remains. When we select the texts that our students read, will we self-censor and avoid potentially offensive material? What are the implications to such a decision and where will it ultimately lead, bland texts that challenge no one?

As it is, students (and many of us) are accustomed to receiving recommendations from Amazon, Netflix, Spotify, Google, news, and other services that suggest material algorithmically derived from what we have consumed, listened to, or viewed in the past. This bolsters the desire and expectation for materials that reinforce the consumers' own beliefs, interests, and worldviews, defensible when dealing with *consumers*, but not students, who must necessarily engage with the unfamiliar and the challenging. The support of such ideological echo chambers is grossly inimical to intellectual growth. The wisdom, sensitivity, and eloquence with which school staff craft a response to this trend has far reaching implications for the role of independent schools in society.

College Outcomes Questionable

There is a media bombardment of sound bites and survey data that question the effectiveness of a college education in fulfilling its traditional role of preparing students to be mature adults who contribute to society, are employed full-time in their chosen vocation, and active in civic life. Independent schools have generally had college preparation as their *raison d'être* and tended to remain outside of the spirited discussion. We content ourselves with the Bureau of Labor Statistics data that annually affirm the higher salaries of college graduates over high school graduates, though we are rather discomfited by the Federal Reserve study that found that "the rate of return on a bachelor's and associate degree is largely the

---

[40] Prior, Karen Swallow. "'Empathetically Correct' Is the New Politically Correct." *The Atlantic.* Atlantic Media Company, 23 May 2014. Web. 09 Mar. 2015.

same and has remained that way for several decades in the U.S."[41] To be sure, parents and students consider the bachelor's an indispensable necessity, for that is often why they come to us, to guide their offspring to a good match school.

As the university has become construed as "an economic entity meant to serve individual and economic interests rather than collective societal interests," we view "the student as customer,…the professor as service provider,"[42] and, in view of our earlier discussion on cultural capital, knowledge, network and credential as the commodity. Arguably, the commodification of education is a natural evolution of capitalism and the prevailing neoliberal ideology that is "Wedded to the belief that the market should be the organizing principle for all political, social, and economic decisions…under neoliberalism everything either is for sale or is plundered for profit."[43] Manifestations of this perception of education include *US News & World Reports* rankings of undergraduate, graduate, and now secondary institutions, Student Opinion of Teaching Effectiveness surveys, which certainly contribute to grade inflation since students use low SOTE scores to punish teachers who bestow low grades, and which can pre-empt tenure, and, of course, sites such as RateMyProfessor.com, StudentsReview.com, and the notorious Yik Yak (which will be discussed in Chapter 7).

There are sweeping consequences of the extension of capitalism to education and the supplanting of the medieval model with the consumer one in higher education. In the college application process, parents commonly refer to the "Return on Investment" rankings of US colleges and universities by Payscale.com and others. Just over 40% of Americans in a Gallup poll rated the "percentage of graduates who are able to get a good job" as the "MOST" important factor in choosing a university.[44] Part of the reason that graduation rates are now measured at the six-year rather than four-year mark is the prevalence of withdrawing from classes that prove to be too challenging. Under 60% of all students who start bachelor's degrees actually complete them in six years or less, leading to proposed

---

[41] Peters, Mark, and Douglas Belkin. "Surprising Findings on Two-Year vs. Four-Year Degrees Return on Investment Holds Steady at About 15% for Recent Graduates." *The Wall Street Journal*. 24 June 2014. Web. 19 Dec. 2014. 10 3 14

[42] Quoting Giroux, 2005, in Turnage, Anna. "Buying the Grade: Professor-Rating Sites and the Commodification of Education," Presented at the National Communication Association 93rd Annual Convention, Chicago, Ill., on Nov. 15, 2007." 21-25.

[43] Ibid.

[44] Calderon, Valerie, and Preety Sidhu. "Americans Say Graduates' Jobs Status Key to College Choice." *Americans Say Graduates' Jobs Status Key to College Choice*. Gallup. 28 June 2013. Web. 19 Dec. 2014.

legislation that intends to reward institutions for higher completion rates. One wonders what kind of social promotion will be in the works to accomplish that feat. Further, "Only one in four employers thinks that two-year and four-year colleges are doing a good job in preparing students for the challenges of the global economy"[45] and just 46% of college graduates in 2014 "say their education has been 'very useful' in preparing them for a career."[46]

In part, this may be attributed to students preparing for an unknown career with unknowable demands. Eighteen to twenty-one year-olds do not know what they will be doing and the vast majority have no knowledge of the demands of any profession. With the exception of co-op programs, our system rather ludicrously puts the cart before the horse. This contrasts sharply with the theoretical Open Loop University project created by Stanford University's Design School.[47] This model proposes that rather than "front-loading" education at the age of 18 for a period (some would say bacchanal) of four years, students enter at any time across the lifespan, returning as needed up to the equivalent of six years for intellectual grounding relevant to their profession or life experience, particularly as it pivots in new directions. While entirely imaginary at this point in time, the concept certainly holds promise and it will be fascinating to see how it evolves.

Shockwaves reverberated throughout higher education with the publication of Josipa Roksa and Richard Arum's *Academically Adrift: Limited Learning on College Campuses* (2011). In their extensive survey, they found:

- 36% of students experienced no significant improvement in learning (as measured by the Collegiate Learning Assessment) over four years of schooling;
- "gains in critical thinking, complex reasoning, and writing skills (i.e., general collegiate skills) are either exceedingly small or empirically non-existent for a large proportion of students;"
- less than one-half of seniors had completed over 20 pages of writing for a course in the prior semester;
- 50% of students' total time each week is spent in social activities, 16% in academic pursuits;
- scholarship from earlier decades suggests there has been a sharp

---

[45] Bauerlein, Mark. "Employers Want 18th Century Skills." *The Chronicle of Higher Education.* 9 Mar. 2010. Web. 19 Dec. 2014.

[46] "The Rising Cost of Not Going to College." *Pew Research Centers Social Demographic Trends Project RSS.* 11 Feb. 2014. Web. 19 Dec. 2014.

[47] See www.Stanford2025.com

decline in both academic work effort and learning…[48]

I add to this my own anecdotal results of having toured well over 150 colleges and universities in the last several years. One of my stock questions to the student tour guides is, "How many pages was the longest paper you have had to write in college?" The usual response was four pages. Only four students, all of whom were enrolled in less selective institutions, had to write papers that were longer. There are actually several dynamics at play here. Despite detection software, plagiarism and essay writing services are prevalent, rendering the exercise moot and providing advantage to those who can pay.[49] Professors don't want to correct and grade longer papers and students' evaluations provide disincentive to do so. And professors do not perceive any "real-world value" to the exercise.[50]

It is imperative to underscore the disparities among college experiences, and they are not necessarily correlated with admissions selectivity. Again, anecdotally, having tutored fourth-year students university students, I have been astonished repeatedly by the paucity of requirements for 400 level courses *in students' majors*. Typical course demands are limited to these: Reading fewer than five non-peer-reviewed articles from popular media (*The New York Times, The Atlantic Monthly, The New Yorker*) **which are provided**, writing two one-page essays, taking two quizzes, a take-home mid-term exam, and a final exam. Of course this cannot be taken as representative, but the fact that it exists in 2015 highlights the panoply of problems in education from the reluctance to elicit rigor and the lack of emphasis on developing research and other information literacy skills to the power of the "Student Opinion of Teaching Effectiveness" survey in influencing instructor behavior with regard to course demands.

Needless to say, Arum and Roksa's is a powerful indictment, and it is directly related to the consumer model. From the students' perspective, the desired outcome is the credential and fun along the way. From the administrators' perspective, the desired outcome is not a lofty ideal, but institutional sustainability.

---

[48] Vedder, Richard. "Academically Adrift: A Must-Read." *The Chronicle of Higher Education.* 20 Jan. 2011. Web. 19 Dec. 2014.

[49] See Bartlett, Thomas. "Cheating Goes Global as Essay Mills Multiply." *The Chronicle of Higher Education.* 20 Mar. 2009. Web. 18 Feb. 2015 and Dante, Ed. "The Shadow Scholar." *The Chronicle of Higher Education.* 12 Nov. 2010. 18 Feb. 2015.

[50] See Blank, G. Kim. "Lets Kill the Term Paper." *The Chronicle of Higher Educations.* 20 Nov. 2012. Web. 21 Feb. 2015;

Enrollment and retention has become a kind of arms race with unprecedented competition. The cost of student recruitment has soared 73% in private colleges from $1,400 per student in 1993 to $2,433 in 2013.[51] A message of "Come here to work very hard and live monastically!" will attract no one. College view books and tours rarely mention the actual *work* of academics. Their focus is laser-like on fun and amenities: rock climbing walls, gourmet food options, wellness programs, lazy rivers, athletics and student activities. Once enrolled, the challenge is retention, and that is where student services comes into play to keep the customers happy and passing their courses, (or else lowering the bar). From 2001-2011, colleges have increased spending on student services between 20 and 30 percent.[52] That category encompasses a spectrum from compliance with ever increasing federal regulations to serious learning support to fluffy diversions. The number of first year students reporting a learning disability has grown dramatically from 6-8% between 1988 and 2000 to 40% in 2000.[53]

Students are happy and supported in their country club colleges, but what happens when they graduate? Arum and Roksa, the same pair of researchers, wanted to find out. In *Aspiring Adults Adrift* (2014), they interviewed 1,000 students two years after college graduation. Among their findings:

- 33% of "those in the labor market were either unemployed or underemployed (working fewer than 20 hours per week or in jobs where the majority of workers had not completed even a year of college)";
- "less than half had full-time jobs that paid $30,000 or more per year;"
- "They were also struggling to be independent:" 24% live with their parents and 74% continue to be supported financially by them;
- The students "are also failing to make successful transitions to adulthood in other aspects of their lives."[54]

The picture is even more bleak when we recall that 71% of all college graduates

---

[51] http://www.naccapresearch.org and "2013 Cost of Recruiting an Undergraduate Student Report." *Noel-Levitz*. N.d. Web. 19 Dec. 2014.

[52] Carlson, Scott. "Spending Shifts as Colleges Compete on Students' Comfort." *The Chronicle of Higher Education*. 28 July 2014. Web. 19 Dec. 2014.

[53] Joyce, Diana, and Eric Rossen. "Transitioning High School Students With Learning Disabilities Into Postsecondary Education." *NASP Communiqué*. Nov. 2006. Web. 19 Dec. 2014.

[54] Arum, Richard, and Josipa Roksa. "Let's Ask More of Our Students-and of Ourselves." *The Chronicle of Higher Education*. 2 Sept. 2014. Web. 19 Dec. 2014.

are shouldering student loan debt with the average at almost $30,000 in 2012.[55] Students are simply unprepared for the economy that is. As we have seen, liberal arts colleges "not only ignore real-world learning in their curricula but even resist it with 'gleeful disdain,'" while gainful employment post-graduation is the goal in mind of the customers.[56]

Let's review. Kagan identified the four traditional objectives of the university thus: "to nourish the life of the mind, to inculcate virtue, to prepare for a profession, and to realize one's obligation to society." Higher education appears not to be effective at improving critical thinking skills or preparing students for the existing labor market or participation in civic life (only 41% of 18-24 year olds voted in the 2012 election, down from 55% in 1972).[57] As for its ability to inculcate virtue, in view of the widespread nature of binge drinking, sexual assault, and academic dishonesty, the best we can do is observe that each of the four objectives has been emphasized in turn, and it's not virtue's turn. (And it isn't likely to be up at bat anytime soon).

Measuring Quality in Independent Schools

Are independent schools doing any better than their higher education counterparts? It's difficult to discern for several reasons. While independent schools revel in their freedom from state-mandated examinations and Common Core, they more frequently than not fail to implement any meaningful substitute and lack any substantive means of assessing their effectiveness. Among all undergraduate students, between 28% and 40% "enroll in at least one remedial course"[58] and remediation is certainly not limited to public school students. In fact, "The average proportion of [California State University] students from public high schools in California who are math proficient exceeds the average proportion from private high schools in all seven years of the sample."[59]

College matriculation lists are not a real proxy because college admissions

---

[55] http://projectonstudentdebt.org/files/pub/Debt_Facts_and_Sources.pdf

[56] Carlson, Scott. "Want a College Experience That Matters? Get to Work." *The Chronicle of Higher Education*. 16 June 2014. Web. 19 Dec. 2014.

[57] "The Youth Vote in 2012." *Center for Information & Research on Civic Learning & Engagement*. 20 May 2013. Web. 10 Sept. 2014.

[58] "Hot Topics in Higher Education Reforming Remedial Education." *Improving College Completion*. National Conference of State Legislatures, n.d. Web. 19 Dec. 2014.

[59] Howell, Jessica S. "What Influences Students' Need for Remediation in College?: Evidence from California." *The Journal of Higher Education*. 82.3 (2011): 292-318.

officers don't have any idea of what transpires in the secondary classroom; they can only presume. They almost never track data on how well students from X Academy do at their college. They tend to gauge the level of rigor of a school by its profile, submitted with almost every application, which details the average or mean SAT/ACT/AP/SAT II scores, curriculum (i.e. the number of higher level courses), special programs, etc. SAT or ACT scores are similarly flawed measures of school effectiveness in view of the well-documented link between scores and socio-economic status.[60] Schools are not absolved of responsibility by countering with the argument that we should only be assessing how well we fulfill our missions, most of which have some statement about college preparation in addition to references to some analog of providing a nurturing community, fostering a love of learning, and developing character. This is in stark contrast to the governmental mantram for public education today: "We only value what we assess;" hence everything can and must be measured. That drive for data appeals to many, including the National Association of Independent Schools.

Criterion 13 of the NAIS *Schools of the Future* initiative mandates that schools make use of "external and internal data in student learning." Fortunately, there is a variety of ways to assess many facets of the school, from student learning to teacher engagement, and the satisfaction of students, parents and alumni. Lyons and Niblock presented many of them in their CAIS presentation.[61] Employee longevity and the percentage of annual giving are used as indicators of engagement and community health, though further discussion of that issue will be found in Chapter 8. To uncover climate issues and reveal how teachers feel about their jobs and their environment, staff should regularly (at least annually) be issued satisfaction surveys, perhaps the Teacher Motivation and Job Satisfaction Survey[62] from Bowling Green University, which can be adapted to the school's particular needs and interests and issued through Survey Monkey or Google Forms. To learn just how well the school has prepared its graduates for life in college, schools often

---

[60] See a) Gow, Peter. "Big Data in Independent Schools: Assessing What We Value?" *Education Week*. 18 Mar. 2013. Web. 3 Oct. 2014.
b) fairtest.org/sites/default/files/optrept.pdf
c) Rooney, Charles, Bob Schaeffer, and National Center for Fair and Open Testing (FairTest). "Test Scores do Not Equal Merit: Enhancing Equity & Excellence in College Admissions by Deemphasizing SAT and ACT Results." FairTest, 1998. 3 Oct 2014
d) Goldfarb, Zachary. "These Four Charts Show How the SAT Favors Rich, Educated Families." *Washington Post*. 5 Mar. 2014. Web. 3 Oct. 2014.
[61] Lyons, Douglas, and Andrew Niblock. "Measuring What We Value: The Excellent Lyons and Niblock Presentation." *21k12*. Jonathan Martin, 16 Dec 2012. Web. 19 Dec 2014.
[62] The survey is available here
http://wps.ablongman.com/wps/media/objects/3984/4080143/forms/jobsatis.pdf

use the Student Tracker with National Student Clearinghouse,[63] which measures alumni's persistence in college and time to degree; survey alumni with instruments created in house; and/or use the NAIS Alumni Survey, which poses questions such as:

> How well did our school prepare you for college in each of the following skills: Writing, Studying, Interpreting Mathematical/Scientific Concepts, Using Technology, Public Speaking, Contributing to Class Discussions, Taking a Leadership Role? [rating scale]
> Being Creative and Innovative, Being Open-Minded, Empathizing With Others, Practicing Sports and/or Exercising Regularly? [rating scale][64]

This is only slightly customizable and schools should be able to add up to two additional questions.

Other instruments should be used while the students are still present at the school. One example is the HSSSE (High School Survey of Student Engagement) "a comprehensive survey on student engagement and school climate issues." Performance task based tests require the students to analyze texts or situations and complete various open-ended activities. Among these are the C-PAS (College-readiness Performance Assessment System), which tests "four key dimensions of college readiness:" cognitive strategies, content knowledge, academic self-management behaviors, and contextual skills and awareness (admissions requirements, cost of college, etc.); the Torrance Test of Creative Thinking, and two products from ETS: the CBAL (Cognitively Based Assessment of, for, and as Learning), which tests proficiency in reading, writing, and math; and iSkills, which tests digital literacy.

The CRWA (College and Work Readiness Assessment) is particularly intriguing. It assigns a real-world role to students (i.e. Vice President of a company) in a situation (i.e. the sales force has identified a low-cost airplane that would greatly expedite transportation to clients) with a challenge (i.e. the model of airplane has safety issues). The students are provided with a document library consisting of emails, technical documents, news items, tables, etc. The students then have 60 minutes to logically respond to the situation, using coherent prose and persuasive arguments based on the data to which they have access. This test is administered in freshman and senior years and purports to measure students'

---

[64] http://www.nais.org/Articles/Documents/CollegeAgeAlumniSurveySample.pdf

growth in "critical-thinking and written communication skills...analysis and problem-solving, scientific and quantitative reasoning, critical reading and evaluation, critiquing an argument, as well as writing effectiveness and mechanics."[65] It is crucial that the school community be educated about the ways the data will be collected and used in order to be open rather than defensive about what may appear, and to commit to making the necessary changes to improve.

Summary

Independent school stakeholders can learn much from our counterparts in higher education and take note that societal expectations for education have shifted dramatically from the antiquated notion of the educated person and Kagan's lofty quartet. Mastery of some accepted and static body of knowledge can no longer be desirable, for it excludes the experience and wisdom of too many and the rapid evolutions in understanding. We must examine where our schools are with respect to the shifting paradigm. We also must develop an authentic culture of assessment to discern the areas that need improvement in order to effectively serve our students and carry out our missions.

---

[65] http://cae.org/participating-institutions/cwra-overview/

Chapter 2

Why Follow the Pack?
Departing From Homogeneous Curricula for College Preparation

...[W]e have constructed an educational system that produces highly intelligent, accomplished twenty-two year olds who have no idea what they want to do with their lives: no sense of purpose and, what is worse, no understanding of how to go about finding one. Who can follow an existing path but don't have the imagination—or the courage, or the inner freedom—to invent their own.
—William Deresiewicz in *Excellent Sheep: The Miseducation of the American Elite and the Way to a Meaningful Life* (2014)

"Don't follow the crowd, let the crowd follow you." —Margaret Thatcher

College Counseling and Life Planning

Many private liberal arts colleges long resisted adding professional schools for business, nursing, engineering, and the like, but in the name of survival have capitulated. Similarly, independent schools must rethink their curricula, precisely for the enormous numbers of students who will be enrolling in those pre-professional schools in college. When our students clamor for Anatomy and Physiology to "prepare for medical school," we often explain that med school is at least five years distant, highly selective colleges prefer to see three to four years of a lab science, and A&P is "fluff." Meanwhile, schools of choice, charter, magnet, and regular public are increasingly attractive for their pre-professional programs like Engineering, Computer Science, Biomedical, Environmental, Marine, and even Veterinary Science, from which students graduate with real-world credentials like Adobe developer, C++, Veterinary Assistant, etc.

We have seen that the original intent of liberal arts was, in fact, to prepare students for professions: rhetor, politician, clergy, lawyer, etc. "There's also an important distinction between preparing students for 'college and career' and preparing them for 'college *or* career.'"[66] In most independent schools, we should be committing to the former; career should not be left out of the equation. The more that students explore career paths *before* college, the better able they are to make a sound judgment about a major.

---

[66] Bidwell, Allie. "Vocational High Schools: Career Path or Kiss of Death?" *U.S.News & World Report*. 2 May 2014. Web. 19 Oct. 2014.

In many years of college counseling, I have seen precious few independent schools offer vocational counseling. Even fewer offer programs like Vistamar's (CA) Life Planning Program, a four-year experience that guides students individually to reflect on their values, strengths, and interests and formulate a post-secondary plan and/or select a gap year program, college or university that can help them to find fulfillment in relationships and meaningful work and be engaged with their community. In part, this is because college counselors in independent schools are typically recruited from teaching positions without any specialized training. They frequently promote liberal arts from their own experience as the best way to learn critical thinking and communication skills, an indefensible assertion in view of the Arum and Roksa work. Further, the prevailing sentiment among this group is that college is a time to explore and that it's not necessary or even desirable to know what one might like to pursue. That was a marginally acceptable approach when students went off to affordable liberal arts colleges, but it certainly is no longer for several reasons.

First, there are more diverse and specialized programs. There used to be a great body of shared knowledge that students used to encounter in college before having to declare their major within liberal arts, and one liberal arts college was not terribly distinct from another in terms of courses offered or required. Now colleges establish niche markets through special programs (Cloud Optimization, Supply Chain Management, Golf Course Management). If students have no idea what career they might start with, they will be unlikely to take full advantage of these programs. Second, the increased competition for employment means that students with significant job-related experience outside of the classroom and who are able to present a portfolio of relevant quality work to an employer have a dramatic advantage. The earlier those students develop a sense of what they might do as a job, the earlier they can get started with experience. Third, the annual cost of college has increased dramatically and only two students in ten finish the degree in four years. Any change in major is likely to cause expensive extra years and opportunity cost in lost wages for those years.

More direction and skilled guidance are certainly required. Independent schools should either have on staff a qualified and credentialed college/vocational counselor or consider outsourcing the service for their students. It is too important to leave to dilettantes. Students choose careers based on familiarity, so exposure to adults in diverse life paths and careers is imperative. Schools must provide ways for students to explore a wide variety of careers, the earlier the better. Beginning even in elementary school, students should be exposed to a broad array of occupational possibilities, especially those that are more imaginative, and to career interest surveys. Secondary school counselors should be familiar with and make use of many resources beyond the typical Naviance product, such as the US Department of Labor's O*NET (free), Gallup's Strengths Finder, Kuder Navigator and many others including The National Career Development Association's *A Counselor's Guide to Career Assessment Instruments*. This should be an integral element of rising ninth graders' program as it should inform their curriculum and the advice provided regarding summer and other enrichment opportunities.

The Curricular Landscape

IB and AICE

The current college preparatory path generally established for students in independent schools allows for little in the way of career exploration—or reflection, or depth of knowledge. The College Board's Advanced Placement has a lock on independent schools, with International Baccalaureate a distant second and Advanced International Certificate of Education (Cambridge) in third. In 2013, 3334 independent schools offered AP courses;[67] students took 3.8M Advanced Placement exams, and 3.35M of those were taken by public school students.[68] 107 independent schools offered the International Baccalaureate Diploma Program, according to the IB Organization; 230 schools (public or private) offered the AICE curriculum.[69] "The number of IB examinations taken increased by 13 percent from 2009-10 to 2010-11 and the number of Cambridge AICE examinations taken increased by 21 percent."[70] While IB and AICE are gaining ground in the US, at this point, colleges are more likely to award college credit for AP courses than IB, and IB more than AICE. The differences between IB Diploma Program and the AICE are explained in depth in a comparison conducted by Florida State University.[71] Briefly, both intend to develop independent learning, intercultural understanding, and higher order thinking and communication skills. Both typically

---

[67] Hu, Winnie. "Scarsdale Adjusts to Life Without Advanced Placement Courses." *The New York Times*. 6 Dec. 2008. Web. 19 Dec. 2014.

[68] 2013 College Board National Summary.

[69] Adams, Caralee J. "Cambridge Academic Program Makes Inroads in U.S." *Education Week*. 3 Dec. 2013. Web. 19 Dec. 2014.

[70] Blazer, Christie. "M-DCPS Student Performance in International Baccalaureate and Cambridge Advanced International Certificate of Education Programs." *Research Brief*. Miami-Dade County Public Schools. Nov 2011.

[71] King, F. J., Faranak Rohani, Derek Hemenway, and Karma Waltonen. "A Comparison of the Certificate of the Advanced International Certificate of Education and the International Baccalaureate Programs in Florida." *Center for Advancement of Learning and Assessment*. Florida State University, Feb. 2001. Web. 19 Dec. 2014.

require students to meet certain criteria and to specifically apply to the program. Both are two-year programs that award credit either for completing the entire diploma/certificate program or earning high scores on externally graded mandatory individual exams.

Initiated as a means to ensure curricular uniformity among secondary schools for offspring of diplomats in international schools, the IB offers a strictly prescribed curriculum controlled by the Switzerland-based IBO and is the most expensive of the three to implement. In addition to the cost of materials and training, each school must pay about $10K annually and must have an IB Coordinator, a Creativity, Action, Service Coordinator, and staff to supervise the Extended Essay (a 4,000 word project on an approved topic). While these are not necessarily full-time positions, considerable time must be devoted to the tasks involved. There are additional fees per student and periodic program evaluation. Any curriculum will advance a particular ideology and the IB intends to offer a "truly international curriculum," transcend national borders, and encourage globalized thinking in the spirit of the United Nations. This is buttressed by links between UNESCO and the IB virtually since its inception in the 1960s. Some schools that have considered implementing the IB have encountered parental opposition largely on the grounds of the costs, the loss of local control, and its associations with the UN, (of which 31% of Americans have unfavorable views).[72]

The AICE was first implemented in 1994, and is administered under the aegis of the University of Cambridge. Like the IB, it is recognized internationally as a high quality university preparatory curriculum, intends to encourage global thinking, and requires proprietary training for teachers, but the curriculum is less prescribed than the IB and allows for students to tailor their classes within certain limits, as there are courses and exams in 55 subjects, though many schools offer just a few. There are two levels of participation, AS (Advanced Subsidiary) and A (Advanced). The cost per school is currently under $1000, in addition to per student fees for exams of $70. As of June, 2017, the certificate will require seven AICE credits, up from five a decade ago. Due to its flexibility, the AICE is growing rapidly.

Faux College Classes and the Reign of the College Board

The College Board's Advanced Placement curriculum is the great juggernaut

---

[72] "UN Retains Strong Global Image." *Pew Research Centers Global Attitudes Project RSS*. 17 Sept. 2013. Web. 19 Dec. 2014.

of secondary education and eclipses both of these programs. Initiated shortly after the Second World War, the story of how AP came to be is an intriguing one, recounted at length in other sources.[73] Briefly, it answered a need for a differentiated curriculum for talented students who found themselves bored in introductory level courses in college. In 1951, representatives from Harvard, Princeton, Yale, Andover, Exeter, and Lawrenceville convened to discuss and plan a new program *"particularly concerned about the superior students* [emphasis in original]."[74] Their recommendations included that schools "encourage more independent study for their brightest seniors" and that a series of examinations be developed that would grant these students advanced placement in college. The first exams were taken in 1954 by students in 27 schools in a pilot study. The students' performance in the twelve participating colleges was compared with that of students who had not taken the exam and the comparison was favorable.

Twenty years later, the AP program expanded greatly, fueled by economic issues that encouraged students to use the AP or the CLEP exams to earn credit and shorten their time to degree. AP exams became a way to strengthen students' college applications by evincing rigor, a way to earn a place in a higher level class, or, conversely, a way for enterprising and confident students to boost their GPA in college by taking an introductory class, which they were led to believe they had already taken as an AP course. In 2007, as a corollary to its rankings of tertiary institutions, *US News & World Report* issued a "Best High Schools" ranking, and used as one of the three determining factors "a College Readiness Index based on the school's AP or IB participation rate – the number of 12th-grade students…who took at least one AP or IB test before or during their senior year, divided by the number of 12th-graders – and how well the students did on those tests."[75] The AP program was thus endorsed as a marker for schools' quality in preparing students for college. AP teachers were accorded a measure of higher status and were often granted special stipends for teaching these classes (when, it could certainly be argued, that the teachers most deserving of stipends were those who had to generate highly differentiated means to assist struggling students, not elite ones).

Particularly in public school circles, the issue of equity inevitably arises in AP discussions because traditionally disadvantaged populations are underrepresented among schools offering the programs and among AP exam

---

[73] http://www.andover.edu/gpgconference/documents/four-decades.pdf
[74] Ibid.
[75] Morse, Robert. "How U.S. News Calculated the 2014 Best High Schools Rankings." *U.S. News & World Report*, 21 Apr. 2014. Web. 19 Dec. 2014.

25

takers. As part of No Child Left Behind and the federal college completion agenda, many districts implement the program as a means to foster a college-going culture, demonstrate the rigor of their curriculum, and help students shorten the time to degree. Some universities award an extra weight to an AP course when calculating GPA, despite the evidence that taking AP courses has no effect on students' performance in college. As a result, public schools implement the AP program as evidence of providing high quality education, teachers often receive a stipend to teach the courses, and some students are dissuaded from taking the exam in order to boost the school-reported numbers of students earning scores of 3 and above, considered passing.

Naturally, all of this is big business for the College Board and it would be difficult to ignore the charge that its actions are "corporate-style revenue grabbing."[76] The AP program provides the College Board with "over half of all its revenues – more than all its other revenue streams (SATs, SAT subject tests, PSATs) combined."[77] Others allege that the College Board itself is a non-profit in name only, citing its lobbying efforts to maintain its monopoly, egregiously inflated executive salaries, "massive profits," as well as its practice of selling test preparation materials, which effectively advantages the wealthy.[78] Further, the $91 fee per test per student certainly adds up for all students, and since federal subsidies have been reduced for students who struggle with the fee, those students are again marginalized.

The College Board recognizes that there is more revenue to be gained from disseminating its AP program far and wide than by targeting it to elites, and at this point in time, that means aligning with the Common Core. In a convenient coincidence, the current president of College Board was the "lead architect of the Common Core standards," the extremely controversial initiative that some say is evidence that "the Gates Foundation's agenda has become the country's agenda in education." [79] Common Core is backed by companies that stand to post astronomical financial gains, like Pearson and McGraw-Hill (test and text publishers), Gates Foundation (Microsoft software packages will train teachers), and Achieve Inc. (Chairman of the Board is former CEO of Intel—all testing for CCSS will be computer-based), by effectively wresting education away from local

[76] Sadler, Philip Michael, Gerhard Sonnert, Robert H. Tai, and Kristin Klopfenstein. *AP: A Critical Examination of the Advanced Placement Program*. Harvard Education, 2010. p.41.
[77] Tierney, John. "AP Classes Are a Scam." *The Atlantic*. 13 Oct. 2012. Web. 16 Dec. 2014.
[78] http://www.aetr.org/the-facts/collegeboard/
[79] Goldstein, Dana. "The Schoolmaster." *The Atlantic*. 19 Sept. 2012. Web. 19 Dec. 2014.

control by the imposition of federal guidelines. AP exams are being revised to align with Common Core. Now more than ever, the College Board AP program is essentially a national curriculum much more aligned with the methods and culture of public schools than independent schools.

It is worth examining our assumptions about the Advanced Placement program (most of which apply to the other programs as well), which are essentially these:

1. AP courses on a transcript strengthen a student's position in college admissions
2. AP courses are the equivalent of college introductory level courses
3. AP courses are the best way to prepare students for college level work
4. AP courses ensure placement of students in higher level courses in college, thus abbreviating the time it takes a student to earn a degree
5. AP courses demonstrate the superior rigor and status of a school

AP courses on a transcript strengthen a student's position in college admissions

Those on the secondary school side of the college admissions equation need to understand that the college side knows that correlation is not causation. There is no intrinsic quality to these advanced *curricula* that transform participants. Rather, it is the qualities of the *participants* that distinguish them. In a study of 67,000 students in Texas, researchers posited that

> Much of those [AP] students' later success in college may be due not to the AP classes themselves, but to the personal characteristics that led them to participate in the classes in the first place – better academic preparation, stronger motivation, better family advantages, and so on. These selection effects will affect any comparison of AP and non-AP students.[80]

And, not surprisingly, just like the SAT, "AP exam performance was closely tied closely to the socio-economic characteristics of the school."[81]

---

[80] Dougherty, Chrys, et al. *The Relationship between Advanced Placement and College Graduation. 2005 AP Study Series, Report 1.* National Center for Educational Accountability, 2006.
[81] https://www.calstate.edu/ier/reports/APreport0601.pdf

On the Common Application School Report (and as part of the application for a great many colleges that do not use the Common App) that the high school counselor must complete for each prospective college applicant, he or she evaluates the applicant's program of studies as "Most demanding/ Very demanding/ Demanding/ Average/ Below average." If a high school offers a smattering of AP courses, perhaps one to five, it would not be onerous for a student to take all of them in order to merit the rating of "Most demanding." On the other hand, if a school offers 20, the student will have to take as many as possible in order to earn that rating, which is a daunting task, one that could render high school a pressure cooker, the case for too many students. To demonstrate the point, in a study analyzing data from more than 45,000 applications to three elite universities, researchers found that

> A student has the best odds of being accepted by an elite college if he or she comes from a high school where no AP tests are taken (and, presumably, where no AP courses are offered)....And at the most competitive high schools—those with more than 1.5 AP tests per senior—the same applicant has 53 percent lower odds of admission.[82]

A student is evaluated within the context of his or her school. To be highly competitive, a student should take the most rigorous courses available, whether labeled honors, AP, or something else. To "game the system," some high schools label all their courses "honors" and eschew ability grouping entirely.[83] Those courses may earn their students an extra weight in GPA calculations by some colleges and scholarship programs, but most colleges will note from the school profile that all courses are "honors" and eliminate the customary added weight. The notion that college admissions officers wouldn't see through this transparent plan is simply disingenuous to the students and parents in the secondary school.

In order to help admissions officers to understand how their curriculum is structured for rigor, independent schools can provide explanations of their proprietary courses and distinctive designations for courses that are writing-intensive, project-based, seminar style, etc. Like it or not, colleges endeavor to

---

[82] Espenshade, Thomas J., and Chang Y. Chung. "The Frog Pond Revisited: High School Academic Context, Class Rank, and Elite College Admission." *Sociology of Education* 78.4 (2005): 269-93. 15 Oct 14.

[83] While the practice of ability grouping and the selection of students for the varied groups is hotly debated, the preponderance of evidence suggests that, for a variety of reasons, heterogeneous groupings penalize the most talented students and may prevent students with serious learning disabilities from receiving the assistance that would help them to succeed.

locate individual applicants' quality within the context of their school and schools that don't rank students need to understand the colleges' perspective. The most cursory understanding of the Academic Index and Converted Rank Score will help schools to appreciate the need for differentiation among students and the degree of challenge provided by different courses. Any rigorous program that sets particularly motivated students apart will advantage them in admissions.

It is instructive to note that, of the original schools masterminding the Advanced Placement program, Lawrenceville and Exeter no longer offer AP courses, though their students may take the exams. Princeton and Yale only recognize scores of 5 in some subjects, 4 in others, none in several others, and allow students to apply those credits toward Advanced Standing or acceleration of time to degree.[84] Harvard only recognizes scores of 5 on several AP exams, none in others, and has adopted a rather complicated policy regarding Advanced Placement, credit and Advanced Standing.[85]

Many renowned independent and public schools including Catlin Gabel (OR), Crystal Springs Uplands (CA), Dalton (NY), Sandía (NM), Shattuck-St. Mary's (MN), and Scarsdale (NY), have eliminated AP in favor of designing their own courses evincing greater depth over the AP breadth. Some similarly-minded folks joined forces in the Independent Curriculum Group, which "emphasizes site-based, teacher-generated curriculum for advanced courses." These schools, some of which charge over $40K per annum in tuition, researched their decisions extensively and would not risk penalizing their students in admissions by jettisoning the program had their research indicated its indispensability. In fact, "Administrators from Fieldston (NY) wrote in 2002 that, after their first year without AP, more students were admitted to highly selective colleges than had been the case for years."[86]

Moreover, *The Wall Street Journal* published admissions officers' responses to the question of how the absence of AP might affect prospective applicants and received the following responses:

---

[84] University, Princeton. "Reference Table for AP Credit Accepted at Princeton." *Princeton University*. 28 Mar. 2014. Web. 19 Dec. 2014. And Yale College. *Table of Acceleration Credit*. Web. 19 Dec. 2014.

[85] "For Faculty and Administrators." *Advanced Standing Office of Undergraduate Education*. Harvard University. Web. 24 Oct. 2014.

[86] Landsberg, Mitchell, and Rachana Rathi. "Elite School Will Expel AP Classes." *Los Angeles Times* 5 May 2005: B1. Print.

College: California Institute of Technology. **Comment**: Does not give credit for AP exams. School gives its own internal exams that allow students to place out of certain introductory-level classes and receive credit for them if they do well.

College: Dartmouth College. **Comment**: Admissions Dean Karl Furstenberg says it's 'perfectly fine for high schools not to offer APs, as long as they are clear about the rigor of applicants' courses.'

College: Duke University. **Comment**: 'If high schools decide that the AP curriculum doesn't serve them well...then what selective colleges are looking for is some indication of the relative rigor of the classes,' says Christoph Guttentag, director of undergraduate admissions.

College: Stanford University. **Comment**: 'Our admission process allows and indeed encourages the flexibility of a high school to design the most appropriate curricular offerings and opportunities for its students,' says Associate Dean of Admission Christian Wire.

College: University of Chicago. **Comment**: The dean of undergraduate admissions says his office doesn't penalize students from schools that offer few or no Advanced Placement courses. 'Success in the exam doesn't mean success as a thinker or success as a future student,' he says.[87]

The complete College Board list of domestic and international university credit and placement policies for AP reveals that the utility of AP is limited to the end results of exam scores of 4 and 5. Some schools, realizing that only the exam scores count, engage their students in exam preparation cram sessions after school or on weekends, and design their classes as they see fit.

College applicants who distinguish themselves from the madding crowd have the greatest advantage. At this point in time, athletic stand-outs have the most to gain; accomplishments both academic and non-academic must be extraordinary to compare favorably with a Division I star. According to the 2013 College Board National Summary, 2.2M students took 3.8M AP exams, with 34% of the total number of test takers earning scores of 4 or 5.[88] That's a large pool of applicants in

---

[87] Chaker, Anne Marie. "Some Private High Schools Drop AP Courses." *WSJ*. 23 Nov. 2004. Web. 19 Dec. 2014.
[88] "AP Credit Policy Search." *Search Credit Policies*. 19 Dec. 2014.

which to establish one's prominence. Logically, a student will stand out from the millions if she or he has published a paper, presented at a conference, or demonstrated deep engagement with a thesis through investigation and synthesis to effectively communicate a final product of note.

AP courses are the equivalent of college introductory level courses

There is an emotionally-charged disparity between what high schools believe to be true about the level of AP courses and the college reality. On the college side, instructors decry the students' level of preparation, particularly in writing, but also in terms of familiarity and facility with the interpretation and analysis of important concepts, especially unconventional perspectives that are given short shrift in the AP program. On the high school side, teachers like to crow proudly about teaching AP and those who serve as exam graders perceive that yeoman's service as another prestigious peacock feather in their cap, confident in their abilities to provide and discern college level work. Let's be clear: they do not provide college level work.

> According to the College Board's assessment based on a nationwide survey in 2000-2001, six percent [of AP teachers] were found to hold doctorates, and about half to hold master's degrees 'in an academic discipline that was consistent with the AP course that they teach.'[89]

This is in no way representative of the faculty profile that students will find in any selective university. The AP program consists of high school instructors teaching high school students high school courses with high school level texts and assignments. Period. Then there are the parents and students who enjoy the status conferred by taking ostensibly college courses as a high school student. This hot air balloon needs to be deflated, albeit with a great deal more care, grace, and sensitivity than I need muster in this forum.

Many students enroll in AP courses without another high school level preparatory class, which means that "At age fifteen or sixteen, they are [led to believe they are] enrolling for college-level study in a subject where their highest level of preparation is middle school." The intellectual maturity of a 9th, 10th or 11th grade student is insufficient to do college level work and comprehend sophisticated concepts and texts. In good faith, as educators we cannot endorse this fiction.

---

[89] Casement, William. "Declining Credibility for the AP Program." *Academic Questions*. 16.4 (2003): 11-25.

It seems patently unreasonable to parents and students when, in the name of ensuring a well-rounded education as defined idiosyncratically and arbitrarily, colleges prevent a student who intends to major in, say, Psychology, from using a 3 on the AP exam in Chemistry in lieu of taking CHEM101, a course in which she has no interest. In truth, the parents discount a significant dimension. By most accounts, 70% of students change their major at least once during their college career. Why? First, students have been exposed to limited options by age 18, and second, a talented, creative active scholar can inspire a student to pursue a field that she had never previously considered or that she regarded with tepid or no interest in high school. The purpose of college is not merely the utilitarian acquisition of a credential, but the opportunity to explore and be transformed at a malleable stage of life. The mind is not merely changed but formed. We do our students a disservice when we encourage a conception of self as clay already dry and downplay the potential in inquiry.

Moreover, a student who takes the AP exam for a subject related to her major, say Biology, as a 10th grader, will forget a great deal prior to the first year of college and should unquestionably retake Introductory Biology in college in order to acquire the strong foundation she will need to pursue advanced studies. Despite revision after revision, the AP courses persist in emphasizing breadth over depth and content over the development of the habits of mind, critical inquiry, and methodologies employed by the disciplines. One professor stated emphatically,

> 'I advise students in the sciences, who need their introductory chemistry, physics, calculus, or biology as a foundation for future work, to start the college sequence at the beginning, unless they get the top score on the AP exam. Otherwise, they risk hampering or crippling themselves in future work. It's just not worth it. This is especially true of calculus, which is a foundation for all the sciences.'[90]

Beyond that issue, whether a high school course can possibly be the equivalent of college level introductory courses depends upon the college.

> Harvard's decision [to accept only a AP score of 5 for credit] was based in part on a study of student performance in second-year chemistry and economics courses, which showed that students who

---

[90] Von Blum, Paul. "Are Advanced Placement Courses Diminishing Liberal Arts Education?" *Arts Education Policy Review.* 110.3 (2009): 25-6.

had earned 4s on AP tests fared significantly worse in advanced courses in those subjects than those who had earned 5s. *Overall, in fact, they did worse than classmates who had not taken AP classes in high school [italics mine].*[91]

High school college counselors are deluged each year with the stories of their newly minted college freshmen who were permitted to skip introductory level college courses and either did and regretted it (or transferred back to the intro level) or opted not to skip them and were glad for it. There are undoubtedly anecdotes of students who are insufficiently challenged in college intro level courses. It is imperative to underscore the disparities among college experiences, and not presume correlation with admissions selectivity.

The lack of program articulation between secondary school and college is an essential issue. Alumni should be surveyed insistently about the ways in which their preparation succeeded and fell short. This data is invaluable. Their freshman year GPA (FYGPA) must be collected (anonymity ensured). School subject area teachers should examine the syllabus of introductory courses of the colleges most frequently attended (and/or aspired to) by graduates in order to ensure articulation. They should communicate with college instructors for feedback on the preparation and performance of their students. This should be a matter of course, not exceptional.

The College Board states that the development of the AP courses and exams is "informed by data collected from a range of colleges and universities to ensure that AP curricula reflect current scholarship and advances in the discipline,"[92] but which colleges? And how much can one exam possibly test? The breadth of possible information is extraordinary. It would be convenient if the College Board were able to accomplish the feat that it claims, but there are impediments, as we shall see.

AP courses are the best way to prepare students for college level work

In the first place, it bears repeating: in study after study, it has been demonstrated that the courses themselves provide no benefit unless students earn scores of 4 or 5. The College Board has no data on how many students are enrolled

---

[91] Trounson, Rebecca, and Richard Lee Colvin. "Rapid Growth of Advanced Placement Classes Raises Concerns." *Los Angeles Times*. 07 Apr. 2002. Web. 16 Dec. 2014.
[92] "Teachers Corner." *AP Central*. College Board.

in AP designated classes but do not take the exam, although some estimates place the figure at 30%, which would place the number of students reaping the full benefit of an AP course at 26% of the total number of students in AP classes.[93] Second, AP exam scores correlate strongly with higher parental education and income, so it's impossible to conclude that AP exposure provides any comparative advantage over an honors level course.[94] Third, even if the AP program prepares 26% of students well to take an exam, it does students a disservice as it

> diminishes opportunity for original advanced courses....for significant immersion in higher-order thinking, independent research, interdisciplinary study, field work, creative out-of-the-box thinking, or deep specialization all of which are considered essential to the coming workforce (Gallagher, 2008; Pink, 2006).[95]

The breadth of coverage is such that AP US History teachers, for example are reduced in many cases to limiting class time dedicated to World War II "to two 55-minute classroom lectures and to cover the New Deal and the civil rights movement in one class."[96] AP language teachers complain that the courses do not sufficiently emphasize oral proficiency. We must provide our students with enriched opportunities and a different sort of preparation to flourish in the new economy.

All secondary and tertiary educators ought to remain skeptical of the College Board's claims about its products. Many studies on the effects of the AP program on freshman year GPA (FYGPA) and college admissions in general date back to the 1980s and 1990s, an era in which the program was a fraction of its size, and AP

---

[93] Based on College Board National Summary Table, 2013. Total number of students taking exams = 3824891 + 30% = 4972358. Total number of students earning a 4 or a 5 = 1288189.

[94] See a) Martin, Duffy 2010 Duffy, W.R. (2010). "Persistence and performance at a four-year university: The relationship with advanced coursework during high school," in P.M. Sadler, G. Sonnert, R.H. Tai, K. Klopfenstein (Eds.), *AP: A critical examination of the Advanced Placement Program* (pp. 139-163). Harvard Education Press, 2010.

b) Geiser, Saul, Veronica Santelices, and California Univ. Berkeley Center for Studies in Higher Education. "The Role of Advanced Placement and Honors Courses in College Admissions." Research & Occasional Paper Series: CSHE.4.04. Center for Studies in Higher Education, 2004.

c) Klopfenstein, K. & Thomas, M. K. *The Advanced Placement performance advantage*: Fact or fiction? American Economic Association, 2005.

[95] Gallagher, Shelagh A. "Myth 19: Is Advanced Placement an Adequate Program for Gifted Students?" *Gifted Child Quarterly* 53.4 (2009): 286-8.

[96] Gibbs, Brian. "The Advanced Placement Numbers Racket." *Los Angeles Times.* 12 Aug. 2014. Web. 19 Dec. 2014.

courses were limited primarily to highly talented seniors, too far removed from the contemporary context to be useful. Further, in the variety of studies that found that students in AP classes performed better in college, the AP courses were not compared with other honors level courses but with standard courses. Certainly it does not require any research to suppose or validate that students who are in advanced classes will perform better in college than students who are not.

The College Board and ETS or one of its partners fund many of the formal studies attesting to the quality of AP courses. Having examined dozens of studies included in this number as well as independent ones that examine the purported effects of AP on subsequent success in college, I find it striking to note in every one of them the researchers admitted shortcomings as they were unable to control for variables including students' family income and level of educational attainment, concurrent exposure to additional accelerated or enrichment curricula, dual enrollment, etc. Let us hope that the vast expansion of the institutional research sector in many universities will result in increased attention to the role of AP credit with college-specific studies of their relevance and efficacy in preparing students for college level work, independent of other variables.

Here is a selection of research regarding the efficacy of specific popular AP courses:

AP English:

"Those who had taken an AP English course and a suitable FYC [first year course] performed significantly better than those who had only AP English or only FYC; both latter groups performed less than adequately on the tasks measured. These results indicate that exempting students from college writing based on work done in high school may be unwise because more instruction in writing at college appears to solidify student learning."[97]

AP Science:

"...it appears as if students reporting low AP exam scores may have gained no benefit from their AP course" and about half of the sample students who scored a 5 on the AP exam did not earn an A in the introductory college level science course, the equivalent asserted by the College Board. The authors theorize about why this may be the case and posited, among other things, that

---

[97] Hansen, Kristine et al. "Are Advanced Placement English and First-Year College Composition Equivalent? A Comparison of Outcomes in the Writing of Three Groups of Sophomore College Students." *Research in the Teaching of English*. 40.4 (May 2006): 461-501.

a. The AP course content is not equivalent to college course content;
b. The AP exams are a criterion-referenced exam (the score is determined in relation to a pre-determined level), but "the criteria may be set too low." In the Physics C exam, for example, students earn a 5 for 56% correct.
c. A single exam cannot test knowledge in a sufficiently comprehensive manner.[98]

AP Calculus
The Thomas Fordham Institute study evaluated the content, rigor, and clarity of several AP curricula and evaluated this AP course a "C" for "Missing or abridged topics of importance [and] overreliance on technology, resulting in a de-emphasis on analytical skills."[99]

AP US History
The Fordham Institute gave AP US a B-: "Unifying themes are tendentious, emphasizing *pluribus* instead of *unum* [and] topics mention very few actual historical events." There is currently a furor raging over alleged political bias in the changes to AP US, prompting the adoption of a resolution by the Republican National Committee denouncing the curriculum as "a radically revisionist view of American history.[100]

On the horizon is another AP product, AP Capstone Diploma Program. Students who participate in this program take a Seminar course, which requires analysis of a variety of teacher-selected texts on a teacher-selected theme, take two performance assessment tasks and an end of course exam, and a Research course, in which students are assessed on

- a reflection log of mentor communication and the research process [15% of score];
- a 5,000 word academic thesis paper [70% of score];
- a 15-minute public presentation, performance, or exhibition and an oral defense of their research and presentation [to include three to four questions

---

[98] Sadler, P. M. & R.H. Tai, R. H. "Advanced Placement® exam scores as a predictor of performance in introductory college biology, chemistry, and physics courses." *Science Educator.* 16.2 (2007), 1 – 19.
[99] Byrd, Sheila with Lucien Ellington, Paul Gross, Carol Jago, Sheldon Stern. "Advanced Placement and International Baccalaureate Do They Deserve Gold Star Status?" Thomas Fordham Institute Nov 2007.
[100] http://blogs.edweek.org/edweek/curriculum/RNC.JPG

from a panel of a minimum of two trained evaluators—15% of score].[101]

Students may earn the AP Capstone Diploma if they "earn scores of 3 or higher in AP Seminar and AP Research and on four additional AP Exams of their choice (that's over $600 in exam fees for the College Board). Students who earn scores of 3 or higher in AP Seminar and AP Research but not on four additional AP Exams will be awarded an AP Seminar and Research Certificate." Some call this a knockoff of the IB's Extended Essay of 4,000 words, others question the value of having a single experience of writing an extended paper in high school; still others will say that it represents a superb innovation.

AP courses ensure placement of students in higher-level courses in college, thus abbreviating the time it takes a student to earn a degree

The policy varies by college and can be viewed on the extensive list maintained by the College Board. Large public universities tend to be more accepting of AP credits than small private, highly selective colleges. Some colleges limit the number of AP credits that can be applied (often not more than one semester of advanced standing), some use AP exam scores for placement purposes, some refuse to count them toward classes in the major. Some won't allow APs to reduce the course load. In Klopfenstein's study of undergraduates at the University of Texas and Eykamp's of University of California, AP units had no real effect on time to degree.[102] Students who earn 5s on the exams tend to be the most motivated and likely to use AP credit to free up the schedule to carry a double major or to ensure sufficient challenge, which is the original intention of AP since its inception.

AP credit will certainly factor into the various programs to address the student loan debt crisis. The government is pressuring universities to shorten time to degree with the threat of cutting federal financial aid or other sanctions for institutions where large numbers of students do not graduate within six years. Many states, including Minnesota, Ohio, Missouri, Rhode Island, and others are actively creating 3-year baccalaureate degree programs. In both cases, AP credits form part of the solution. In contrast, it is unclear what the future holds for AP in

---

[101] "AP Research." – *A New Advanced Placement Course.*
https://advancesinap.collegeboard.org/ap-capstone/ap-research N.d. Web. 19 Dec. 2014.
[102] Eykamp, Paul W. "The Effect of Advanced Placement Credit on Time to Degree at the University of California." Proc. of AIR 2003 Forum Changing Our Attitudes, Expanding Our Latitudes, Tampa, FL. Print.

private colleges. With the financial straits of some small private colleges, enabling students to graduate in three years may represent too great a loss of revenue and may lead to restrictions on the one hand, but help in recruitment on the other.

Pragmatic financial constraints notwithstanding, many educational leaders question whether abbreviating the time a student spends in higher education is even a worthy enterprise. If we aspire to inculcate a lifelong love of learning in our students, a utilitarian approach to university studies and truncating them by allowing high school courses to effectively count twice, once toward the high school diploma and simultaneously toward a college degree, is not the message we want to transmit, though it does seem to be in keeping with the *Zeitgeist*.

AP courses demonstrate the superior rigor and status of a school

It is crucial for independent school leaders to ruminate on the fact that public schools began implementing the AP program to attract and retain students who might otherwise have left for independent schools. By 2013, "Approximately 132,500 teachers taught AP classes in nearly 14,000 public high schools."[103] AP courses and exams are appropriate for public schools, which are all too familiar with standardized testing, because students' efforts on the AP are distilled in a three-hour exam. Any standardized test facilitates comparison among large numbers of students who are churned through the industrial style of education; thus, for large schools and those that primarily serve marginalized populations, AP can demonstrate rigor and offer an alternative to motivated students to "escape the chaos" and be with others like them, often in smaller classes with what they perceive to be "better teachers." Various providers, ranging from state-sponsored to no-cost MOOCs [Massive Open Online Courses] to for-profit online providers are also offering AP courses, further expanding their reach, and some would argue, diluting their quality.

Independent schools that serve more advantaged groups and that seek to distinguish themselves as offering a superior *educational and curricular* alternative to public and charter schools can no longer cite AP as a mark of quality because the program is so ubiquitous. Remember, AP began as a luxury elite brand (think Bentley automobile) available to the few, who paid a premium for it. As it spread, it became aspirational (BMW), a program that many schools were proud to offer or aspire to offer and that still offered some discernible comparative advantage. At

---

[103] "10 Years of Advanced Placement Exam Data Show Significant Gains in Access and Success; Areas for Improvement." *The College Board*. n.d. Web. 19 Dec. 2014.

present, however, AP is a mass-market brand (Honda), a functional, serviceable, generally reliable product. Independent schools should offer better.

Tony Little, the outgoing Head Master [sic] of Eton in the UK, recently decried high stakes testing as an outmoded system:

> 'It strikes me that we are peculiarly uninventive about the way we go about assessment. You look at a child [in an exam] sitting on their own for two or three hours, not talking to anybody - penalised if you do - because that's the way in which you get an exam grade. Only then to go into the world of work and work as a team.' He added assessments through team work and discovering 'real-life' answers were a 'far more valuable way to assess young people than what is fundamentally a Victorian approach to exams'.[104]

Standardized exams represent the status quo. If we expect parents to pay a premium for education, our schools had better deliver a premium experience.

Perhaps most incongruous is the fact that we promote AP exams while marketing ourselves as blithely exempt from state mandated tests, one of the characteristics that enhance our marketability. We claim to offer families and staff an alternative to drill/bubble fill and cram/pass/forget teach-to-the-test education. It is an egregious inconsistency in our message to submit to the practice of teaching to the test in independent secondary education with AP courses, especially if we sincerely believe that we have the capacity to offer a better alternative. If a school community does not believe it has the capacity to offer an educational experience superior to that of public schools, it needs to stop wondering why enrollment is down and/or question its very *raison d'être* (or *droit d'exister*), revisit its mission, and reflect on whether the tuition is justified merely by smaller classes and a sense of community, but not a superior curriculum. Rather than subscribe to a curriculum-in-the-box, independent schools should be at the forefront of curricular innovation that evinces creativity, flexibility, and deep engagement and should offer other highly rigorous courses demonstrably superior and transformative and/or that result in quality student products. Several ways of doing that will be discussed in the next chapter.

---

[104] Furness, Hannah. "End Ritualised Focus on Exams, Says Eton Head." *The Telegraph*. 4 Oct. 2014. Web. 19 Dec. 2014.

39

"Real" College Classes: Dual and Concurrent Enrollment

For decades, schools have been offering students the opportunity to take college level courses while still in high school, almost always in 11th and 12th grades, and the movement is growing. In 2010-11, "1,277,100 high school students took courses for college credit within a dual enrollment program and approximately 136,400 high school students took courses for college credit outside a dual enrollment program."[105] There is significant evidence that dual enrollment has a positive impact on FYGPA and college completion, especially considering that many of the students who participate in dual enrollment are traditionally marginalized populations. Currently, there are three principal means of delivery: dual enrollment, which entails students taking college courses either online or physically at the campus; concurrent enrollment, in which students take college courses at their own high school, usually with high school teachers; and the Early College High School initiative, an offshoot of concurrent enrollment, in which students complete two years of college credit while in high school. Then there is the category of high school students who simply enroll in college courses independently, not through the aegis of their school.

Formed in 1997 to ensure that concurrent high school/college enrollment programs are as rigorous as college courses, The National Alliance of Concurrent Enrollment Partnerships accredited 89 concurrent enrollment programs as of April, 2013. The organization provides a wealth of information and research on the efficacy, structure, and financing of these programs. At first glance, concurrent enrollment courses share some of the features of AP courses that draw criticisms in that they are taught by high school teachers to high school students on a high school campus, but 87% of tertiary institutions offering dual enrollment reported that "the instructors' minimum qualifications were the same as those required for college instructors" and 85% stated that the curriculum, syllabus and textbooks are the same as those utilized by their college students.[106]

University admissions offices regard participation in these programs highly because it demonstrates students' elevated level of motivation to take the most rigorous courses available. How universities treat the credits is a separate issue and varies. According to a study by the College Board (!), "in Florida, 94% of dual

---

[105] Marken, Stephanie, Lucinda Gray, Laurie Westatt. *Dual Enrollment Programs and Courses for High School Students at Postsecondary Institutions: 2010–11.* National Center for Education Statistics. Feb 2103.

[106] Marken, ibid.

enrollment students earn postsecondary credit compared to 41% for AP students."[107] Not surprisingly, public universities are generally amenable to accepting and applying the credits. Private colleges tend to treat the credits as they would other college transfer credits, which means that the credit will transfer, but not the grade. The most selective private institutions tend to be less inclined to accept any transfer credits and, by extension, any college credits earned through these programs. University of Pennsylvania, for example, stipulates the following, which seems rather retrograde:

1. The course must be taught on the college campus by a member of the regular faculty.
2. It must be open to enrollment by and graded in direct competition with regularly matriculated undergraduates at the college.
3. It must consist of the normal curriculum published in the college's catalogue and cannot be a distance learning course of any type.[108]

Nevertheless, it must be noted that, at one time, the English class offered through the University of Connecticut Early College Experience program (in operation since 1955) required students to write extended papers of approximately twenty pages in both semesters. This far surpasses any exigencies of the AP, IB, and AICE programs, so it seems illogical to accept credits from AP exams and not from other universities through a dual or concurrent enrollment program. I hypothesize the rationale to be that AP exams are standardized, while college courses are not.

The principal considerations with dual enrollment are cost, transportation schedule, transportation, and separation from the community. Obviously, the latter three are not considerations with online dual enrollment. The cost of dual enrollment depends on the institution. It can range from nominal fees to the full regular cost per credit hour. According to the NCES study, about half of the tertiary institutions surveyed reported that participating students' families paid the tuition; the other half reported that students paid no tuition, a substantial benefit, to be sure. Schools interested in dual enrollment situations in the fee-based category would need to ascertain whether some arrangement might be made with the university regarding discounts and payment of tuition and fees and survey parents who are already paying tuition to the high school to determine whether they might be amenable to paying the additional tuition.

---

[107] Wyatt, Jeff, Brain Patterson, and F Tony Di Giacomo. "A Comparison of the College Outcomes of AP and Dual Enrollment Students | In Progress | Research and Development." College Board. 28 June 2014. Web. 19 Dec. 2014.
[108] "AP, IB and Pre-College Credit." - *Penn Admissions*. n.d. Web. 19 Dec. 2014.

Transportation is certainly an issue. Some schools transport students at common class times; others identify options for students from carpooling to public transit; and others stay out of the issue entirely. The schedule can be a challenge since college courses are often longer and offered at times that make accommodating them in a high school student's schedule problematic or impossible. Evening (and online) courses can often be a better fit.

When students engage in dual enrollment as a small group, the effect can be a strengthening of their ties with one another. On the other hand, individual students who embark on several courses on their own can feel alienated from their peers as they miss out on bonding opportunities with their classmates, expeditionary learning, etc. For some students, it should be noted, this is not a loss but a secondary gain, and their independence should be encouraged.

Summary

We in independent schools must carefully consider the message our actions communicate. Some questions to ponder:

- In what ways do we emphasize college admission as the goal, rather than the transformational and holistic school experience?
- In what ways are we encouraging the acceleration of students' time in college and why?
- In what ways might we be allowing organizations, including the College Board and universities to hijack our students' education?
- With dual enrollment, are we promoting the notion that a university experience, even community college, is superior to the one students will have in our own classrooms with our teachers and students?
- By supporting yet another program available through public schools, are we undermining our ability to effectively promote the comparative advantage of our institutions as worth the tuition?

The most vital question of all is do we confidently believe—and can we prove—that what we do provides deep, challenging, and transformative experiences that set students on the road to recognizing their responsibilities to the larger community and constructing a purposeful life, that lead students to a lifelong love of learning, and forge meaningful bonds with adults and peers in a nurturing setting? Do we deliver on whatever else our mission statement might affirm? If so, have the proof and be sure that the community and prospective families know and trust your assertions. If not, there is much work to be done to re-examine the mission statement and all that proceeds from it.

Chapter 3

What Did You Do During the Information Revolution?
Harnessing Disruptive Innovation

In 1996, Kodak had a market cap of $28 billion with 140,000 employees. In 2012, it went bankrupt. That same year, another company in the photography business called Instagram was purchased by Facebook for $1 billion. The company, which had been founded only a year earlier, had just 13 employees.—Peter Diamandis

Cassandra or Chicken Little

Let's begin with a story. I began working in libraries in 1985, in the days when reference librarians answered questions ranging from a recipe for blueberry muffins to commodities market figures in the 1880s. Then the Information Age dawned. I likened it to the Protestant Reformation because in the late 20th century, the public no longer needed librarians to mediate information just as in the 16th, the public no longer needed clerics to mediate grace. In the mid-1990s, I predicted that the Internet would present a profound threat to libraries; my colleagues called me Chicken Little and found the very idea absurd.

Fast-forward to 2015 and sure enough, funding has been cut for many libraries and the way that the next generation conceives of libraries is dramatically different — if they think of them at all. With the average cost of an ebook at less than $7, many users prefer to purchase rather than borrow. Librarians have struggled to find ways to remain relevant, which they have done with varying degrees of success. They tried organizing the web, evaluating the best websites and organizing them into directories like the taxonomies we used to catalog books; their efforts were largely ignored. They tried converting the online catalog into a place where people could read and discuss books; readers chose Amazon and Goodreads, etc. to access a broader community. They tried offering virtual reference services to answer questions through simultaneous chat, text, or other means, but most of those services have also ended; they just weren't needed to the extent that justified funding.[109]

In academia, some librarians have taken to roaming the stacks with iPads,

---

[109] See Coffman, Steve. "The Decline and Fall of the Library Empire." *Information Today*, Apr. 2012. Web. 18 Dec. 2014.

asking if they can help. They develop outreach programs to teach students how to conduct searches with greater precision and recall, make themselves available for research consultations, and even deliver physical books to dorm rooms. They circulate a wide variety of digital items, from newspapers to music. (Of course there are other librarians who still expect the people to go to them, still charge annoyance fees, set all kinds of limits and constraints, and treat the public with a certain disdain). What they have not done, however, among other things, is develop the means of suggesting titles so accurately as the algorithms of Amazon or Netflix. Amazon now features a lending library that will provide access to more books than most library systems can house.

I had entered librarianship with revolutionary zeal. I still sincerely believe in its anti-consumerist mission: if we all shared certain items in common the way that we do library books, we would buy less stuff and the world would be better for it.[110] With the rise of neo-liberalism, market forces have taken over and the publishers of books and music challenge the "first sale doctrine," which gives the right to the entity that first purchases an item to do as it wishes with it. This tenet was nullified for digital content, which means that publishers can limit the number of times libraries may circulate materials and the rights to the items, which are *leased*, not owned, so the items can evaporate for a variety of reasons. There is another hidden truth. Librarians purchase books based on intuition and circulation patterns, but 40% of the books purchased never circulate and another 40% circulate fewer than three times.[111] That is hard to defend and gave rise to a new trend called Patron Driven Acquisition, which calls for books to be borrowed from other sources or purchased only when a patron requests it.

The funding of libraries has also changed. The common good as a motive for funding is passé. Diversification of funding streams has become imperative. Online catalogs routinely link to retailers with a tiny fraction of sales going back to the library. That's just the beginning. Corporate underwriting, partnerships with local businesses, fee-based programming, research and genealogical services, retail outlets, pledge drives, and sizeable advancement/grant writing teams are all part of the modern library's functions.

Why this story? It illustrates the effects of disruptive innovation on a revered

---

[110] See *The Story of Stuff*, storyofstuff.org, a provocative if somewhat strident book to use with students or as an all-school read to encourage reflection on patterns of consumption.
[111] Roncevic, Mirela, and Sue Polanka. "Patron Driven Acquisition in Libraries." *No Shelf Required*. 28 Oct. 2011. Web. 18 Dec. 2014.

social good with a long tradition in American life. Like teachers, librarians were passionate about their contribution to the common good; they downplayed or ignored the massive changes that were striking at their foundation, and attempted vain and ineffective ways of using the new tools at hand. Some allege that librarians' mistake was not acting sufficiently quickly or dramatically, but it was a lost cause, like that of coopers, tinkers, and hatters. From 1990 to 2009, the number of librarians shrunk by 31%[112] and, as Stanford political science professor Terry Moe asserts in his book, *Special Interest,* the number of teachers is likely to shrink significantly as well. Further, emergent technologies can change the landscape dramatically by modifying or even terminating essential practices that people in a profession have long taken for granted, like the annulment of "first sale," — or of face to face teaching and learning in a classroom setting for online education, already a requirement in Florida, Alabama, and Michigan and under consideration in at least ten other states.

Online Learning

Those who haven't taken an online course are far more likely to be critical of their potential than those who have. Doubtless there are online courses that allow for little to no interaction, that aren't effectively scaffolded or structured, that have poor content, etc. However, researchers are busily defining best practices for online education and great strides are being made. I found the first course I took online in the late 1990s to be stimulating, challenging, and vibrant. It was a graduate school class; the lectures were synchronous and students were able to ask questions throughout. Students submitted assignments and read, critiqued, and commented on the other students' work. The quantity and quality of interaction in this online class surpassed most face-to-face classes I had in four years in three small private colleges.

Since that clearly auspicious initiation, I have taken many courses of varying quality and degrees of engagement, stimulation, and challenge, some featuring asynchronous lectures, others synchronous. The greatest barrier I encountered and continue to struggle with was the learning management system (LMS). The information architecture is often so broadly accommodating that the lack of standardization among instructors regarding where to locate content can impede enormously the student's ability to locate necessary content and assignments, etc.,

---

[112] US Census data cited by Beveridge, Sydney, Susan Weber, and Andrew Beveridge. "Librarians in the U.S. from 1880-2009." Oxford University Press Blog. 20 June 2011. Web. 16 Dec. 2014.

buried several layers of nests deep or in a place that only made sense to the instructor, who has had little guidance in online course design.

While online learning may not have taken over yet, the cycle of technology takes time to develop momentum and when it does, it can be like a boulder rolling down a hill. Like many other technological products, when they first emerged in the 1990s, ebooks produced an uproar in the library world and promptly flopped, allowing libraries to return to business as usual, but the diffusion of innovation and the technology cycle are such that new technologies rarely find an appreciative audience immediately. They must demonstrate their comparative advantage over the existing means of achieving the same thing. They need to be compatible with peoples' needs and beliefs, and easy to use, try, and observe.[113] This relates to education in various ways. When I stopped teaching on the college level in 2000, I noted the practice of video recording instructors' classes, not renewing the instructors' contracts, and using the recording in combination with graduate teaching assistants to facilitate discussion, grade assignments, and attend to administrative details. That practice was a small-scale version of what was to come: massive open online courses. Since MOOCs burst onto the scene in 2011, more than six million people have signed up for one with diverse motives including to supplement traditional classes, to earn credit or a certificate, to continue professional education, to try out a subject, or to hear a specific professor's lecture.[114]

In the minds of those stewarding public funds, far worse than books that sit on the library shelf is the extravagant waste of time and resources incurred by a teacher repeating the same lesson up to five times a day. Multiply this by thousands of teachers repeating a lesson millions of times. Certainly the content of courses like U.S. History and Calculus is largely the same from school to school. There was a reason for this duplication before the advent of online education, but it will take quite a bit of persuasion to persist in this practice.

Somewhere a federal, state or district bureaucrat is thinking: Why not find a few excellent teachers, the kind who might be featured on a Great Courses DVD, and connect students around the country or the world via online means? It can significantly democratize education by ensuring quality and standardization of the material, which the government seems to like, creatively and expertly structured

---

[113] Rogers, Everett M. *Diffusion of Innovation*. New York: Free, 1995.
[114] Selingo, Jeffrey. "MOOC U: The Revolution Isn't Over." *The Chronicle of Higher Education* 3 Oct.14.

and delivered according to the very best evidence-based pedagogical practices. This can follow paths already in place for a national curriculum, since No Child Left Behind, Common Core, and other initiatives certainly demonstrate the efficacy of linking "optional" participation to funding. Administrative details like attendance could be performed by IP address or some other means. The current teachers, who are always complaining of being overburdened, would be relieved from a great deal of preparation and could devote their time to supporting students' understanding of the content. Perhaps the most ambitious could structure engaging continuation activities. In any case, there would be a need for far fewer of them to pay, benefit, and pension. Eventually, expensive school buildings and facilities could be repurposed since students can learn from anywhere. Our imaginary bureaucrat has a point, for the current system is undeniably inefficient.

Naturally, the politicians will see and sell the fact that superlative online courses can significantly democratize education by ensuring that any student with Internet access can participate. Or they can go in the opposite direction, with the best courses available at astronomical cost. A star teacher might be identified for specific subjects by each district or state or even the nation as a whole. As the consummate teachers and exceptional courses become apparent online, they will dominate, like Kim Ki-Hoon in Korea, whose in-person and online test prep courses earn him $4M annually.[115] Such teachers can emerge and work from anywhere in the world, entirely independent from any institution.

This is not some wild dystopian vision for education. As noted earlier, the number of homeschoolers is growing exponentially, and the growth of online courses is expected to expand that market further. Though other surveys place the figure much higher (7.1M),[116] according to the National Center for Education Statistics, in 2012, 5.5M, a quarter of all undergraduates were enrolled in online courses, 2.6M of them were taking all of their classes exclusively online, with enormous differences by region, with 23% of the students in the Plains states and only 7% in the Far West and New England in the exclusively online category.[117] Thus, readers in those latter regions may not fully grasp the shift that is so evident to those of us on the front lines.

Nova Southeastern University in Florida offers every one of its courses in

---

[115] Ripley, Amanda. "The $4 Million Teacher." *WSJ*. 3 Aug. 2013. Web. 16 Dec. 2014.

[116] Spies Blair, Barbara. "Babson Study: Over 7.1 Million Higher Ed Students Learning Online." Babson College. 15 Jan. 2014. Web. 18 Dec. 2014.

[117] Ginder, Scott and Christina Stearns. "Enrollment in Distance Education Courses, by State: Fall 2012." *Web Tables*. U.S. Department of Education. June 2014.

three formats: face-to-face, hybrid, and online. Several states already require high school students to take an online course prior to graduation, ostensibly to ensure that students are capable digital citizens, but also to help schools meet class size requirements. As a result of the Digital Learning Act requiring all students in Florida to take an online course, in June, 2013, Florida Virtual School reported 1.7M "successful semester completions."[118] Currently, the courses are structured very much like bricks-and-mortar ones, but that is almost sure to change.

Make no mistake about the rigor and quality possible in the online format. The level of engagement of an online course can be exhaustingly intense, with daily assignments like discussion board posts, replies to other students' posts, instant pop-up quizzes to assess understanding of lectures or readings (or videos, etc.), essays or projects that are individual or collaborative, and evaluating other students' work. Classmates are not limited to the local environment but may hail from anywhere in the world, contributing a glorious diversity difficult to achieve otherwise. There is no hiding in an online course, for unlike bricks-and-mortar classes where a record of participation is often impressionistic and ephemeral, online students' participation is durable and visible for evaluation by the students, instructor, and administrators in the case of grade arbitration. And the potential for individualization is enormous. Programs like ALEKS in mathematics already use artificial intelligence to identify and target students' areas for growth with greater precision than a classroom teacher who has 100 students to track can.

One of the early issues with MOOCs was plagiarism. Students could have someone else write their exams and assignments, but to preclude the possibility, providers are now commonly using keystroke analysis to ensure that the student is in fact the one doing the work. Exams are taken by the student in front of a webcam.

The benefits of online courses are not to be reaped solely by higher education or public schools, of course. Online education offers extraordinary comparative advantage over the status quo. It is portable, inexpensive (once developed), scalable, and available 24/7. Elective courses that normally couldn't be offered due to the lack of critical mass, interest, schedule or instructor can be taken online, exponentially expanding students' options. Many online courses offer students the ability to begin on demand at any time and allow them to work at their own pace. Students who demonstrate fulfillment of some established objective, perhaps a portfolio of coursework coupled with experiences of various kinds,

---

[118] https://www.flvs.net/areas/contactus/Documents/Florida_Virtual_School_Summary.pdf

might earn digital badges. Badges can stand on their own, i.e. Web Design, or serve as benchmarks toward a larger goal, for example accumulating Badges in Sitemap Organization, Web Design, UX, and Social Networking leads to a Certificate in Search Engine Optimization. Badges can also link to the syllabus and the work that the student completed to earn it. Independent school staff are creating their own online courses, of course, but they can't very well compete with the quality of a course professionally produced by universities like MIT or Harvard or the companies already in the education business, for whom production costs are upward of $500 per minute for a 60-minute course[119] to $325,000 for a MOOC.[120]

Online education is driving one of the most disruptive forces in higher education: the surge in unbundling, in which students take courses from various providers rather than just one. I unbundled my own undergraduate and graduate school education in the 1980s and 90s by taking courses at several different universities. My diverse motivations mirror those of students today: to acquire different perspectives in my major field, save money, expedite the time to degree, work more hours, and live and conduct research abroad. Secondary school students are already expressing the desire to unbundle and receive credit for summer experiences, college courses, and classes they take online.

Independent schools would be foolish not to leverage the online learning revolution. If anything, independent schools might jump the curve by identifying the best teachers and courses. Schools are currently utilizing language programs in the interest of expanding offerings without hiring more faculty. While it may be that schools that can pay the most might negotiate exclusive rights to these courses, current practice indicates otherwise, with Stanford and MIT offering free courses, often only charging a fee for a certificate. I suggest keeping a close eye on how this develops since providers are still determining how to make money from this platform. Stanford's Gifted and Talented/Education Program for Gifted Youth and its Online High School are two distinct models. The former is entirely online for K-12, while the second offers online classes full-time, part-time or single courses with intensive on site summer residencies. Many independent schools offer courses through consortia like Malone Schools Online Network, Hybrid Learning Consortium, Global Online Academy, Online School for Girls, Online High School for Boys, Hybrid Learning Consortium, and Virtual High School Collaborative.

---

[119] Corbett, Todd. "How Much Does It Cost to Produce an Online Elearning Course?" *Xcelus.* 12 Feb. 2013. Web. 16 Dec. 2014.
[120] "*TC Study Finds MOOC Reality Not Yet Meeting High Expectations.*" Columbia Teachers College. 15 May 2014. Web. 16 Dec. 2014.

Others continue to emerge. The courses range from specials like "Asian Studies: Impact of History on Current Culture" and "Entrepreneurship for Musicians" to the usual slate of AP courses.

Many teachers already integrate the online experience by including Khan Academy and YouTube videos and flip their classrooms so that students watch a video outside of class time and work collaboratively on activities carefully structured by the teacher or projects during class time. Online courses can be similarly blended with small group discussions conducted through virtual facilitators or by teachers in person, in learning centers, or in schools.

There is one significant exception to the types of experiences that are most congenial to online learning, notably the laboratory sciences. Students should not be permitted to take the lab portion of science courses online. Period. The only exceptions might entail dissection, certainly an ethical dilemma which many schools resolve by eliminating it, and any physical disability that precludes participation in a lab. Virtual labs are utter nonsense: click to lift the pipette; click to fill the flask; click to project Ball 1, etc. This is absurd and obviates the rationale for labs in the first place. Students must have the tactile experience of the lab and the ability to make errors and account for them. There is no substitute for beakers and burners experimentation, and this brings us to what could one day be the core of the school as we shall come to know it.

Online courses are here to stay and offer overwhelming comparative advantages. School staff must determine ways to use them wisely, not prohibit them. Unequivocally, the motivation for online courses in the independent school must be the pursuit of *quality*. When executed and implemented appropriately, their potential to serve the students is extraordinary. That they stand to save the institution inordinate amounts of money is a felicitous by-product. Crucially, staff need to find the means for the face to face experience to be **clearly superior, indispensable** and **not replicable** online, such as expeditionary learning, global education, community and project-based learning, internships and externships, in short, **experiences** that must be had in real time and place. We shall explore what that looks like next.

A Day in the Life of the School for the New Millennium

Some students and staff are exercising in the gym as early as 6 AM. Others arrive in time for breakfast at 7. Some classes begin at 8 AM, though it is mostly the younger students who are present. By 9 AM, many students are gathered in "huddle spaces" for collaboration on projects; others are settled in at workstations for online classes, with teachers available nearby for assistance and supervision. These classes are based on mastery and students move through them at their own pace. Students are assessed prior, during, and following instruction through a variety of means, provided with narrative feedback, and given ample opportunity to demonstrate their learning. Some students blaze through a course in a few weeks, while others take months.

Throughout the day, younger students tend to remain in or around the building, while older students trickle in and out. Lunch is served for a full hour and students have enough time to eat lunch and join an exercise class or shoot hoops. Some students are animatedly working in groups monitored by a facilitator. Students are not over-programmed and have plenty of time to work, study, reflect, socialize, and be physically active if they choose. Some more traditional classes meet for 90 minutes every other day or twice a week; others meet for several hours or a full day to enable in-depth and off-site work. Some students leave at the more traditional hour of 4 PM, while others remain to collaborate, consult with teachers, or return for classes that continue into the evening, but all students have left the building by just after 9 PM. There is little homework to be done.

The notable features of this school of the 21st Century include:
- Extensive autonomy and choice
- Blended formats of instruction
- Flexible schedule, physical activity and downtime
- Innovative use of space
- Collaboration
- Individualized instruction
- Authentic assessment
- Projects with real-world application integrated into the curriculum

This is not an impossible dream but a reality in various permutations in hundreds of schools around the country, like D9 in Oregon, Next in South Carolina, School of Environmental Studies in Minnesota, Fusion Academies around the country, Center for Advanced Research and Technology in California, and many others.

51

In the for-profit sector, "learning centers" are sprouting up everywhere; there are currently ten within a thirty-mile radius of my suburban home. They typically use online curricula and tutors to present the material initially or to enhance students' understanding, and/or to assist with assignments. Many operate year-round. Students have diverse reasons for using these centers. They may be students who have rigorous athletic or professional obligations, or who experience learning, attention or other challenges that are not well-served by regular school environments. They benefit enormously from the individual or very small group environment that caters entirely to their schedules and learning needs. For most of these students, these centers are their school, though some attend to augment homeschooling or to receive extra help with regular school classes or to recover credits for classes failed. The key to their success is individual attention and differentiation.

Autonomy and Self-direction

Traditional education has been based on an authoritarian model in which staff have wielded all of the power regarding the determination of what students would learn, how they would learn it, how their progress would be assessed, etc., quite effectively disenfranchising the student with respect to every facet of his or her formal education. It is at cross-purposes to the ultimate goals of education that the student learns to submit passively rather than to take charge of what, how, and why he or she wants to learn. Moreover, it is assumed by and large in tertiary institutions that students are able to determine their program and be responsible for their own learning but they have had no prior opportunity to develop these skills since secondary schools do not foster them.[121] In the workplace, professionals are expected to make decisions independently, to take responsibility for their actions, "to learn more effectively without the constant presence or intervention of a teacher,"[122] and be accountable to those who receive the employer's services, all of which are practices encouraged by self-directed learning.[123] Students' autonomy and taking responsibility for their own learning should be initiated early on through "project work, laboratory enquiry activities, learning contracts and other forms of

---

[121] Before starting college, students and their parents would do well to read Ken Bain's classic *What the Best College Students Do*. Harvard, 2012, about how to derive the greatest benefit from the experience.

[122] Boud, David, ed. *Developing Student Autonomy in Learning*. Kogan Page, 1988. Second Edition. E-book.

[123] Boud, David and Joy Higgs. "Bringing Self-directed Learning into the Mainstream of Tertiary Education." *Learner Managed Learning: Practice, Theory and Policy.* Ed. Norman Graves. HEC, 1993. 159-73. Print.

negotiated learning and open-ended assignments" so that it is well-developed by the time they enter universities.[124] Such initiatives must be *fundamental* to curricular design, rather than supplemental.

Renowned professor of education Malcolm Knowles wrote of the sociological rationale demanding the restructuring of education for autonomous learning:

> Traditional education has been based on the premise that the central purpose of education is to produce knowledgeable persons,....with the concepts, values, and skills required to function reasonably well....in a world of relative stability,...on the basis of what they had learned in their youth. But this assumption is a myth in a world in which the half-life of a fact or a technical skill or a value or an attitude is shrinking year by year. The new assumption about the purpose of education...is that it is to produce autonomous *lifelong* learners...the development of the skills of self-directed inquiry rather than the inculcation of subject-matter content.[125]

Knowles went on to state that tertiary institutions should therefore be "primarily educational brokers...linking autonomous learners with appropriate learning resources." Of course, nearly thirty years later, that is precisely what online resources do, from YouTube videos that teach how to frame a house or MOOCs that teach coding. Instead of learning by being taught in a classroom, students must learn to learn, by first determining what they need to know, where and how to find helpful resources, and assess their learning.

Further, the kind of learning that self-direction produces is deeper, characterized by "mastery of concepts and a firm hold on detailed factual knowledge in a given subject area," rather than "low-quality learning...geared to short term requirements, [focused] on the need faithfully to reproduce fragments of information."

> Deep learning "occurred most often in contexts characterised by freedom in learning, less formality, good teaching input, a good social climate and clear goals. By comparison surface or rote learning approaches are more likely to occur where there are heavy

---

[124] Ibid.
[125] Ibid.

workloads."[126]

This seems fairly self-evident, until we realize how frequently teachers test students on rote learning and conduct classes with rigid top-down structures and rules that penalize students for petty behavioral and legalistic issues like tardiness or failure to skip a line on the paper or create the proper margins. This is a flagrant misuse of the teacher's power, has no basis in best pedagogical practices, belittles and disempowers students and quite effectively serves both to encourage the acceptance of authoritarian structures in which students have no ability to participate or change and develop strong feelings of aversion to learning in general. The fact that in more selective colleges, students have considerably fewer such restrictions than in community colleges demonstrates that the practice clearly reflects and reinforces privileges of class.

Management guru Peter Drucker wrote that our age will be notable to historians not for its technology, the Internet, or any of the other things that might spring to mind, but rather for its "unprecedented change in the human condition." Until the modern era, individuals' work followed from jobs their parents had and jobs were divided by gender. Now, in contrast, with the rise of the knowledge worker, for the first time in history, people have choices, many careers over a lifetime, and will need to manage themselves. "And," Drucker insists, "Society is totally unprepared for it."[127] That's just the beginning. In the fourth quarter of 2013, 90% of the new jobs created in Britain were classed as self-employment.[128] Beyond Drucker's celebrated knowledge worker, the sharing and on-demand economy exemplified by Uber and Airbnb encourages individuals to essentially be their own companies, capitalize on their assets (e.g. knowledge, car and an extra room), build their brand through an online presence that conveys something of value to some segment of the population and that is supported by associations with other strong brands, positive user reviews and/or engagement in forums.

Educators certainly aren't going to prepare students for this reality by training them to conform to the rigid order and structure that was suited to preparation for participation in an industrial economy. Instead, we must train our future knowledge worker/individual brand to manage and regulate themselves, connect, collaborate, determine market needs and creatively respond, etc. We can

[126] Quoted from Boud and Higgs, p. 8, in Entwistle, N. J. and P. Ramsden. *Understanding Student Learning.* Croom Helm, 1983.

[127] Drucker, Peter F. "Managing Knowledge Means Managing Oneself." *Leader to Leader.* Peter F. Drucker Foundation. Spring 2000.

[128] "On Their Own." *The Economist.* 12 Apr. 2014. Web. 03 Jan. 2015.

best help students when they have a say in what they study, how they learn, and how they assess mastery. When students feel they have agency, they learn better. Learning contracts are a brilliant means of accomplishing this. We shall see an example of one later in this chapter, but briefly, in a learning contract, the overarching learning objective is broadly defined and the student determines or negotiates how he or she will demonstrate mastery of the objective.

There is yet another basis for ensuring that students have more choice and control over their education and environment. In her splendid book, *The Art of Choosing*, social psychologist Sheena Iyengar cites a number of studies that demonstrate the importance of choice and control to wellbeing. The Whitehall Studies, for example, of more than 10,000 British civil servants, found that, after accounting for other factors, "employees in the lowest pay grade...were twice as likely to die from heart disease" as workers in the highest-grade. Why? Scientists found that "the less control people had over their work, the higher their blood pressure during work hours." In comparison with the better-paid workers who had a great deal more stress and responsibility, but more autonomy, "they experienced more back pain, missed more days of work due to illness in general and had higher rates of mental illness." In effect, they exhibited "the human equivalent" of stereotypy, the kind of desperate self-soothing behavior of animals in captivity.[129]

Our students usually have their entire days prescribed for them, as well as when to sit (usually for far too long), when to rise, even when to use the toilet! They are beset daily by trivial rules and regulations and constant consequences. There is surely no wonder that 11% of adolescents have a depressive disorder by age 18,[130] 42% of college students report anxiety and 36% report depression as a "pressing concern."[131] Instead, imagine a classroom in which students and staff together formulate broad norms of conduct by which they will abide, the students encourage and check one another toward compliance for the common good, and the students and staff treat one another with mutual respect.

Many schools' mission statements and service programs profess the aspiration that students will contribute to the community. As we shall see in the discussion of service learning in Chapter 7, serving the community is not limited to making sandwiches in a soup kitchen. It is drilling deeper to discern the causes of

---

[129] Iyengar, Sheena. *The Art of Choosing*. NY: Twelve, 2010., p. 15.
[130] "Depression in Children and Adolescents (Fact Sheet)." *NIMH RSS*. Web. 29 Dec. 2014.
[131] "College students' mental health is a growing concern, survey finds." *American Psychological Association*. 44.4 (June 2013). 29 Dec. 2014.

that which challenges or threatens the common good, understanding the structures that undergird the system for good or ill, and being active participants in making the world a better place for their having been in it. We educators share the responsibility of engaging students in that process and we should certainly be assessing whether we are doing this well.

In *Bowling Alone,* Robert Putnam reports that community participation has dropped by 40% since the 1960s. The rate of voting among 18-29 year olds dropped from 29% in 1974 to 21% in 2014.[132] We should not be surprised that this is the result when our schools are run in a way that is top-down, with technology serving as a kind of opium of the masses, and individual students having little to no say in what happens during the school day, far less their academic experience in general. Students should have ample opportunities for leadership, for collaboration, and for participating in and appreciating the democratic process. The weekly Democratic Meeting at Brooklyn Free School affords such a venue:

> The Democratic Meeting is the heart and soul of Brooklyn Free School. Once a week the entire school comes together to make announcements, voice concerns, discuss problems, and work together to improve the daily functioning of the school. During these meetings, students learn democracy by practicing democracy. Meetings are chaired or moderated by students. Anyone can create an agenda item or topic to be discussed. Proposals are made and can be passed with a two-thirds vote in favor. Everyone who regularly teaches at or attends the school, from the five-year-old students to the oldest staff member or parent volunteer, has one vote.[133]

While the Free School movement may be too revolutionary in its democracy for many school administrators, it is imperative that they be aware of students' capabilities for self governance, far beyond the usual titular student government that doesn't dream of making any real change or wielding any real power and that the administration holds in firm check.

---

[132] http://www.civicyouth.org/quick-facts/youth-voting/

[133] http://www.brooklynfreeschool.org/our-program/ Listen to the students in action at http://www.thisamericanlife.org/radio-archives/episode/424/kid-politics?act=3#play; transcript at http://www.thisamericanlife.org/radio-archives/episode/424/transcript

Blended formats of instruction

The combination of online and face-to-face instruction can be subtle or revolutionary. The old way of doing this is integrating audio-visuals or software into class time. The newer ways of blended learning allow for the classes to be flipped, with lessons accessed online at the students' convenience and class time reserved for practice, help, and/or activities; or for classes to meet less frequently, which frees up time for students to engage in experiential activities beyond the school's walls, possibly leading to a much freer and flexible schedule.[134] Schools are also gamifying coursework and developing Skype global classrooms to work with sister, consortium, or partner schools in other countries.

On the tertiary level, this is already leading not only to the aforementioned unbundling, in which students take courses from a variety of sources like community college, MOOCs, and face-to-face courses, but also to an educational *bricolage,* in which students compile a portfolio of work combined with real-world experience. While some institutions like Charter Oak College and Exelsior College have sponsored competency-based credentials for decades, many universities are exploring further expansion in that area, particularly for adult learners. Demonstrating competency through diverse means may increasingly trump the credit hour since students clearly do not absorb information by osmosis or just by being present in a seat. Their ability to demonstrate competency through portfolio assessment, examination, projects, etc. is far more valuable.

Shattuck-St. Mary's School (MN) has an innovative model described on its website and reprinted here with permission:

Why Blended Learning at Shattuck-St. Mary's? [By Courtney Cavellier]

Blended learning provides new opportunities for individualized instruction for students, while preserving the best of classroom instruction.

• Teachers can use twice-weekly course meeting time for activities, like discussions, guided practice with concepts, and hands-on projects, and use online components for information delivery.
• Teachers can differentiate through one-on-one sessions, student-led study

---

[134] Currently one of the best books on innovative practices in education: Bowen, José Antonio. *Teaching Naked: How Moving Technology Out of Your College Classroom Will Improve Student Learning.* Jossey-Bass, 2012.

groups, and online components.

• Blended learning meets the needs of all kinds of students as students can adjust for their individual strengths and weaknesses in different disciplines. Students can adjust the pace and time commitment, depending on their comfort and competency. Students who need more time in an area can seek out their teachers for additional support; students who want enrichment can move quickly through course material and seek enrichment opportunities in disciplines of interest under the mentorship of their teachers or focus on other disciplines that are more difficult for them.

Blended learning is truly a college preparatory model.

• The leap from a fully structured 12th grade year to a first year schedule in college is significant, and the traditional high school schedule does not provide a transition that gradually prepares students for this leap.
• In blended courses, students prepare for the college model of classes while still within the structure of boarding school. In college, classes rarely meet daily! In blended courses, students are expected to engage during class and independently manage work during the rest of the week, with the ongoing support of their teachers.
• Students learn how best to manage their time on days which are less structured, but with the same daily access to faculty they have always had.
• Advisors are on active-duty, overseeing progress and letting go over time.
• Students are ready for the new challenges of college through increased independence in 11th and 12th grade.

Blended learning opens up the weekly high school schedule to allow students to explore and develop new areas of academic interest and collaborate with peers as part of their whole academic experience.

• Students have time to delve into established interests and explore new areas of interest.
• Students have time to share passions, talents, and work with others and to collaborate and grow with peers.
• Students have time and increased opportunities to give back to the community.
• In a fully blended model,...students have time to hold an internship opportunity in Faribault or other cities; participate in extended community service commitments; focus on independent research projects, including scientific research; or work in the weCreate Center, developing innovative products, solving

complex problems collaboratively, or exploring and developing their skills in a variety of multi-media studios.

Blended learning facilitates the development of 21st Century Skills, which our students will need to succeed in the world ahead.

- We *do not know* what the world will look like 10 years from now, when our students are beginning their careers. Our responsibility remains to facilitate their development into adults who will succeed in the world, which means we need to adapt the academic experience to the preparation they need.
- Blended learning provides increased opportunities for collaborative problem solving, creativity and innovation, and digital, media, and technical literacy.
- Blended learning enhances our long-established commitment to the development of critical thinking and critical reading skills, strong oral and written communication, and strong mathematics skills.
- The increased independence required by blended learning helps students develop the resilience and adaptability necessary to succeed in an ever changing world, where new careers and jobs emerge faster than schools and colleges can adapt.

Blended learning is a new approach to teaching and learning, and we are excited to watch our school grow as the world around us changes. Our upper school students need rigorous college preparation that includes the instruction of our teachers, increased practice with the independence required of them in college, and opportunities to develop the skills that will best prepare them for success beyond the arch. [135]

Students in this blended learning experience at Shattuck-St. Mary's are experiencing authentic agency. They learn to be independent and proactive, they develop the time management skills so important to success in college and beyond. They are likely to have less stress. They have the opportunity to collaborate, explore interests, engage in internships, and be responsible for themselves, an enormous advantage over students whose every minute is programmed for them.

Today's students are likely to take online courses at some point, whether in college or beyond, so it makes sense to acclimate them to the format. Students can

---

[135] www.s-sm.org/live/files/83-why-the-blended-learning-model

access instructional material and collaborate with their colleagues via smart phone at their convenience, which can lead to delicious flexibility for the schedule.

Schedule

Until such time as more schools arrive at the vision portrayed in the Day of the Life vignette, blended learning can free up the schedule enormously to accommodate imaginative and experiential programming, but even without any online component, schools' schedules can be far more functional than they are currently. Schools reveal their gridlock of imagination when they adhere resolutely to the eight period a day model and spend years mulling over other options, unable to make the change when there is an endless array of better ways to schedule classes, dozens of templates available, and thousands of pages of research supporting the advantages to longer class periods when preceded by training for teachers in using the time effectively.

Some schools elect to implement a 4 x 4 plan, in which students study four courses in the fall and four other courses in the spring. There is the less common trimester 2 x 2 plan. Subjects such as Math and World Languages that scaffold strongly and depend upon retention of previously apprehended information may suffer in these plans since students might not have the practice time they need during the off semester unless there is creative reinforcement, perhaps online. The Copernican plan remedies this neatly with two courses each trimester for half the day and World Languages and Math held for half the day. More common is the A/B plan, in which students study four courses on A days alternated with another four on B days. Naturally, there are infinite permutations of these to accommodate individual schools' cultures and needs and to achieve the objectives of improving learning and school climate, and increasing engagement, achievement, and collaboration.

The increased instructional time permits students to delve more deeply into concepts, focus attention, and engage in projects, creative activities, and experiential learning off site. Stress is mitigated since students need to prepare for fewer classes each day, the pace of the school day is relaxed, and discipline improves because there are fewer transitions. Students and teachers have increased time for collaboration. While science and art classes particularly benefit from time for lab and project work, all subjects certainly can.[136]

---

[136] See a) "Block Scheduling: Innovations With Time." (1998). *Brown University Education Alliance*. Web. 5 Jan. 15;

The Importance of Daily Downtime

There is an enormous body of research dating back nearly a century to support breaks between complex cognitive tasks. Benefits range from social, emotional, and cognitive development, as documented by the American Association of Pediatrics[137] to the ability to "increase productivity, replenish attention, solidify memories and encourage creativity."[138] All students benefit from having a scheduled preparation period, study hall, or time built into the day to prepare for assignments and assessments, to review material and reflect on their understanding, to ask questions about material that they may not fully grasp, and to learn time management skills. At the very least, students should have an extended lunch period that permits time to wait in line, obtain a meal, sit and converse with peers, and perhaps get some physical exercise, the benefits of which to academic performance (and general wellbeing) are well known.[139] Upon its implementation, students' achievement often improves dramatically because they are able to complete assignments while supported academically at school and spend their time after school on extra-curricular events, athletics, and family time. With less homework, students are more likely to get enough sleep, which dozens of studies show to be the root cause of poor achievement, behavioral issues, ADHD, and various other factors that impede students from realizing their potential.

It is imperative to understand that if the preparation period becomes an opt-in (students must register for it) rather than an opt-out class, meaning that the default value is not to have one, students who opt to take it will be penalized in the college admissions process for choosing an "easier" slate of courses. If the default is to have the preparation period and students must petition for permission to opt out, there is no such penalty. Even extremely motivated students benefit from the preparation period. They are able to complete assignments, collaborate with peers, confer with teachers, read, and have precious downtime. Driven by college

---

b) Queen, J. Allen. *The Block Scheduling Handbook.* Thousand Oaks, CA: Corwin, 2003. Print; c) Zepeda, Sally J., and R. Stewart Mayers. "An Analysis of Research on Block Scheduling." *Review of Educational Research* 76.1 (2006): 137-70.

[137] Ginsburg, Kenneth. "The Importance of Play in Promoting Healthy Child Development and Maintaining Strong Parent-Child Bonds." *American Association of Pediatrics*, Jan. 2007. Web. 7 Jan. 2014.

[138] Jabr, Ferris. "Why Your Brain Needs More Downtime." *Scientific American Global RSS.* 15 Oct. 2013. Web. 07 Jan. 2015.

[139] Several articles dealing with the ways that physical activity support academic performance can be found on the Spark website: http://www.sparkpe.org/physical-education-resources/academics-physical-activity/

admissions anxiety, some parents and students will insist on students taking an extra course in lieu of the preparation period, and those cases must be handled sensitively, in ways appropriate to the individual student, and with explanation about the admissions process and the value of downtime to learning and wellbeing.

...But Not A Whole Summer

Beyond the issue of the daily schedule is that of the calendar year. Considerable research has been conducted for over a century, with more current studies from leading research institutions including Johns Hopkins,[140] the Rand Corporation, the Wallace Foundation, and many others, indicating that students who do not engage in educational activities over the summer experience learning losses and return to school in September at least one month behind where they were in June and two or more months behind in mathematical computation skills.[141] There is enormous interest, especially among charter schools, in year-round schooling, in view of the fact that the agrarian planting and harvesting impetus no longer applies. There are currently over 3,000 year-round public schools in the US, enrolling 10% of public school students.[142] It merits further consideration by independent school stakeholders.

Aside from year-round schooling, many public schools require extensive summer curricula for students to complete independently, though it is often limited to those preparing for AP courses, rather than the students who may need the practice most, an untenable choice in view of the research. In order to ensure that students continue to progress academically during the summer, students should be expected to complete some assignments that are specific preparation for classes and others to develop their skills. (See descriptions of Summer Assignments in Appendix Section III). The online math program, ALEKS, utilizes artificial intelligence to create an individualized program of instruction to build precisely those skills that a student most needs to develop—and tracks when students log in and for how long they work. It is ideal for use during the summer. An online interface can be set up to permit students to log in to a summer assignment portal and ensure that they meet benchmarks to completion

---

[140] McLaughlin, Brenda, and Jeffrey Smink. "Why Summer Learning Deserves a Front-Row Seat in the Education Reform Arena." *School of Education at Johns Hopkins University-Why Summer Learning Deserves a Front-Row Seat in the Education Reform Arena.* Spring 2010. Web. 17 Mar. 2015.
[141] Cooper, Harris, et al. "The Effects of Summer Vacation on Achievement Test Scores: A Narrative and Meta-Analytic Review." *Review of Educational Research* 66.3 (1996): 227-68.
[142] http://www.statisticbrain.com/year-round-school-statistics/

along the way, rather than in a rush in the days before classes resume. With adequate discussion of the rationale and the promise of support on-site, through email, Skype and phone, summer assignments can become an expected and valued part of the academic program, one that presents considerable comparative advantage for the extensive academic preparation of students.

Innovative Use of Space

The way that space has been configured in schools and corporate offices has been cyclical and reflected the method and philosophy of the enterprise. Early schools were constructed for safety, permanence, and endurance. With the progressive era, the desire emerged for more air, light, connection to the outdoors and circulation through the building and indeed, the absence of doors and the ability to observe classroom activity remains integral to the philosophy in a number of progressive schools. In some schools and classrooms, the orientation of the desks shifted from squarely teacher-centric to the discussion circle (including the Harkness method) with students facing one another, to desks and chairs on casters to enable frequent reconfiguring for pairs and group work. With so much technology in the classroom, the needs of today's schools have shifted again to include glare reduction, better noise abatement, desks with electrical outlets, and high-speed networking. Security, indoor air quality, and sustainability in terms of building materials and energy consumption are further concerns.

As individualized instruction through distance learning expands, students need places to work both independently and alongside other students who all access the same instructional aid. Libraries have already changed dramatically since the Internet, e-books, and online databases exponentially reduce storage needs. Many have been transformed into maker spaces or information commons, where students may have quiet space to work and group space to collaborate, where they may access more specialized equipment like 3-D printers, or meet with librarians for research and information literacy instruction.

The open plan in offices like Google's is finding expression in the design of new schools with more flexible, multipurpose and open space, yet the history of open plan office space has not been a happy one and gave rise to cubicle farms in the late 1960s. Noise, privacy, and concentration remain persistent concerns, but the influence of Silicon Valley on design is far-reaching. Cornell Tech, a collaborative enterprise between Cornell University and Technion-Israel Institute of Technology, to be located on New York City's Roosevelt Island, is planning to have "large, uninterrupted spaces" with few classrooms and no faculty offices, just office zones with workstations with "huddle room" enclosures, in "an attempt to break down traditional academic boundaries." [143] Revitalized and reformed pedagogy necessitates a similar shift in the design of the space where it occurs.

Collaboration

There are innumerable benefits in both classroom and eventual workplace to students developing the ability to collaborate and work effectively with others on a team. [144] Students working in small groups take more responsibility for their learning, perform at higher levels, experience deeper learning, retain more information longer and are more satisfied with their classes. The effectiveness of students teaching other students or submitting their work for critique to peers has also been documented time and again. Working in groups also exposes students to other perspectives and challenges their own interpretations. In addition to working on projects, there are many resources available to integrate cooperative and collaborative experiences into the traditional classroom. [145]

There is a great deal for students to learn as they cultivate the skills to wisely select team members (i.e. ability rather than affinity); determine strengths and weaknesses and how best to distribute tasks; understand group process (forming, storming, norming, performing); manage and resolve conflicts; hold one another accountable; motivate, monitor, and evaluate one another; and maintain collegiality throughout the process. In early experiences of group work, parents often attempt to insert themselves and demand staff intervention over some distress, often a perceived inequality in workload or responsibility, and staff must be extremely sensitive but emphatic regarding the importance of students learning to deal

[143] Wolfman-Arent, Ari. "How Do You Plan the Campus of the Future? Try Not To." *The Chronicle of Higher Education.* 18 July 2014. Web. 05 Jan. 2015.

[144] See a) Baumeister, Roy F., and Mark R. Leary. "The need to belong: desire for interpersonal attachments as a fundamental human motivation." *Psychological bulletin* 117.3 (1995): 497.
b) Cohen, E. G. Restructuring the classroom: Conditions for productive small groups. *Review of Educational Research* 64.1 (1994): 1–35.
c) Nestojko, John F., et al. "Expecting to Teach Enhances Learning and Organization of Knowledge in Free Recall of Text Passages." *Memory & Cognition* 42.7 (2014): 1038-48.
d) Webb, N. M. Peer interaction and learning in small groups. *International Journal of Educational Research,* 13 (1989): 21–39.
e) Vygotsky, Lev. S. *Mind in society: The development of higher psychological processes.* Harvard University Press, 1989.

[145] See Karre, Idahlynn. *Busy, Noisy, and Powerfully Effective: Cooperative Learning Tools in the College Classroom.* Greely, CO: U of Northern Colorado, Dept. of Speech Communication, 1994. Print. This is equally as useful in the secondary classroom as it is in college.

independently with issues as they arise and intervene only when absolutely necessary. The group work assessment rubric in Appendix Section VI can be extremely helpful at benchmarks or final reckoning.

Learning to work collaboratively and develop soft skills is essential as teamwork is part of today's employment landscape. Different experts work together, often virtually, each bringing his or her own perspectives and strengths to bear on a problem or opportunity. "Increasingly, teams are considered the engines of innovation and creativity that lead to future products and services."[146] The ability to function effectively as part of a self-regulating team is vital for success in the 21st century.

Individualized Instruction

The independent school community has long emphasized its ability to provide individualized instruction and attention to students to help them reach their fullest potential, and the expectations of both parents and students in that regard continue to rise. We know that experiencing success in personally meaningful work affects students' achievement.

> One of the strongest predictors of children's performance in school is individual differences in their perceived control....Experimental studies show that changes in children's perceptions of efficacy, contingency, and control do in fact produce changes in quality and persistence of problem solving and performance on academic tasks (e.g., Diener and Dweck 1978; Dweck 1991; Schunk 1991; Seligman 1975).[147]

Any of us blossoms when we feel we have control and we feel successful. Surely we should endeavor to provide that for our students.

There is such an array of computer-assisted means of differentiating tasks

---

[146] Schramm, Jennifer and Steve Williams. "Innovative Work Teams in a Challenging Business Environment." *Society for Human Resource Management*. 2009. Web. 6 Jan 2015

[147] Skinner, E.A., M.J. Zimmer-Gembeck, J.P. Connell, J.S. Eccles, and J.G. Wellborn. "Individual differences and the development of perceived control." *Monographs of the Society for Research in Child Development*. 63.2/3 (1998): 1–231 Quoted in Yeh, Stuart. "Understanding and Addressing the Achievement Gap through Individualized Instruction and Formative Assessment." *Assessment in Education: Principles, Policy & Practice* 17.2 (2010): 169-82.

and content to tailor them to individual students' abilities that there is no excuse for one-size-fits-all education. Online videos, activities, and entire courses may be used for further enrichment. Another means of differentiating instruction involves the integration of the consistent practice of assessing students' understanding prior to, during, and after instruction.

A highly effective student-centered method of differentiating within the classroom is Kathie Nunley's Layered Curriculum, which features a learning contract that "integrates the three keys: choice, accountability, and increasingly complex thinking."

> To write a layered lesson plan, the teacher simply takes the main concepts, tasks, and skills that need to be taught in a lesson and divides them into three layers based on the complexity of the task, along the lines of Bloom's Taxonomy. Simple, basic concepts go into the C layer; more complex thinking skills in the B layer; and the most complex, higher level thinking skills go in the A layer....Each layer provides a menu of assignment choices that represent different learning styles, abilities, and disability accommodations. Students can choose which assignments they'd like to complete...work their way through the increasingly complex layers, and all assignments require an oral defense. [148]

Example of a Layered Curriculum Unit

Bacteria (Kingdom Monera)

NAME_____DUE DATE_____Points possible: 100

C Layer: Section I- Basic Understanding (65 points maximum)

1. Take notes from daily presentations. (5 pts. /day. MUST BE PRESENT)
2. Watch the DVD on bacteria. Take notes. Include information on bacteria shape and arrangement and ways to prevent bacteria growth (15 points)
3. Using materials of your choice, make a three-dimensional model of a prokaryotic cell. (10 points)

---

[148] Nunley, Kathie F. "Giving Credit Where Credit is Due." *Principal Leadership*. 3.9 (May 2003). Web. 7 Jan 15.

4. Make 15 vocabulary flash cards using the vocabulary terms from this unit. Be able to define the terms IN YOUR OWN WORDS. (10 points)
5. Read Chapter 20 in HBJ. Be able to answer all the "Reviewing the Section" questions. (15 points)
6. Using construction paper and plain paper, make a 10-page children's book on 10 ways to prevent bacterial infections. Illustrate your book. (15 points)
7. Answer question 15-20 on page 312 of the HBJ book. (10 points)
8. Write two paragraphs, one on ways bacteria are helpful to humans and one on ways bacteria are harmful to humans. This MUST be done in a language other than English. (10 points)
9. Pass a quiz on the shapes and arrangements of bacteria. (10 points)
10. Research three types of bacterial infection: botulism, tetanus, and strep throat. Write a small, half-page report on each. List your sources of information. (15 points)

B Layer: Section II- Labs (15 points each) Choose one. These must be done in class!

1. Which surface in the school contains the most bacteria? Which the least? Using a plate with agar, swab and streak between 5 and 7 sources of bacteria around the school. Describe your colonies using the correct terms. Compare and contrast them.
2. Does hand washing reduce bacteria numbers? Prove your hypothesis using fingerprints and a plate with agar.
3. Do current face cleansers reduce bacteria present on the face? Use a plate with agar, face cleansers, and the *Staphylococcus epidermis's* from the tip of your nose. Describe the colonies.

A Layer: Section III- Use an A-Layer Assignment sheet to analyze one of these issues. (20 points)

1. What issues are we currently facing due to the overuse of antibiotics?
2. Would a campaign to encourage hand washing reduce the rate of illness at our school?
3. What role should government play in making our meat safe to eat?

Grading Scale: 86+ = A, 71-85= B, 56-70 = C, 40-55 = D

NOTE: You will have a 50-point exam on this unit on
_____.

(More sample units are available at http://help4teachers.com). Reprinted with permission from Dr. Kathie Nunley.

The advantages to this system are clear. Through the learning contract and layering, students understand the overarching learning objective and have the opportunity to determine how they will demonstrate mastery of it. They have the ability to select their assignment (see other examples of alternative assessments in the Appendix Section IV), and teachers may permit students to generate their own tasks in lieu of or in addition to those listed. Students using Layered Curriculum evince far more self-efficacy, interest, and engagement than those merely taking quizzes and tests.

Authentic Assessment

Observe an athletic team at practice with a skilled and nurturing coach. The students are enthusiastic, attentive and eager to follow the coach's specific recommendations, which can be critical, but are viewed in the spirit of helping students to improve. Students are cheered on by coach and peers when they make the recommended alteration to achieve greater individual and team success. Compare this with the usual system of grading, in which students receive instruction, take a test, receive a grade, repeat. There is no opportunity for the student to receive specific recommendations regarding areas for improvement, nor is there incentive, since the next unit looms. Also lacking is any social dimension, which is developmentally so important to adolescents.

There are thousands of pages of peer-reviewed research recommending a dramatic shift from the practices that have persisted through the ages, and yet we aren't applying it for the same reasons that we fail to implement so many other best pedagogical practices. First, it has been well documented that teachers teach as they were taught,[149] though it should be noted that educators who are committed to constant improvement in their professional practice seek to add skills to their skill

---

[149] Oleson, Amanda, and Matthew T. Hora. "Teaching the Way they were Taught? Revisiting the Sources of Teaching Knowledge and the Role of Prior Experience in Shaping Faculty Teaching Practices." *Higher Education*. 68.1 (2014): 29-45.

set. Second,

> Although influential organizations and education thought-leaders have reached a general consensus about the benefits of formative assessment, teacher education and training efforts lag behind. As research has shown, teachers get little training or support in assessment and often turn to their untrained peers for information (Black & Wiliam, 1998; Shepard, 2000; Stiggins, 2001, 2002).[150]

We in independent schools must deliver on our promise to offer our students a better quality experience than they can receive elsewhere. We must do the very important work of assessment better in particular, since it has enormous potential to build up or to tear down. When executed well, it can help students to improve their skills and learn how to learn. Poorly, it can be punitive and destructive, turning them off to a subject, to the school, or to learning and causing them to lose faith in their abilities and worth.

> Instead of encouraging true learning, the current practices have other effects, summarized by Alfie Kohn in his essential essay "From Degrading to De-Grading."

> Grades "reduce students' interests in the learning itself....preference for challenging tasks....and....the quality of students' thinking." They aren't "valid, reliable, or objective," they "encourage cheating," "spoil relationships" [of all kinds: teachers-students, between students, with parents, among teachers, etc.] and they "distort the curriculum."[151]

None of this should come as a surprise. Simply put, grades are not the most effective means of achieving the objective of *learning* that we educators claim to set for them. "The tests used by teachers encourage rote and superficial learning even when teachers say they want to develop understanding; many teachers seem unaware of the inconsistency."[152] Rather than serving as a feedback loop that enables students to improve and teachers to reach them more effectively, grades often serve to comply with classroom administrative functions and ratify students' beliefs in their inability to learn.

---

[150] Greenstein, Laura. *What Teachers Really Need to Know about Formative Assessment.* Alexandria, VA: ASCD, 2010. Print.

[151] Kohn, Alfie. "From Degrading to De-Grading." *High School Magazine* 6.5 (1999): 38.

[152] Black, Paul, and Dylan Wiliam. "Inside the Black Box: Raising Standards through Classroom Assessment." *The Phi Delta Kappan* 80.2 (1998): 139-48.

Formative assessment is the performance of a variety of formal and informal means of assessment prior to instruction and during instruction in order to modify instructional strategies to improve students' achievement of learning objectives. Its value is well established in the research and yet it is not performed with any consistency in schools. A required reading for educators, the review by Paul Black and Dylan Wiliams of over 250 studies on assessment concludes

> There is a body of firm evidence that formative assessment is an essential component of classroom work and that its development can raise standards of achievement. We know of no other way of raising standards for which such a strong prima facie case can be made.[153]

Teachers use formative assessment to improve their teaching strategies and scaffold appropriate learning experiences for students. Students learn to use teachers' assessments and develop their own ways of evaluating their personal skills and knowledge. As Greenstein states in *What Teachers really Need to Know about Formative Assessment,* her superb book that belongs in every professional development collection, formative assessment

- Allows for purposeful selection of strategies
- Embeds assessment in instruction
- Guides instructional decisions
- Emphasizes learning outcomes
- Makes goals and standards transparent to students
- Provides clear assessment criteria
- Provides feedback that is comprehensible, actionable, and relevant
- Provides valuable diagnostic information by generating informative data

Formative assessment helps teachers
- Consider each student's learning needs and styles and adapt instruction accordingly
- Track individual student achievement
- Provide appropriately challenging and motivational instructional activities
- Design intentional and objective student self-assessments
- Offer all students opportunities for improvement[154]

---

[153] Ibid.

[154] Greenstein, Laura. *What Teachers Really Need to Know about Formative Assessment.* Alexandria, VA: ASCD, 2010. Print.

Similarly, the assessment of students before instruction is imperative yet infrequently performed, which is curious since, as Greenstein indicates, "pre-assessment is a routine part of most people's jobs": taking vital signs in a doctor's office, performing diagnostic tests in an auto repair garage, checking inventory in retail. Pre-assessment reveals "predispositions, values, and beliefs" and the sources from which those were acquired, helps both teacher and student to be more conscious of what they already know, and guides planning. It also "activates prior knowledge" to help students make connections to what they already know.

Formative assessment takes place during instruction as well to guide and support teaching and learning. When conducted collaboratively, formative assessment can develop students' abilities to reflect upon and evaluate their own progress and changes in their "predispositions, values, and beliefs." Teachers help students to identify areas that need additional work and develop opportunities to address them. There are many effective ways to perform assessment. Greenstein's book details fifty discrete techniques for use prior to, during, and following instruction.

Portfolios and rubrics represent other best practices related to assessment. When students compile portfolios of their best work, they, their teachers, and their parents are able to authentically document progress over time far more effectively than a test, which, like a snapshot, merely demonstrates performance at a single sitting. Well-constructed rubrics demonstrate the criteria for success and the learning target. They reduce the subjectivity of evaluation and provide students with a much clearer understanding of performance expectations. They can be an indispensable part of the learning culture and an excellent means to foster students' efficacy and control. Sample rubrics for many types of activities are available in the Appendix Section VI.

Summative grade comments, those issued at the conclusion of a term, are a tradition in independent schools. (Guidelines from a fifty-year veteran of independent schools are provided in Part II of this chapter). They are an expected and valued means of communicating with parents about the progress of their students but they are also a vital means of demonstrating that adults at the school truly know the student, hold him or her in positive regard, and are committed to helping him or her attain success. Rather than the boilerplate comments that public school teachers may simply select from a menu, in independent schools, the writing of narrative assessments is a well-regarded art.

71

It is a mere baby step not the imagined giant leap to substitute these narratives for letter or number grades. Narratives provide students (and parents) a clear prescription for what and how to improve. Students learn to regard assessment as "a useful tool for growth, rather than simply a teacher-determined statement on 'how they are doing.'"[155] Frequent feedback is considerably more helpful than assessment that occurs only at the end of the term, which educators call "summative."

It is not, by and large, that school administrators dispute the merits of changing the current system of letter grades on pedagogical grounds. They merely feel that there is no choice due to the requirements of college admissions. Let me be clear: **the use of grades is not an imperative for college admissions**. Period. Narrative assessments can be used and in fact are used in some schools. College and university admissions offices adjust, and not just the small private colleges. I have had this discussion with state flagship universities and they have assured me that they want the best-qualified students and they will review narrative comments in lieu of letter or number grades.

The curious outlier in my poll was a state scholarship program that required a GPA in order to consider students. It is here that the system truly reveals its absurdity. When I explained that our school's educational philosophy eschewed grades, the representative insisted that the agency needed a grade or GPA, which could be derived from a single class. I asked if a grade from another institution would count. Affirmative. I then pressed as to whether a student who earned an A in a single online AP course could count that as a GPA of A plus the added weight for the AP. Affirmative again. I checked one last time for understanding: that is, a student in a high school that doesn't issue grades, only narrative assessments, but who takes a single online AP course and receives a grade of A will have a higher GPA for the purposes of the scholarship than a student in another high school who has taken twelve AP courses and earned all A- grades? Affirmative, she assured me. Clearly this is a system that is ripe for gaming and a major overhaul.

It bears reiterating: there are high schools that do not issue grades and their students go on to even the most highly selective colleges and universities. Among these there is a variety of procedures. Some use only narrative assessments. Some use narrative assessments and then convert these to a GPA. It can be done and should at least be a matter for consideration.

---

[155] Bagley, Sylvia S. "High School Students' Perceptions of Narrative Evaluations as Summative Assessment." *American Secondary Education.* 36.3 (2008): 15-32.

Part II: Effective Communication With Parents: General Guidelines for Writing Effective Summative Narrative Assessments/ Grade Reports

By Wellington J. Ramsey, III © 2015
Reprinted with permission

Teachers' written comments are a direct communication to your students and their parents. They are one measure of your professional competence. The comments you write often say more about you than they do about your students. Parents and students have a right to clear, correct, concise, and meaningful comments which touch upon the student's strengths as well as weaknesses, positive aspects of the student's progress as well as negative ones. A few points to remember:

1. Comments should be faultless in mechanics: sentence structure, spelling, capitalization, and punctuation.
2. Comments should be free of triteness, clichés, and sarcasm.
3. Effective comments, whenever possible, should focus on four major areas of the student's performance. Obviously, your comment can expand beyond the four to include, for example, a humorous anecdote highlighting the individual's performance. From the standpoint of practicality, not every comment can include all four areas, but if writers will consider all four and include as many as possible, the quality of their comments should improve.

   a. Academic accomplishments: measured against the curriculum including an expansion or explanation of the numerical achievement average.
   b. Attitude: including interest in the subject matter, relationship with classmates, and relationship with the teacher.
   c. Motivation: including enthusiasm, academic maturity, and academic stamina.
   d. Behavior: including your first-hand observation of the student's behavior in your academic class – a specific example wherever advisable.

We all know that attitude, motivation, and behavior are frequently interchangeable parts, one often functioning like a mathematical subset of another, but the purpose of dividing them into separate entities is to give the writer an opportunity to have at least four major areas of the student's performance to focus on.

Finally, and perhaps most importantly, if you write in your comment that a student is having some difficulty, it is definitely prudent on your part to offer some form of remediation, e.g., student conference, extra help, parent conference, recommending a tutor, changing sections, etc. We have all read comments that paint a grim academic picture without offering any solutions. My first reaction as a parent when I read such a pessimistic account was: "Well, what are you going to do about it?"

How Do I Start?

Having read the guidelines for writing good comments, you are probably saying to yourself "That's all well and good, but where do I start?" This question is more likely to be asked by a teacher who is facing the process for the first time; however, many experienced teachers I interviewed during my research admitted that they had had the same problem.

For the beginner, I recommend a rough draft. Few of us have the talent to blaze away for five or ten minutes and produce a finished copy that fulfills the guidelines previously mentioned. Although a somewhat tedious task, revision and editing of the rough draft will culminate in a more polished comment, and it will save the writer time in the long run.

- **Start making notes on each student early in the trimester.**
- Start filling in the top section of the grade report as early as possible.
- Start your rough draft as early as possible.
- Never wait until the night before they are due to write your final comments.
- Your topic sentence should make the most positive statement you can create about your student, if possible.

I cannot emphasize too strongly what a time saver this "student notes" ploy is. Teachers who have those notes readily available - and use it daily - already have thirty to forty percent of their comments at their fingertips. Why? Because an anecdote will enliven a comment faster and more effectively than any other strategy; also, the note or notes on that particular student will jog the writer's memory about that student's performance during the quarter. Filling in the top section of the grade report in advance, if possible, is a tremendous time saver. Final copies written at the eleventh hour usually read like eleventh hour comments.

Placement of a positive statement in your topic sentence accomplishes two things: first, it focuses your thinking on the admirable qualities or successful attainments of the student. By so doing, you will create an optimistic tone to your comment that will help you to offer enlightened remediation later in your comments. Second, the reader's first perception is that "...this teacher really knows my child...." Whatever negative aspects of the student's academic accomplishment, attitude, motivation, or behavior you bring up later, you have established a beachhead of rapport with the reader.

To avoid monotony and for stylistic purposes, you may wish to delay the positive statement until later in the body of your first paragraph, but the impact will be lost if you wait until the third or fourth sentence.

If there are any problem areas, these are better discussed later, perhaps in a second paragraph if you are writing a two-paragraph comment. We all know that some students are far easier to write about than others. We tend to write less about the highly motivated, straight A and more about the trouble-making, poorly motivated student.

- Plan ahead
- Start taking notes early
- Start with positive comments
- Include remediation whenever advisable

Your conclusion, whenever possible, should be optimistic. After all, you are a capable professional, and even though Johnny may be having some problems or difficulties, you can suggest some probable solutions that will begin to alleviate the problems. You can be guardedly optimistic in your last paragraph without predicting immediate or long-range success.

General Guideline: How To Avoid Writing Poor Comments

1. Poor comments are categorical judgments, absolute condemnations.
2. Poor comments are literary exercises on the writer's part.
3. Poor comments are confined to pat phrases or clichés.
4. Poor comments are an outline of the course.
5. Poor comments are biased by other teachers' remarks.
6. Poor comments are discussions of behavior of which you have no first-hand knowledge or observation.
7. Poor comments are psychological observations.
8. Poor comments are predictive of success or failure.
9. Poor comments are critical without suggestions for remediation.
10. Poor comments are those that make unsupported allegations.

11. Poor comments are those written at the eleventh hour.
12. Poor comments are those that compare a student to a sibling or to another student.

The above is an excerpt from Wally Ramsey's 34 page *Guide to Writing Comments*, which is used by independent schools across the country. It provides wise guidance and tips, examples of best [and worst] practices, and useful words and phrases. To acquire copies, contact Wally directly at WallyRamseyIII@comcast.net

Summary

The dramatic shifts in the education landscape provide independent schools with an unparalleled opportunity. Free from governmental constraints, we can adapt with great agility and implement practices and programs that will truly prepare our students for the realities of the 21st century. We must help students to learn to exercise autonomy responsibly and to collaborate effectively. We must be flexible and inventive regarding instructional formats, schedule, and space. With our freedom comes the responsibility to model evidence-based best practices in curriculum, especially individualized instruction with real-world applications, and authentic assessment to provide feedback that helps students learn and grow.

Chapter 4

Part I: What Can You Do Better Than Anyone?
Developing Signature Student-Centered Programs

The key to competing and surviving…is to focus your business into a niche or pocket where you can leverage your strengths in the local marketplace. —Michael Bergdahl

Looking Toward the Future

Librarians are only one of many professions that have experienced a severe downturn. Technology and outsourcing have replaced and will continue to replace many others, as has been the case for centuries. It has affected professions thought untouchable, like attorneys. Of the 44,000 law school graduates in 2012, only 56% found stable employment in law.[156] (Fittingly, alumni have litigated against law schools for failing to inform them of the employment reality prior to enrollment; perhaps doing so is their only opportunity to practice their skills).

As co-hosts of NPR's *Planet Money,* Alex Blumberg and Adam Davidson addressed a group of students with some advice:

> "The basic rules of the economy are changing. The safe career path is no longer so safe." They advised students to be nimble in their career plans and to accept the challenge to figure out "how you can add value" in the new economy. "You have absolute choice but no security," Davidson said, "You don't want to compete with a robot." Instead, he suggested that students look to careers that will require capacities of creativity, insight, or emotional intelligence. "Do things that are very human."[157]

In a similar vein, Robert Reich, Secretary of Labor during the Clinton administration, wrote an insightful article for *The New York Times* about the kind of education we need in the coming years. He discussed the radical shift in the new

---

[156] Weissmann, Jordan. "The Jobs Crisis at Our Best Law Schools Is Much, Much Worse Than You Think." *The Atlantic.* 9 Apr. 2013. Web. 16 Dec. 2014.
[157] Boss, Suzie. "In China, Students Come Face-to-Face with Global Issues." *Edutopia.* 25 Mar. 2014. Web. 16 Dec. 2014.

economy that has quite effectively "exploded the old job categories into a vast array of new niches, creating a kaleidoscope of ways to make a living."

> Yes, people need to be able to read, write and speak clearly. And they have to know how to add, subtract, multiply and divide. But given the widening array of possibilities, there's no reason that every child must master the sciences, algebra, geometry, biology or any of the rest of the standard high school curriculum that has barely changed in half a century.[158]

The economy has changed and hence how we prepare students to participate in it must change with it, and equally dramatically. Beyond that, as intellectual historian Daniel Rodgers points out in *The Age of Fracture* (2011), the market is the contemporary dominant metaphor for society. All that was once fixed is no longer. Further, in this dynamic environment, it is no easy feat to make the intellectual and imaginative leaps that are necessary. I know this from experience and I shall share a few personal anecdotes to illustrate the point.

Breadth, Depth and Liberal Arts Redux

For decades, I adamantly opposed the increasing specialization that is encouraged on various levels. The increase in schools of choice often means that students in grades six through twelve select a "major" in some field, from dance to computer science, in which they take most or all of their electives. On the tertiary level, I found the myopia astounding, especially in those colleges with open curricula. One junior described her field of inquiry *over four years* as "how theater spaces make audiences feel." This instantly registered in my mind as a Venn diagram with circles for Psychology, Architecture, and Theater, with her concentration as the Reuleaux triangle, that tiny overlapping intersection in the center. I asked about her background in the three fields and scorned her intellectual hubris when she revealed that she had none.

That was precisely the wrong reaction, conditioned by old paradigm thinking. The student was fascinated by her topic and it served as the springboard to exploration of the other fields as they pertained to her quest. That student had conducted hundreds of hours of research in those fields to answer her question. It

---

[158] Reich, Robert. "One Education Does Not Fit All." *The New York Times*. 10 July 2000. Web. 16 Dec. 2014.

was what we in information science would extol as the perfect educational matrix because the student was engaged in a quest of personal relevance; had to define the information problem and its parameters; gather resources; evaluate and confirm or disconfirm their validity; form a hypothesis; proceed through the deep intellectual work of thesis, antithesis, and synthesis; extrapolate; and create a professional product presenting her original work. She learned far more about her topic, as well as Psychology, Theater, and Architecture, than she quite likely would have from taking a smattering of courses. Scientists and scholars of all stripes have engaged in the same procedure for centuries to make glorious discoveries, but we are tied to the idea of the credit hour as the demonstration of engagement in a rational and systematic course of study. What utter nonsense.

We may be devoted adherents of the merits of a broad foundation of knowledge, but when we look to that powerful metaphor of the market, we see specialization is intertwined with capitalism. The repudiation of the division of labor was one of the major stumbling blocks of Marx and Engels' utopian ideology, for there appears to be no means to deny (or circumvent) its contribution to the rise of modern industrial society. The fact is that in higher education, as in society, the more specialized the study (or the scholar or the worker), the more significance accorded. And we all use our specialized knowledge, work, studies, and experience of life as a lens to view the world. Those lenses bend the light of information to focus narrowly, but they can also help us to see more clearly and broadly. Think about your lenses. From where do they come? How do they influence you?

I was fortunate to be a dedicated, intellectually omnivorous student in a high performing public high school in affluent suburban Connecticut with superb teachers. Over thirty years later, I still remember a great deal from tracing human history from the Neolithic Revolution through the Middle Ages, several of the short poems we had to memorize weekly as well as many of the exquisite literary pieces we studied in Spanish, a great many of the features of European history, including the paintings representative of specific periods, and much more. It is only recently that I was compelled to realize to my utter shock that my experience of remembering so much is rather uncommon.

Perhaps because I enjoyed my classes and teachers (though I hated everything else about the school—a dreary 70s concrete monstrosity with half the classrooms windowless), as an educator, **I promoted the goal of exposing students to the same things in order to ensure they had the cultural capital and the foundation for being an educated person, according to my**

definition. Students may never experience a World History class again after high school, so, I reasoned, it is our duty to expose them to, among other things, Athenian democracy that they may see the philosophical underpinnings of our own government; the Printing Press, so that they understand the role of technology and innovation in systemic social change; and to fine works of art like Jacques-Louis David's *Marat*, so that when they see the painting, they locate it within the context of the French Revolution. They may never have a Biology class again, so they must experience field science collection and laboratory analysis. The world is becoming more global and we cannot rely on the old imperialistic expectation that others should speak our language, so it is our duty to ensure that they can communicate in at least one other language. And students must understand that service is the rent we pay for living. I valued these things in my own life experience, so I felt they were important to promote in schools to our students.

Again, this was thinking rooted in the old paradigm. By overvaluing my experience and wanting to share it universally, I made the classic error akin to teaching how and what I was taught, one of the central problems with education. It no longer makes sense to cultivate in students some arbitrary body of knowledge once valued by the *ancien regime* to prepare them to participate in the old economy and its categories, or to operate from the premise that memorization was essential in order to be able to recall knowledge that was scarce and difficult to access. As Reich asserts, "…[T]oday's high school students…won't all be doing the same things, and they won't be drawing on the same body of knowledge."[159]

Tony Wagner makes the point that the modern high school curriculum is rooted in the early 20th century, **when information resources were scarce and difficult to access**, with libraries often distant and encyclopedias rare. Further, **"knowledge was also more stable or enduring** than it is now," when the information in books is so often obsolete before it is published. For both of these reasons, memorizing facts made sense in order to retain and apply useful knowledge later.[160] This is no longer the case on either account.

With a smart phone in hand, a student can access exponentially more information than the greatest scholars ever could. It is patently absurd to persist in teaching as if students didn't have this capability, and yet we do. We have them memorize all kinds of things that are easily found within a minute (and forgotten almost as rapidly). Good heavens, what on earth *for*? We must ask ourselves that

---

[159] Reich, op cit.
[160] Wagner, Tony. *Making the Grade*. Routledge Falmer, 2003., p. 20.

question. Our emphasis must be on developing their ability to gather, evaluate, and analyze various sources efficiently and effectively, confirm their accuracy, establish a thesis, examine the contradictory views, extrapolate and synthesize, and be able to craft an original narrative product in a logical and professional way. Information literacy is key.

It is easy to "do school" the way that schools have done for decades, but when what we have been doing fails to account for new realities, when the fate of so many independent schools is tenuous, when parents are paying for an experience that is superior in every way to that supported by their taxes, when the prevailing attitude toward education is one of a commodified credential, it is time to examine more deeply and precisely what we are doing and why. If we are willing to do the hard work of being deliberate, keeping up with and figuring out how to develop and integrate imaginative ways of preparing students, our efforts will be rewarded. We teach our children that with freedom comes responsibility. The freedom of independent schools implies an extraordinary opportunity and responsibility to be leaders in engaging in constant and nimble innovation and developing and providing excellent, creative, individualized student-centered pedagogy, among other things.

We must be agile in implementing change and we must both anticipate proactively and respond reactively to emerging trends. The recent campaign launched by Bill Gates and other leaders in the technology field, for example, underscores the desperate need for computer programmers and increased computer science education. Many nations like the UK and Estonia introduce students to coding in primary school. Students are less likely to major in a subject in college to which they have had no previous exposure.

The market demands that independent schools surpass the norms of neighboring public schools, exceed the standards for college admission and ensure students' success in highly competitive institutions nationwide as well as state-sponsored universities, but it is imperative to understand that the paths that lead to that destination are extremely diverse. Admissions officers seek students who distinguish themselves from others and demonstrate industrious use of time and energy.

School stakeholders need to understand the latitude that secondary schools have is actually enormous, far beyond what they read on university admissions websites, which typically state that they "seek students who have successfully performed in a rigorous high school curriculum that includes three lab sciences, three years each of Math, ideally with some exposure to Calculus, Social Science, often including US History, and study of one language other than English, and four years of English." **That is not a hard and fast rule, except for some state flagships, and it does not mean that these need to be taught as individual subjects in order to be acceptable to universities.** Some examples include the combination of English and Social Science or History in American Studies or Humanities. Math, Science, and Social Science and even English can be combined into Economics or Statistics or a Research course or even Entrepreneurship. So long as the school provides the rationale and can prove the rigor of the course, universities are amenable to *and appreciative of* such innovation.

My least favorite question at Open House for prospective families is, "How are you preparing students for the State University's lecture halls with 500 students and standardized tests; aren't you doing too much hand holding?" While our coddled students are often highly successful at large universities, the fact remains that the universities' ways are not and should not be ours. State U is charged with churning tens of thousands of students through the system, expose them to knowledge, test their ability to demonstrate that knowledge, usually through standardized tests, and provide them with a credential. Arun and Roksa proved that what is going on in higher education is not at all praiseworthy. College professors almost never have any training whatsoever in pedagogy, learning disabilities or differentiation, and they most often use the lecture format of knowledge transference, based on unenlightened 12th century ideas about learning.

Certainly we should not emulate the dysfunction of higher education. We need to do the best job that we can with the resources and knowledge available to us. We must remember that students' time with us in our schools may well prove to be the most significant and transformative experiences that they have of vibrant and dynamic teaching and learning and of close-knit supportive community. For many, it may also be their last exposure to certain bodies of knowledge, so we must take our responsibility seriously to engage them deeply and provide them with the salient tools, not merely discipline specific tools, but the skills to develop and stimulate critical thinking, communication, collaboration, and creativity that they will need no matter what their path may be.

We need to consider what we are teaching and why we do it the way that we do and how to change it to more appropriately meet the needs of the 21st century student.

Student-Centered: What Does *That* Mean?

A student-centered school focuses on the needs and interests of the students, rather than on traditional or conventional ideas of how students should learn. It implies significant rights *and* responsibilities on the part of all members of the community. A student-centered philosophy means that:

❖ Students are responsible for their learning as active agents, rather than passive recipients of instructors' teaching.

Students determine their learning objectives first in collaboration with the instructor and colleagues and soon develop them autonomously. They engage with subject material not through lectures but through activities and research-based projects that demonstrate real-world relevance, complexity, depth of knowledge, and that respond to students' own interests.

Students are expected to take the initiative to seek out research and activities to develop mastery of the material and understand a topic better. This may be done independently or in collaboration and interdependence with other students.

❖ Teachers are facilitators who structure learning experiences and provide guidance and some resources to enable students to actively engage with the subject material.

More than a sage on the stage, teachers are expected to be a guide on the side who will encourage students to want to learn more.

❖ School employees and students treat each other with mutual respect.

Interaction should be characterized by honesty, caring, trust, and positivity, not patronizing, punitive, and niggling rules.

Do what veteran teacher Alexis Wiggins did and follow students throughout their day to see just how much time they must remain immobile.[161] You may be shocked.

---

[161]Strauss, Valerie. "Teacher Spends Two Days as a Student and Is Shocked at What She Learns." *Washington Post*. 24 Oct. 2014. Web. 19 Dec. 2014.

How are your students spending most of their day: sitting and passively listening or up and about, active agents in their learning?

Where on Bloom's Taxonomy (a hierarchical framework of cognitive skills: Knowledge, Comprehension, Application, Analysis, Synthesis, Evaluation) are the students spending most of their intellectual energy? Are they constructing meaning or are they instructed in the meaning?

Are the students evaluated on their abilities to understand and synthesize or to memorize and regurgitate?

Are they collaborating or isolated?

We must not continue in traditional paths without examining what we are doing, comparing it with the research, and implementing change. Independent schools have the opportunity to be at the forefront of innovation. We have a moral obligation to be educational leaders because our families believe in our product and process, pay our tuition, and sustain our organizations in the trust that we are providing the best possible opportunities for their children. We must deliver on that contract.

Learning from projects, inquiry, and expeditions

Say the word "project" and many are likely to envision an analogue of any of the following: a shoebox diorama housing action figures dressed as Wampanoags and Pilgrims at the First Thanksgiving; a poster board or website about a historical figure featuring various excerpts printed off the Internet; a term paper with plenty of information cut and pasted from websites; a half or full day dedicated to making the preparations for sending a camera far enough above ground to snap some great photos. These examples don't really reflect what we mean by project-based learning.

Project-based learning (PBL), or problem-based learning, is a term that can mean different things to different populations, but in general, it means that students learn by doing and by constructing meaning. Teachers spark students' curiosity and scaffold and facilitate opportunities for students' original research projects. Students pursue workable topics that respond to real-world issues and are guided to formulate a research strategy and methodology, perform extensive research, apply methods of quantitative and qualitative analysis, make connections with experts in the field and community leaders (when appropriate), and present their research in a professional way, which may be in front of a class, at a school-wide symposium open to the public, at a competition or a national conference, or in a published format. They develop sophisticated skills that are interdisciplinary and discipline-specific and are turned on to learning. PBL can also integrate place-based education, which encourages students to make meaningful connections and to develop an understanding of their role and responsibilities within their communities. Many independent schools affirm as part of their mission their commitment to inculcating a sense of civic responsibility in students and this is an outstanding means to achieve that goal.[162]

PBL can take shape in many ways that range from entirely teacher-driven to entirely student-driven. Simulations that teachers create for AP Government classes are one example. A teacher presents a problem with all its nuances and challenges and assigns students to different roles (i.e. House Judiciary Committee, the President, State Attorneys, special interest group lobbyists, etc.). The students then research the problem extensively and interact from the perspective of their assigned role. Teachers may insert "curve ball" contingencies into the scenario that further develop students' reasoning abilities.[163] PBL can also be an adaptation of the Google 20% project, in which students work 20% of class time, or one day a week on a project of their own design, as they do at Brightworks School (CA).[164]

Or it can resemble the class of the 9th grade Biology teacher who determined that among her principal objectives were that students realize their agency, become excited about science and understand the scientific method. Students worked alone or in teams of up to three members and brainstormed the topics that they would investigate over the course of the year. The school librarian and the teacher jointly taught initial class meetings to introduce students to the research process. Students became proficient in using subscription databases, searching Google Scholar for peer-reviewed articles (and what that meant), evaluating the quality of a website,

---

[162] For more information on place-based education, see http://www.promiseofplace.org Our Curriculum Matters http://www.ourcurriculummatters.com; Antioch University New England's Center for Place-Based Education http://www.antiochne.edu/anei/cpbe/

[163] A superb resource on PBL is Duch, Barbara J., Susan E. Groh, and Deborah E. Allen. *The Power of Problem-based Learning: A Practical "How To" for Teaching Undergraduate Courses in Any Discipline*. Stylus Pub., 2001. Print.

[164] "3M started it in the 1950's with their 15% project. The result? Post-its and masking tape! Google is credited for making the 20% project what it is today. They asked their employees to spend 20% of their time at work to work on a pet project...a project that their job description didn't cover. As a result of the 20% project at Google, we now have Gmail, AdSense, and Google News." Petty, Kate. "What Is the 20% Project in Education?" *The Tech Classroom*, n.d. Web. 19 Jan. 2015.

85

and gathering information from a variety of other sources, including experts in the field. To a casual visitor, the class appeared chaotic, as students were using their phones, leaning over to view several laptops at once, or walking around. Closer observation, however, revealed that students were speaking professionally to Fish and Wildlife officers and university professors; others were strategizing their next steps in research or modifying their methodologies; and still others scurried around the room to confer with other students or the teacher.

Summaries of a few of the student research projects that teacher inspired and guided appear in Appendix Section VIII. Two students presented *as adults* at national professional conferences, where the adult attendees assumed their work to be doctoral level. One group of students shared an interest in large felines and, after consultation with the local zoo about its needs, constructed a study of tigers and jaguars involving direct observation, coding, statistics, and other activities. Collectively, they spent hundreds of hours on their projects and achieved the course objectives, transformed by their participation. English Language Learners who normally struggled with reading did the same activities as highly proficient readers, but used different resources. The magic in this classroom was palpable. Imagine the difference in the student experience of this environment and that of a traditional classroom with the teacher in front and students sitting quietly in their chairs.

When students learned of a local cancer cluster, they hypothesized about the role of unregulated private wells and the quality of the water used for drinking, cooking, and bathing. Their teacher used the Get Wet! (Groundwater Education Through Water Evaluation and Testing) program, which instructs students in the methods of well water testing and provides the materials and equipment they need. The students discovered high concentrations of certain chemicals and proceeded to issue surveys to residents regarding their well maintenance practices. They discovered that residents were mismanaging their wells, filtration systems, and septic systems. Further student research discovered that these homeowners' actions were generating carcinogens in their drinking water systems. This led to a community-wide program to educate residents in proper care for their wells and to partnering with community power brokers to lobby for greater awareness of the problem and the necessary measures to put an end to the uninformed practices. These students were able to address a real-world problem and affect positive, lasting change in their communities.[165]

---

[165] Thigpen, Tyler. "Taking a Relationship-Centered Approach to Education." *Education Week*. 10 Sept. 2013. Web. 9 Nov 2014

In another example, teachers collaborated in the summer before classes started to create the interdisciplinary Zora Neale Hurston Project. Students traveled to the local home and gravesite of the extraordinary author, anthropologist, and African-American Zora Neale Hurston. The students took black and white photos of her home, drew and painted on site in the style of the Harlem Renaissance, and learned to play musical pieces from the time period, instructed by professional musicians. In the style of the anthropologist, the students collected oral histories from local Civil Rights activists, explored African-American history in the area, gathered archival materials, and created video essays demonstrating deep reflection upon their findings. One of the objectives with this project was to raise students' consciousness about issues of social injustice and the richness of local ethnic history, but the results greatly surpassed the expectation: the students truly were transformed. Local dignitaries as well as several of the activists interviewed attended the public presentation of the visual artwork and the video essays interspersed with jazz performances by students beside the professional musicians. The experience was far more powerful than anyone had anticipated.

Clearly, these are the kinds of life-changing experiences that independent schools should be offering to students. They can—and should—be relevant to students' experience and the community that surrounds them. For boarding schools, it offers a particularly effective means to connect town and gown.

There are conditions that are congenial to these exciting educational experiences. First, educators need to know that students are able to accomplish far more than adults generally believe. Any educator who attends the Intel International Science and Engineering Fair, the Junior Science and Humanities Symposia (JSHS), the BioGenius Challenge, National History Day, and other public exhibitions of student work is treated to an earth-shaking reality check that reveals the kinds of work of which students are capable when engaged and inspired to collaborate to achieve remarkable results. Expectations for students must be high. Second, educators need to be both humble and realistic about educational outcomes. There will be some curriculum that won't be covered (and quickly forgotten, if we are realistic), but the tradeoffs in terms of providing life-changing and memorable experiences cannot be underestimated. They would do well to focus on the "big ideas," which combined with students' inquiry frequently "lead to, and often exceed, overall curriculum expectations (Natural Inquiry 2011)."[166]

---

[166] From a content-rich and superlative document on inquiry based learning that deserves wide dissemination from the Canadian Ministry of Education: Student Achievement Division. "Inquiry-based Learning." *Capacity Building Series* 32 (2013). Ontario Ministry of Education,

Next, flexibility in terms of schedule is quite important; extended class periods enable in-depth engagement. Schools should consider whether the interdisciplinary nature of the engagement warrants combining classes and/or counting classes for multiple credits, e.g. a Humanities class that explores Social Science and English themes might count for both. The methods and materials used and the student products, *not* seat time, should inform the decision. Trusting in students and educators and offering freedom to explore and experiment are like water and light to plants, necessary conditions to successful PBL. The quality of students' products should speak for themselves. If they don't, the educators should be able to explain why and the changes that need to happen.

PBL also prepares students for the reality of the 21st century. In order to "develop and motivate knowledge workers," Peter Drucker recommends four things that organizations should do: "Know people's strengths, Place them where they can make the greatest contributions, Treat them as associates [not subordinates], Expose them to challenges," all of which is exactly what PBL does.[167]

Project-based learning and college admissions

The most common reason that independent schools give for not implementing programs such as these is college admissions, and that reflects yet another grave misunderstanding of the process. Colleges strive to admit the best students who demonstrate a high level of ability, motivation, and engagement. **By occupying students with AP courses, a school is essentially rendering them just another student amidst the 2.2M other students taking AP exams, rather than enabling them to stand out with an impressive portfolio of work, perhaps a record of state, national, or international presentations or awards, publication, or sustained engagement over time with a project that has had a positive impact.** In fact, this is the type of work that top students are able to present to colleges. A leg up in college admissions is only the tip of the iceberg.

By offering the kind of experiences described above, schools offer students incomparable advantage through deep intellectual engagement and emotional investment in their education, the opportunity to realize their ability to affect positive and lasting change, to grasp their responsibilities within the larger community, and to develop insight into their strengths, gifts, and interests for

---

May 2013. Web.
[167] Drucker, op.cit.

potential paths in adulthood. Students also develop subject mastery, skills in collaboration, communication, problem-solving, critical thinking, and so much more. Seniors in the first two graduating classes of the school I led with a PBL philosophy were admitted to such highly selective universities as Cornell University, the Universities of Florida, Michigan, California-Berkeley, and many more.

Courses that apply the principles of project-based learning can be denoted on the transcript as such (i.e. *PBL). Descriptions of the specific course methods and projects that students are engaged in should appear on the school website. Staff involved with college guidance, admissions, marketing, and communications must all observe what happens in the courses as well as the students' products in order to be able to clearly explain and exhibit the strengths of this method of education in person and in marketing materials, since many are likely to be unfamiliar with it. College counseling staff can encourage visiting college admissions officers to observe a class or, at the least, should have samples of student work ready to demonstrate the rigor of the coursework.

Better Learning Through Inquiry

> Memorizing facts and information is not the most important skill in today's world. Facts change, and information is readily available — what's needed is an understanding of how to get and make sense of the mass of data. Educators must understand that schools need to go beyond data and information accumulation and move toward the generation of useful and applicable knowledge...a process supported by inquiry learning.[168]

As we all know, *teaching* something is not the same as *learning* something. It is a reasonable assumption that every student has been taught at some point that the earth orbits the sun, yet the National Science Foundation reports that 25% of Americans surveyed affirmed that the sun revolves around the earth.[169] Schools unwilling to shift to PBL would do well to consider a modification of it in the form of inquiry-based instruction, promoted by the National Council of Teachers of English, National Science Teachers Association, and various others, a method that

---

[168] http://www.thirteen.org/edonline/concept2class/inquiry/
[169] http://www.nsf.gov/statistics/seind14/content/chapter-7/chapter-7.pdf

can be implemented to great success in even the most textbook-driven schools.[170] To start, it is most useful to have a team of two, a librarian and a subject area teacher, or, ideally, three (a librarian, subject area teacher, and an additional subject area teacher or a specialist, like the educational technologist or an arts specialist), and could extend to include an additional subject matter expert from the community or museum (virtually or in person).

The team collaborates to create a dynamic and intriguing invitation to inquiry, to spark students' curiosity and guide the students to build background knowledge, discover and explore the ideas that are interesting to them, and locate resources to probe. Students reflect and consider their learning and identify the questions they wish to pursue. This builds on Donna Ogle's KWL (What I Know/What I Want to Know/What I Learned) framework educators are likely to be familiar with. Individually, in groups, and supervised by the educator team, students decide the direction of their inquiry, gather and evaluate important information, and reflect on what they are learning, perhaps in a journal format. Most importantly, students go beyond the facts to make meaning and create an original product to share what they have learned. Finally, the students reflect on the process, the product, what they have learned, their hypotheses, their successes, errors, and areas for improvement or further exploration, and the findings that are most meaningful to them and why.[171]

There are many ways of engaging students through inquiry. Using Bloom's Taxonomy is a good starting place to help evaluate educational objectives and elevate the level of instruction. Teachers should consider ways that they might integrate features of Bloom's Question Stems,[172] The Big6 (Define the information problem, determine the best sources, locate the sources and information within, extract and use the information, synthesize the information, evaluate the

---

[170] See the work of Carol Collier Kuhlthau et al., especially Kuhlthau, Carol Collier. "Guided Inquiry: School Libraries in the 21st Century." *School Libraries Worldwide.* 16.1 (2010): 1 and Kuhlthau, Carol, Leslie Maniotes, Ann Caspari. Guided Inquiry Design Framework. 2012. Web. Kuhlthau describes the pivotal role of the school librarian in the 21st century as an information professional uniquely qualified to lead the teaching of information literacy in all of its iterations and collaborate in the classroom to guide the process of inquiry.

[171] Joyce, Marilyn Z., and Julie I. Tallman. *Making the Writing and Research Connection with the I-search Process: A How-to-do-it Manual.* Neal-Schuman, 1997. Print. And Eisenberg, Michael, Robert E. Berkowitz, and Michael Eisenberg. *The Definitive Big6 Workshop Handbook.* Linworth Pub., 2003. Print.

[172] http://www.meade.k12.sd.us/PASS/Pass%20Adobe%20Files/March%202007/Blooms TaxonomyQuestionStems.pdf

effectiveness and efficiency of the information),[173] and the I-Search project (What I Knew about this topic, Why I Am Writing This Paper, The Story of the Hunt, and What I Learned [or Didn't]).[174]

Research as Essential Skill

The information landscape has shifted dramatically since the days of searching in solitude for scarce and sequestered resources in the effort to write the obligatory ten-page research paper in high school. So has the curriculum. With the current emphasis on standardized testing, many students never have the opportunity or guidance to develop their research skills. At the dawn of the Information Revolution, we engage in research constantly:

- To be informed voters (What is my senator's voting record?) and savvy consumers (What's the top-rated air purifier?)
- To optimize our leisure time (What's the best sushi restaurant nearby? When is the cheapest flight to NY and where to stay?)
- To scratch an information itch (What film featured Dennis Farina and Gene Hackman?)
- To learn or improve a skill (What's the secret to the chaturanga asana in yoga? How do I make authentic French macarons?)
- To trace family history (When did my great-grandfather arrive in the USA?)
- To find long-lost friends, and to achieve any number of other objectives.

While the media describes this generation of youth as "digital natives," their actual digital literacy is abysmally low with ineffectual search strategies (as employers continually complain), a tendency to become "infoxicated" quickly after a cursory glance at only the first page or two of results of a basic Google search, and rarely, if ever, a Boolean search (using terms like AND, OR, NOT, NEAR, and quotation marks for exact phrases, etc.) or an advanced search with delimiters (such as format, publication date, terms in the URL etc.).

In teaching media literacy, librarians often use sites such as California's Velcro Crop ["severely stressed by drought, disease, and pests"] and Feline Reactions to Bearded Men[175] to demonstrate that appearance alone, along with the

---

[173] "Welcome to the Big6." *Big6.com* n.d. Web. 10 Oct. 2014.

[174] Assaf, Lori Czop, Gwynne Ellen Ash, and Jane Saunders. "Renewing Two Seminal Literacy Practices: I-Charts and I-Search Papers." *Voices from the Middle* 18.4 (2011): 31.

[175] http://www.umbachconsulting.com/miscellany/velcro.html and http://www.improb.com/airchives/classical/cat/cat.html. Accessed 27 Dec 2014

presence of a literature review, tables, graphs, works cited, academic tone, etc. are not reliable indicators of trustworthy content. In many years of using these and other examples, I can attest to the fact that the number of so-called "digital native" high school students who deem these bogus articles to be factual is easily over 90%. It is critical that students (and staff) understand how to locate and identify quality research and the significance of peer-reviewed literature, articles submitted to and evaluated [rigorously, one hopes] by a body of the authors' peers.

Contrary to what we are led to believe, students do not absorb these skills through osmosis. We must teach our students to access wisely the abundant and competing resources at their disposal to formulate logical and effective search strategies, evaluate sources' comparative value, define a thesis (and, in some cases, antithesis), synthesize, extrapolate, and compose an original product, which might take any number of creative formats.

Capstone and Cornerstone Projects

The increasingly common practice of capstone projects in schools both public and private and on levels both secondary and tertiary is reflected in the new College Board product, the AP Capstone Diploma, mentioned earlier. The State of Connecticut, for example, is already on board to require a senior capstone project (not AP) of all graduating seniors. Several public school systems as well as many colleges and universities across the country have had such programs for decades. These programs typically demand that students demonstrate competency or mastery of specific learning objectives or broader academic achievement. They can include traditional academic products such as a thesis and oral defense (as in the AP program), multimedia presentations, gallery exhibitions, performances, physical products, and portfolios. After an extended search of hundreds of models for a comprehensive, clear, logical capstone framework that reflects the research in information literacy, I selected a particularly outstanding one from Weymouth Public Schools to adapt and include in Appendix Section V.

Prior to implementing this program, schools need to understand that a capstone project will not enhance a college application (which is often part of the impetus) if it is elaborated entirely in the students' senior year. While **capstone** projects typically occupy seniors, **cornerstone** projects function differently. Students may start and finish a cornerstone project in each grade, but it is more typical and desirable to begin work on a **cornerstone** project in 9th or 10th grade and make some major professional presentation of the completed work in junior year, with additional data collection and perhaps an internship in the senior year with final exhibition. Thus, the cornerstone timeframe entails protracted and deeper engagement. It is more strategic in that it facilitates the presentation of the project as part of a college application. (Even schools planning to implement the AP Capstone, which is intended to occupy the junior and senior years, would do well to have students begin it in the sophomore year to reap the full benefit). It is important to note that students are not required to continue their cornerstone project in subsequent years and may pursue new interests in each successive year.

Expeditionary Learning

There are imperative learning objectives that simply cannot be achieved so effectively in the classroom as outside of it. Field trips have a singular power to

- Enrich and expand the curriculum
- Expand students' awareness of their own community
- Strengthen observation skills by immersing students in sensory activities
- Augment students' knowledge in a particular subject area
- Provide a new way of learning abstract information[176]
- Excite, motivate, and inspire students to learn
- Lead students to an experiential appreciation of arts and culture

Further, in a large scale (including nearly 11,000 students and 500 teachers) randomized-control trial, researchers concluded that field trips

> Contribute to the development of students into civilized young men and women who possess more knowledge about art, have stronger critical-thinking skills, exhibit increased historical empathy, display higher levels of tolerance, and have a greater taste for consuming art and culture.[177]

In survey after survey, adults report that their most memorable experiences in school took place off school grounds on field trips, yet "museums across the country report a steep drop in school tours" and "A survey by the American Association of School Administrators found that more than half of schools eliminated planned field trips in 2010-2011," largely due to financial constraints,

---

[176] Nabors, Martha L., Linda Carol Edwards, and R. Kent Murray. "Making the Case for Field Trips: What Research Tells Us and what Site Coordinators have to Say." 129 Vol. Mobile: Project Innovation, Inc, 2009.

[177] Greene, Jay P., Brian Kisida, and Daniel H. Bowen. "The Benefits of Culturally Enriching Field Trips." *Education Digest* 79.8 (2014): 4.

the emphasis on standardized testing, and a shift in attitude of the purpose of such trips from enrichment to reward (i.e. a trip to an amusement park as a reward for an increase in test scores).[178]

Expeditionary learning can mean anything from a walk to the park next door to collect insect samples to a trip to the local art museum to a month-long trek through Peru. Expeditionary Learning is also the official name of an organization that arose from a collaboration between Outward Bound and Harvard Graduate School of Education, with acclaimed methods, materials and professional development programs that may be adapted in various ways to achieve the goals of individual schools and need not be adopted wholesale.[179] Above all, expeditionary learning is engaging pedagogy. This is what I envision:

The sophomores have voted for the theme "From Farm to Fork" from among a selection that they generated. After mind-mapping the theme for all that it refers to and may lead to, students propose and set about planning a series of lessons and trips. They will keep a journal in which they will reflect on the issues that they encounter on this journey. They will learn about the supply chain, how the food they eat reaches their plates. They will travel to local farms, speak with migrant farm laborers about their lives, meet with other farm workers and owners and hear about their challenges in bringing quality food to market in a timely fashion and at a reasonable price point, working with and in competition with large agribusiness companies. The students will observe produce picking and packing as well as animal "harvesting" and butchering. They will speak with supermarket and farmers' market managers as well as chefs about the issues related to their work.

They will design projects that respond to personal interests. One team, for example, plans to conduct academic research to formulate an appropriate hypothesis and develop background knowledge, make supermarket observations and survey customers in various neighborhoods to draw conclusions about the relation between immigration, cultural identity, and food.

Students will work weekly in a soup kitchen and dine with residents to hear their stories. They will interview Food Bank workers, managers and users, as well as the local and regional managers of retail markets to learn their reasons why they donate or why they don't. They will meet with a representative from Health and

---

[178] Greene, Jay P., Brian Kisida, and Daniel H. Bowen. "The Educational Value of Field Trips." *Education Next* Winter 2014.
[179] See http://elschools.org

Human Services about the challenges and successes associated with the food stamp program. They will work in the school lab advised and guided by a food scientist in her lab (done virtually) to determine how the nutritional values of foods are calculated. They will work with a nutritionist to determine the quality of their own diets and understand the relationship between diet and health.

The students will map "food deserts," places in the community where low-income residents do not have ready access to food and create a guide to help those residents locate and identify healthy options in the languages of the residents. They will organize a food drive for the Food Bank and a campaign to persuade the retailers that do not currently participate in donating to the Food Bank to do so. The students will create a public gallery exhibition and oral presentation reflecting on what they have learned through the year and possible extensions for further exploration.

It goes without saying that this is an extraordinary opportunity for students to learn about an aspect of their daily lives that ties them to the lives of so many others. Students locate themselves in a community and come to understand the complexity of the constellation of issues related to culture, health, social services, entrepreneurs, small businesses, and conglomerates. They collaborate, think critically and creatively, dialogue with adults on diverse life paths, and empathize with or at least become familiar with the challenges that they encounter. They comprehend their agency, their ability to affect positive change. They present their findings to the community as experts. They are transformed.

Even if only comprised of the occasional trip to enhance a particular lesson, expeditionary learning should be integral to the independent school experience. Such trips entail careful planning not merely for logistical issues but in order to derive the full benefit from the experience. In order to be successful, school staff should determine clear learning goals for the trip and communicate these to students and families. Students are adequately prepared to appreciate the purpose and highlights of the trip and participate in activities, have site-related questions ready, and be prepared to respectfully and attentively listen and respond to the replies. A pre-assessment will help staff to determine what students already know and anticipate. Depending on the site, a "site-quest," which prompts students to seek out specific features and answer *higher order* questions, not merely identifying questions, will generally aid students to be more aware of the value of the site. Assessment may be conducted in collaboration with site staff and followed up with more formal summative assessment to determine whether the learning

95

goals were met.[180]

Signature Programs and Certificates

Schools' signature programs should leverage the resources in the school and local community in the same way that expeditionary and project-based learning do. A few examples include Scattergood Friends' (IA) sustainable agriculture certification; various schools in proximity to the ocean with special diplomas in marine biology; schools in areas with vibrant art scenes, a community of craftspeople, and/or an art school with arts-related diplomas and public exhibition of their work. Several schools establish relationships with area businesses to offer internships tied with advanced research or projects. Students might earn a certificate for projects within courses coupled with guided or independent study perhaps collaborating with experts relating to an intractable community issue such as homelessness, the digital divide, low voter turnout, low participation in recycling programs or an environmental issue like a watershed, a habitat, a conservation area, etc.

Asking staff individually about whether they have a special interest, talent or idea for a program or project that they have would like to share and realize can lead to first-rate signature programs that genuinely inspire students. The obvious downside is that, should the staff member(s) leave the school, the program is likely to dissolve, often despite the best intentions to keep it running. Nevertheless, a few years of wonderful should trump the possibility of the program's demise.

There is a strong drive toward fostering global citizenship in independent schools and signature programs can serve that goal. Several schools with area studies certificates require that a student demonstrate advanced proficiency in a language, participate in an academic study abroad for at least a summer (far more than a two-week excursion) or a semester, and create a significant research project related to some aspect of the culture. Students in these programs demonstrate sustained engagement with a subject and a level of expertise acquired through systematic study.

In order to be truly successful and respected, the rigor of special certificate or diploma programs should be clear and indisputable by external and internal observers, as well as the staff involved with marketing the school, including

---

[180] Nabors, M. L., L.C. Edwards, and K. Murray, K. Making the Case for Field Trips: What Research Tells Us and What Site Coordinators Have to Say. *Education* 129.4 (2009).

college counseling staff. Merely taking a course or two beyond what a student would expect to do in the process of meeting graduation requirements should not be sufficient to earn a certificate. Intentional participation, significant effort, reflection, the production of a comprehensive project and its public presentation are essential features. Students' processes and products should be readily accessed on the school website.

Global Education

While the Grand Tour of Europe was a certain rite of passage for young men of privilege in the 19th century and American Field Service exchanges of students began in 1946, independent schools' widespread interest in experiential global education is quite recent. Common motivations are exploration and adventure, enhancing language skills and college applications, marketing the school, and developing global citizens. NAIS has identified it as a priority and more and more schools are integrating global education in various ways, often through trips, sister schools that might entail long and short term student exchanges and frequent communication, study abroad for a term or year, and partnerships of various types. Cape Henry Collegiate (VA) has a full year science course that culminates in significant fieldwork in Panama with the Smithsonian Tropical Research Institute. The Challenge 20/20 Initiative of NAIS is quite promising as it connects schools virtually in the US with schools around the world "to identify local solutions to a global problem," such as climate change, water deficits, natural disaster prevention and mitigation, etc. This avoids the pitfall inherent to international programming by establishing encounters with empowered concerned global citizens on equal footing.

Partnerships should be formed in thoughtful and deliberate ways. To some, a program pairing a school in Wyoming with a "sister school" in South Africa is broadening because it exposes students to another culture; to others, it is unjustifiably arbitrary, but that begs the question of why anywhere? Students in a school in Baltimore pair with a sister school in Japan and learn Japanese, a language spoken by 122 million people. Some argue that it is far more useful to partner with a school in Latin America and learn Spanish, spoken by 414 million people, and of certain use in the U.S. on a daily basis in many communities. The rationale and the issue of pragmatism and utility are valid concerns and should be discussed. Not every opportunity that presents itself is worthy of pursuit.

How to ethically send students to poor countries has been a personal preoccupation of mine for decades. Having spent considerable time in Mexico,

Colombia, Chile, and Trinidad, West Indies, once as Coordinator of a university's program abroad with homestays, I have come to see the ubiquitous practices of band aid assistance and, especially poverty tourism—"travel as a means of experiencing what it's like to have very little, but within the embrace (and insurance net) of a safe, commercial venture, and easy access to an industrial-size tub of hand sanitizer"[181] as misguided and reflective of a dangerously disingenuous naïveté.

The contact must be executed with enormous sensitivity in order to avoid perpetuating ethnocentrism and the binary categories that social scientists label the in-group or Self, which "embodies the norm whose identity is valued" and the out-group Other,

> defined by its faults, devalued and susceptible to discrimination....Although it seems that the Other is sometimes valued, as with exoticism, it is done in a stereotypical, reassuring fashion that serves to comfort the Self in its feeling of superiority.[182]

Regardless of how discreet and muted they believe their privilege and political, social, and economic power to be, school groups can too easily inadvertently bolster students' colonialist mindsets, American exceptionalism, and the paternalist racism exhibited in President William Howard Taft's reference to "our little brown brothers." To make matters worse, the tourists often romantically conclude that despite the crushing poverty, the natives are "happy" and, often, "closer to nature" in the way of the noble savage.

Wealthy people who travel to poorer countries in order to see how the poor live dehumanize them and in essence tour poor communities as they would a human zoo. The all-too-common goal of fostering in comparatively privileged young people an "appreciation for what they have" by seeing the Other with less both diminishes the natives' dignity and uses them as a means to an end.

Service projects with the goal of "ministering unto" harbor these problems and more. With considerable poverty proximate to any independent school in the US, school staff must consider and justify why it should be preferable to pick out

---

[181] Murungi, Miriti. "A Brief Guide to Fetishizing Poverty During the World Cup." *Soccer Gods*. 15 June 2014. Web. 22 Dec. 2014.
[182] Staszak, Jean François. "Other/Otherness." In *International Encyclopedia of Human Geography*. Elsevier, 2008.

the mote from the eye of the other than the log in one's own. Justifying voluntourism or "poor-ism" and the selection of the Dominican Republic or Tanzania or Tijuana for service projects is absurd merely on the grounds of wanting to make a difference. Too many of these high school programs entail paying $3000 per student for an adventure / hopefully resumé-boosting / fodder for application essay experience that does precious little good for the local community but plenty for the arranging agency and corporate tourism infrastructure. It is staggeringly objectionable that these experiences are often structured in such a way that students work for a few days and spend the remainder of their time enjoying splurge experiences like safaris or even excursions which feature ample opportunity for shopping. Care must be taken to avoid situations in which "locals and their communities become props in your vacation"[183] and students merely drop in and out of circumstances that are inescapable and formidable for those mired in them. Such schemes must be examined closely, for they may even work at cross-purposes and prolong injustice and poverty. In fact, several books have been written recently about the ways that service workers often become unwittingly complicit in quick-fix schemes that serve to buttress corrupt governments.[185]

School staff must match the service opportunity to students' actual skills, language or otherwise. One group of boarding school students with no skills in driving a nail, laying bricks, or framing a house was led to believe that they were constructing a building in an impoverished community when local workers were actually undoing and redoing their work at night.[186] There are various ways to match the right students with the best fit opportunity. One small group focused on watershed research might head to one destination for fieldwork; the Habitat for Humanity Club brings its skills to a construction project site in another; the Future Physicians Club, already certified in first aid and trained in basic care travels to help in a clinic; a language club travels to a place where the language is spoken. Depending upon how staff structure the experience and the students' own

---

[183] Murungi, op cit.

[185] See a) Gonzalez, Deborah. *A Survey of Best Practices of Global Service Learning Programs in UGA*. University of Georgia. July 2009. Web. 15 Mar. 2015.
b) Easterly, William. *The Tyranny of Experts: Economists, Dictators, and the Forgotten Rights of the Poor*. Basic, 2014.
c) Easterly, William. *The White Man's Burden: Why the West's Efforts to Aid the Rest Have Done So Much Ill and So Little Good*. Penguin, 2006.
d) Munk, Nina. *The Idealist: Jeffrey Sachs and the Quest to End Poverty*. Anchor, 2013.
e) Schmidt, Annette and Walter Van Beek, eds. *African Hosts & Their Guests: Cultural Dynamics of Tourism*. James Curry, 2012.
[186] Biddle, Pippa. "The Problem With Little White Girls (and Boys): Why I stopped being a Voluntourist." *Pippa Biddle*. Blog. 18 Feb 2014. 22 Dec14.

propensities, its impact on students can range from the aforementioned confirmation of presumptions of cultural superiority to the desired questioning of the factors that gave rise to and maintain economic inequality and injustice, and what can be done to mitigate them. The complex power dynamics involving concepts of the Other and the wealthy White person "ministering unto" have to be carefully and sensitively navigated. It is absolutely crucial that students be led to engage in guided reflection on their experience. It should never be presumed that they will do so on their own, for reflection is not automatic.

The question of who gets to participate is complex. Some schools arrange trips for entire grades, for example every year the juniors travel to China and the seniors travel to Ghana. Global programming veterans William Fluharty and W. Joseph Vogel assert that this may not be the best course of action since "the benefits per student *increase* as the group size *decreases.*"[187] The contact that students have with the natives is obviously likely to be greater in smaller groups. Homestays are excellent ways of interacting with natives in their daily lives, but these are extremely onerous to arrange for large groups, though equal exchange programs between schools facilitate this considerably.

It is also appropriate to some academically oriented programs for students to compete for available spots on the basis of a series of academic assignments and oral presentations related to the work they would undertake there. Schools' commitments to economic equity mandate facilitating access for students who are unable to pay through fundraising, seeking sponsors for students, requesting that parents paying for their own student's trip and a portion of another student's, or establishing separate scholarship funds just for trips. Students should be assisted with budgeting for and during the trip to avoid the all too frequent occurrence of the student who squanders all of his money the first day, the student on full scholarship who splurges on an inexplicable spending spree, and the compulsive shopper, among others.

In his dissertation, "Independent and Global: School-wide Global Education in Two Independent Schools," Bob Ogle (Head of Pacific Ridge School, CA) underscores the importance of having clear goals for the program and provides a useful framework of considerations.[188] The Global Education Benchmark Group

---

[187] Fluharty, William G. and W. Joseph Vogel. "Beyond Sight Seeing: Maximizing Your Students' International Experience." *Independent School.* Print. Spring 2013.
[188] Ogle, Robert Wallace, "Independent and Global: School-wide Global Education in Two Independent Schools," (Doctoral dissertation, Columbia Teachers College, 2010).

intends to assist independent schools with establishing objectives, benchmarks, assessment (i.e. the Global Competency Aptitude Assessment), risk management, and more.[189] GEBG has just published the iBook Global Education: A Roadmap to Program Development, which may prove helpful.

Despite all of the caveats, when executed in a deliberate, thoughtful, and meaningful manner, global education is an excellent way for independent schools to develop students' competence and confidence in collaborating with others around the world to make the world a better and more just place, to spark their curiosity and appreciation for diversity and exploration, to be transformed by stepping out of their comfort zones, to cultivate empathy and deep understanding, and to learn to be comfortable with the unfamiliar. It also can represent a significant comparative advantage over other area schools.

Leadership Programs

I take a dim view of most of the programs companies create to develop their people. The real development I've seen of people in organizations, especially in big ones, comes from their being volunteers in a nonprofit organization where you have responsibility, you see results, and you quickly learn what your values are. There is no better way to understand your strengths and discover where you belong than to volunteer in a nonprofit. — Peter Drucker

Prospective independent school parents often ask about leadership opportunities for students as though they were experiential commodities to acquire. This is not a helpful way to frame the situation and ignores the evidence the field of leadership studies presents.

Leaving aside the age old conundrum of whether leaders are born or made, students become leaders by setting an example, not by telling others what to do. Students lead when they experience an internal spark, take the initiative to achieve some goal and inspire others to follow them, not when they are *assigned* some role. Murray Bowen's Family Systems Theory posited that "a child learns his leadership principles, skills, and roles in his family and translates it organizationally to the groups in which he/she later participates as an adult."[190] Further, Howard Gardner,

---

[189] www.gebg.org Accessed 23 Mar. 2014.
[190] Gottlieb, David G. *The Application of Bowen Family Systems Theory to the High School Principalship.* ProQuest, UMI Dissertations Publishing, 2001, p. 50.

of Multiple Intelligence fame, examined leaders and leadership in his *Leading Minds: An Anatomy of Leadership*. Gardner found recurring themes in young leaders:

> Excellent speaking skills, and "keen interest in and understanding of other people," a perception of authority figures as peers and a "willingness to confront them," a sense of entitlement, confidence, "concern with moral issues," and a large personal network comprised of "hundreds of individuals, rather than a dozen or a score, by the time she has reached her majority."[191]

If we accept Bowen's work and Gardner's ideal type, which correlate strongly with those presented by others in the field, public speaking might be the one facet of leadership that the school is best equipped to cultivate.

Project-based learning can help facilitate leadership on a basic level since students take turns managing projects, but not surprisingly, just as some students have an innate ability for visual art, others simply demonstrate a natural capacity for the skills of storytelling and relationship building that comprise leadership and other students gravitate to them and follow. We can put other students in leadership positions in groups, in clubs, or some other situation and train them in group dynamics and management techniques, but if they can't tell the story in a compelling way, aren't interested in others or are too undifferentiated (meaning they have an undeveloped sense of self), immature, apathetic, unmotivated, narcissistic, etc., they may derive no benefit and their group or organization can suffer. Followership is an essential part of leadership and it is to students' advantage to learn how to support the group.

False Choice: College vs. Career Preparation

> Given the immense scientific, technological and socio-economic development, either in progress or envisaged, which characterizes the present era, particularly globalization and the revolution in information and communication technology, technical and vocational education....those aspects of the educational process involving, in addition to general education, the study of technologies and related sciences, and the acquisition of practical skills, attitudes,

---

[191] Gardner, Howard, and Emma Laskin. *Leading Minds: An Anatomy of Leadership.* Basic, 2011.

understanding and knowledge relating to occupations in various sectors of economic and social life....should be a vital aspect of the educational process in all countries (UNESCO, 2001).

Career and Technical Education (CTE) is not what it used to be. Exciting things are happening in this sector, particularly in the STEM fields, health care, energy, information technology, and various others. Bergen County Academies (NJ), for example, has labs for cell biology, nano-structural imaging, nanotechnology, and stem cell research. BCA has impressive staff; most hold doctorates and have worked for many years not as teachers but as scientists in labs and are highly qualified to guide and assist students in research. Much of the remarkable instrumentation results from partnerships and in-kind grants from companies and includes various types of microscopes (including electron), various types of spectrophotometers, a differential scanning calorimeter, thermal cyclers and real-time PCR, UV-Vis spectroscope, and so much more. With courses such as Research Applications in Molecular Biology and Genetics, Research Virology and Gene Therapy, and Entrepreneurial Science Project, in which students create a biotechnology start-up company, students conduct extraordinary research, explore STEM careers, garner attention and awards on national and international levels, and, of course, gain admission to highly selective colleges. That is what CTE (and a *real* STEM program) looks like in the 21st century.

As discussed in Chapter 2, liberal arts colleges and universities have by and large accepted the need to offer vocational and pre-professional programs but independent schools have resisted, clinging to the traditional path to prepare for college preparation by developing a broad base of knowledge. Since 1980, the percentage of students earning bachelor's degrees in business has remained steady at 20%, Computer Science and Engineering (this is the combined category used by NCES) 8%, and Natural Science and Math (another combined category) also at 8%.[192] Meanwhile, "schools of choice," charter, magnet, and regular public schools are increasingly attractive to students and their families for their pre-professional programs in Business, Engineering, Computer Science, Biomedical Science, and many other fields, which to lead to matriculation in highly selective universities.

Revisiting that stable and sizable federal statistic indicating that 20% of bachelor's degrees are awarded in business, it would seem imperative that schools engage students in business skills. Entrepreneurship incubators and programs

---

[192] NCES. Table 318.20

103

modeled on the popular television show *Shark Tank* are cropping up to great acclaim, but most of these involve mere dabbling for a few hours over the course of a few weeks. Contrast that experience with Springside Chestnut Hill's (PA) Center for Entrepreneurial Leadership or Hawken's (OH) program and the difference is clear in the commitment, rigor and quality of a thoughtful, deliberate, and systematic approach.

At Hawken, students in the Entrepreneurship program learn the basics of business operations using Steve Blank's Lean LaunchPad method used at Berkeley and Stanford. Students read prodigiously and meet with CEOs of area businesses and non-profit organizations, who present a dilemma that they are offering the students the opportunity to solve. In teams of three, students spend three weeks addressing the organization's issue and then present their solution to the organization's leadership. They address two additional organizations in the subsequent six weeks.

Then the students use what they have learned about business, user experience design (UX), the principles of design thinking (empathizing with a user, defining the problem, thinking about ways to address it, creating a prototype and testing)[193] to create their own business or non-profit for an additional five weeks. The students interview people in the larger community, test their hypotheses about their product or service on real users, establish a value proposition, conduct market research, and pivot as needed to pursue more fruitful paths.

This program is extremely rigorous and accounts for half of students' course load for the semester. They receive English, Math, and Social Science credit. Students devote two half-days and one full day each week for a semester to the program. This is the kind of transformational experience that makes students want to come to school because they see the relevance and meaning of their work and they experience control and efficacy. It adds immeasurable value to the independent school experience and prepares students for the real world as well as college. Learning to be entrepreneurial in order to be contributors and creators in the new economy, rather than just consumers, is a quintessential 21st century skill.

Independent school students clamor for vocationally-oriented classes, perhaps most commonly Anatomy and Physiology to "prepare for medical school," and perhaps we offer one or two, but our common reply is to point out that:

---

[193] See Virtual Crash Course in Design Thinking by Stanford's Design School
http://dschool.stanford.edu/dgift/

a) Yes, we know you want desperately to be a physician some day, but 30%-60% of students who enter college with that intent change their mind
b) Medical school is at least five years distant
c) For *undergraduate* admissions, your first priority, you should demonstrate exemplary performance in solid lab classes in Bio, Chem, and Physics, not Anatomy/Phys, which is seen as a fluff elective
d) Engineering majors have the highest admissions rate to medical school of all majors
e) Various other perfectly reasonable and dismissive adult replies.

This is no longer an adequate response to the demand for career-oriented and practical education. Independent schools must endeavor to provide diverse routes to respond to students' interests and plans; public schools often do so quite well. Public schools may not supply the education on-site but often facilitate or adjust students' schedules to accommodate certification in fields like emergency medicine, surgical technology, nurse assisting, radiography, etc. These experiences may or may not lead to careers in health care, but at the very least give students the sense of what such careers entail, and corroborate or invalidate the students' perceived interest in the field. The most effective of these programs entail curricula designed in collaboration with community partnerships that also facilitate work-based learning experiences, such as clinical rotations and internships.

Part II: Facilitating Place-based, Original Research for the Individual Student, the Classroom, and the Community

By Dr. Teresa Thornton, PhD.

Education that is exciting and engaging must be personally relevant to the learner. Although this is an inherent truth at all ages, the focus in science and STEM education has been at the secondary and middle grade levels. Independent schools, unencumbered by state mandated outcomes and standardized tests have been able to make science process skills relevant to these grades through encouragement of independent and community-based research projects. This additional flexibility allows for room in the curriculum to foster relationships with professional mentors, community leaders, and research facilities eager to share their knowledge and equipment in a meaningful way. When educators integrate process skills in daily coursework and a concurrent long-term project, students are offered the opportunity to study what they desire while they are learning course content and practicing process skills.

I. Original/Independent Research
The Set-Up

The course begins with the nature of science. Students are requested to read a minimum of five peer-reviewed journal articles and discuss what is defined as truth in science. They are exposed to real world examples of bias and poor science. They are then asked to think about something they are truly interested in learning, any topic.

Choosing A Topic

Students are encouraged to view their favorite pastime from a perspective of gathering data. They are requested to think about what they love from a scientific point of view by asking, "How can I measure this?" The beauty of science is that it underlies all things; almost anything can be turned into a research project. Once a general topic is chosen, Google Scholar is used to determine existing research on the subject and to hone in on specific details of the thesis statement as well as realistic methods. For instance, a student interested in video games found a great deal of existing peer-reviewed journals addressing the lack of women in college programming courses. It occurred to him that there had been only one girl in any of his computer science classes, so he decided to determine why girls in his school had not signed up for programming courses. Thus he was able to formulate an appropriate literature review and methodology. A lacrosse player who worked out in a group that performed the exact same workouts on the same days, decided to evaluate how body type effects muscle mass gain. Initial measurements and mass was taken, body types of all participants were determined, and food intake was managed and monitored. In order to formulate a thesis and complete a literature review, preliminary research for the literature review was performed to determine how different muscles based on somatotypes react to both weight lifting and cardio workouts. Behavioral observations in animals and humans, environmental chemistry projects, transect studies, and social science surveys are the simplest to develop; however, limitations to research methodologies are numerous in secondary education.

The Limitations of Methodology

Working with students under the age of 18 poses particular hurdles. Legally one might not want to have students do door-to-door surveys, work in potentially polluted areas, or work with unhealthy chemicals. Safety is, of course, first priority. However, the real limitations come from finding equipment and

106

appropriate population samples. Medical, psychological, neurological, and other human centered research is restricted by HIPAA Laws, and facilities do not want to share confidential patient information with a secondary student. People who suffer from disease have either been overused in testing or do not take high school research seriously. This was a hard lesson as students exhausted avenues to try and survey targeted populations; one was focused on breast cancer and another on social anxiety disorder. The student interested in breast cancer attended public breast cancer functions soliciting participants. She posted an electronic survey on chat forums, sent them to hospitals, research facilities, universities, and even tried her own web page. The responses from most of these avenues were expected. What was not expected was the nastiness and vitriol directed at her for trying to collect data on forums. She was directly insulted, dropped from more than one forum, and blocked from others. She was able to sample a total of 75 women, but she was interested specifically in women who developed breast cancer from injuries. Less than 23% of her sample population was acceptable, not enough to perform parametric statistics. Her superlative literature review and communication with researchers in the field had professors requesting her data, but no one was willing to share their human subjects.

The same was true for a student interested in social anxiety disorder. She exhausted potential connections to population samples. She followed a similar path as the breast cancer student, but in the end she had only five diagnosed participants. She too, created a literature review that caught the attention of a graduate student at Drexel University who also requested her data with the promise of sharing their population, but in the end it was for naught. She did, however gain a valuable education regarding research limitations and refocused her paper on her comprehensive attempt to collect data on a sensitive issue relating to human illness.

There has been greater success in enlisting biochemistry laboratory internships and mentors in local colleges, universities, and private industry. Facilities dependent on grant monies and donations are encouraged to include educational outcomes in their deliverables.

Finding a Mentor

Professionals want to share their career expertise (Thornton, 2011) and most organizations have education objectives built into their grant deliverables or mission statements. Focusing on governmental and non-governmental organizations (NGOs), community clubs, private businesses, large corporations, and local universities or colleges, one can find assistance or referrals to individuals that desire to be mentors. However, contacting mentors too early in the process may sour them to participating.

Students should complete a literature review that is on par with the contact made. In other words, do not send a middle grade paper that is not referenced properly, without appropriate punctuation and form to a professor at your local university. Make sure that the research paper is well written and even has an authored reference to the mentor sought. It would be poor form and may feel insulting that a person thinks so little of another's valuable time as to expect them to assist a child who did not do his or her best, or a teacher who is not diligent. Professionals may not be asked to evaluate the grammar and punctuation, but they may evaluate the relationship on which they are about to embark through writing skills. It is the only real way to show them where in the comprehension process the student lies. That said, the student should have a fairly good understanding of the subject matter when they, or the teacher, reach out for collaborators.

Funding

Finding money may be a bit more challenging in institutions that have limited budgets or parameters on the kinds of "gifts" that can be accepted. Private schools are not always eligible for grants offered to public schools or they may not be able to receive funds that come from organizations deemed a conflict of interest. Yet the companies that are willing to give time, human resources, and expertise are the very same that may be able to financially support some research projects. Associations, NGOs, or any other business that has some sort of ties to the student's discipline of study or to students/education in general are also prospective funding sources. They may also supply equipment or some other need that could defray costs. This kind of funding may be piecemeal, but it is very effective.

Keeping the Focus

Data collection can be daunting for young people. Scheduling fieldwork can be hectic while pursuing sample populations for surveys and interviews are more sporadic and may appear laggard. Using mentors and social networks to assist in finding assistance is a great resource. However, if there is a period of stagnation while waiting for the next step in the process, students can begin to seek conferences and journals where their research might be published or accepted in poster/talk format. It is encouraging to sometimes see the light at the end of the tunnel even though a student may be at a midpoint. There are also many opportunities for students to present preliminary results or research to local groups and organizations. This can encourage others to share their social networks (Thornton & Leahy, 2012). Everyone loves to be an expert in their field, and most want to help young people learn more about their shared interest (Thornton, 2011).

Distributing the Information

As stated above, there are many organizations, associations, groups, and clubs that have specific interests and would be delighted to have a young person share their research. A student interested in the experiences of female lawyers might connect with the Women Trial Lawyers Association. A student performing groundwater research might want to contact The Groundwater Foundation. Additionally, there is a plethora of journals specific to each discipline and a few that focus directly on student research. To name only a very few:

- Journal of Young Investigators: www.jyi.org/
- International Journal of Student Researchers: www.ijsronline.com/
- Journals of Student Researchers: jofsr.com
- Journal of Emerging Investigators: www.emerginginvestigators.org/
- Zebrafish: www.liebertpub.com/zeb/

Don't discount professional journals. If the research is performed under the purview of professors and professionals, and the student can assert how her/his research will further the discipline, professional journals will be happy to support up-and-coming young scientists. It is about quality, not age.
For more information regarding specific steps in a research project see:
http://drthorntonscourses.webs.com/honors-research-syllabus   and
http://drthorntonscourses.webs.com/hr-project-expectations

II. Multidisciplinary Science

Multidisciplinary research in the classroom is teacher-directed in that the teacher picks the subject that the class is going to study. For instance, during a unit on genetics one might choose to have the class study genetically modified organisms (GMOs). However, students will choose which aspect they would prefer to learn. Environmental issues like GMOs are perfect for this kind of class involvement in that it contains elements of social justice, economics, politics, environmental chemistry, population dynamics, ethics, and human health. Each one of these topics can be divided and dissected in small groups. There is certainly enough information regarding GMOs and all of these topics (*and more!*). Each

109

group will choose their area of interest. They are all required to perform research on valid web sites, newspapers, journal articles, wherever reliable information can be found. The idea is to dive deep into the one discipline among the many and be able to teach others what they have learned. The students devise a lesson at the length the teacher determines. It can be a simple PowerPoint with references and appropriate images, a presentation with an activity that helps the class master what the group has learned, or it could have a community component whereby students devise a plan for their neighborhood in which they help the community solve a particular problem. It should be noted that if students were to take on a community-based project it would behoove them to make it sustainable. Whatever the matter, carrying it on allows for either long-term data collection or the ability for other students that come after that class to continue with the project. This builds community-school relationships that foster social capital allowing for other opportunities; be it funding, expertise, equipment, or opportunity.

III. School Centered, Community-Based Research

Creating a program that fosters place-based, kinesthetic learning is simple in theory. There are specific parameters one can follow, but the effort and determination required to complete this kind of research in a sustainable matter requires the founder(s) to believe in the subject matter. And, although funding does affect the timeline for objectives and deliverables, funding should not limit passion. I have seen a funded project bloom in two years and when the funding failed the program died. I have seen other programs with smaller successes over a long period of time in which founders drew funding from multiple sources and grew their programs slowly.

The following is a worksheet I created for conferences. It helps the reader/participant think about where to begin and how to move through the process of starting a community-based research program. It is divided into three parts: volunteerism, practice, and objectives.

The Theory

Many professionals have listed the desire to share their expertise as a reason to volunteer with other organizations. When dealing specifically with students, volunteers stated that they wanted to increase their community's level of education through the youth, as well as make a connection within the community through the school. These motivations can be harnessed with any environmental concern in your neighborhood provided you follow a few basic ideas:

1. Make sure you are asking volunteers to perform specifically what they do for a living (i.e., a GIS expert can help students create maps).
2. Ask volunteers to invite others that they feel may be interested in participating.
3. Make sure that your demands on a volunteer's time are flexible, specific, and clear from the onset (i.e., an hour of time doing X before a specific date)
4. Invite your volunteers to be a part of the process. Ask them how the goals of their organization, or how their personal goals can be met through their participation. What would they think is a valuable input to the program?
5. In order to complete #3 and #4 make sure your program has clear objectives, specific roles and goals for the volunteers, and an opportunity for the participants to see outcomes in a reasonable time.
6. Also, make it clear how their participation in the program, or the program itself is beneficial to the community, the environment, and to education.

The Practice

1. What is an environmental concern in your neighborhood or county?
   If you are not already aware of a problem in your community, you may Google an environmental concern you find interesting. Also, calling the local health department is a good start if you are completely at a loss for ideas.

2. Determine which organizations in your area would be stakeholders for that concern. In order to facilitate a comprehensive educational experience, be sure to include multiple disciplines. Make a list of the names of organizations and their contact information.

3. Decide how you will market this to schools or your principal/department chair? How does it benefit that organization? Look for other organizations or schools that have been successful in this discipline doing work that is similar to your interest. Don't forget the possibilities of collaborating with NGOs, ENGOs, universities, or other organizations presently trying to move in the same direction. You don't always need to reinvent the wheel.

4. Do you want to develop curriculum that goes along with this program? Teachers often like a set program, especially those in K-8. Programs that have state and national standards, activities, and lesson plans that help THEM understand the information or process are often more successful.

5. Do you want to make that curriculum public?

6. Will you include your stakeholders in curriculum development?

7. What role would you like your volunteers to assume? Do you need help with set-up of the program or do you simply want those volunteers to fill in predetermined "slots."

8. How will you secure funding for supplies? Collaborations often have better chances of obtaining grant funds. Organizations are also very generous if the outcomes fit their missions.

9. Can you facilitate this as long-term research or do you need to acquire facilitators? Organizations like conservation districts have education deliverables as part of their grants. Community organizations and local government departments also have educational deliverables or community service as part of their job descriptions or department goals. How can you tap into this?

10. What is the time frame from beginning to end? Be specific. Will this be a summer program or a school year program?

Relevant Objectives:

STEM and STEAM are the buzzwords of the time. A school-centered, community-based program fits perfectly into STEM/STEAM education guidelines:
1. A curriculum driven by problem-solving, discovery and exploratory learning that requires students to actively engage a situation in order to find its solution
2. Nature of technology; engineering design; and systems thinking, maintenance and troubleshooting incorporated into the science and mathematics curricula
3. Innovative instruction allows students to explore greater depths of all of the subjects by utilizing the skills learned

4. Technology provides creative and ingenious ways to solve problems and apply what has been learned
5. Independent and collaborative research projects embedded in the curricula
6. Collaboration, communication, and critical thinking skills threaded throughout the curricula
7. Opportunities for mentoring by business, industry, and research organization leaders

Community-based research can also be a form of service learning whereby students can take the lead on specific sections or responsibilities. Most college bound students need community-service hours. Helping create a sustainable program in their community that encourages social networking and social capital can only benefit their neighbors, their lives, and their college applications!

IV. Tell Them What You Told Them

As educators with diverse demands on our time, independent schools offer the autonomy to explore scholarly passions. For those who love the sciences, be it social or classic, research offers the opportunity for both students and teachers to explore the ideas they desire to learn. The format can be individual, class wide, or community-based, but the passion is the same.

Summary

Parents have traditionally sent their children to independent schools because they perceived a comparative advantage. Most of us who work in independent schools are confident that we provide that, but if we persist in offering the same curricular options as public schools, simply stated, we aren't. We must find ways for independent secondary schools to be far superior to other options. We must invent experiential programs that leverage our unique resources in terms of staff, location, partnerships, and whatever else we might exploit. We must be thoughtful and deliberate about the various facets of what we are doing, whether in the classroom or in the local or global communities, in order to truly prepare students and our institutions to flourish in the new world, not the old.

Chapter 5

Why Do I Have to Memorize When I Can Find It On My Phone? Reconsidering What To Teach in the Information Age

Education is, after all, a backward-looking enterprise. Although a school's mission is to prepare children for the future, it can only do this by teaching them about the past—not just history, but the assembled body of knowledge in each subject. We can only teach what we know. Moreover, much of the curriculum is, if not fixed, slow-changing, and many independent schools pride themselves on their devotion to enduring truths and established traditions.... Continuity, more than change, is a core value in school life. —Robert Evans[194]

Preparation Suitable for the 21st Century

In previous chapters, we saw that education has always had the intention of preparing students for professional life: in government, law, clergy, medicine, etc., which led to the clear conclusion that, whatever we who love school and education may feel, the loftiness ascribed to the notion of elevating knowledge for its own sake is misguided. The fact is that pre-professional training tracks have taken over the university and, increasingly, high schools. We may rage against "Burger King-have it your way education," but after postmodernism's deconstructionism, that which the culture traditionally valued now seems arbitrary and baseless. Arguments for maintaining the *status quo* are specious. We had better adjust and offer "pre-" pre-professional education and far more individualized education. We must continually reassess our stakeholders' desires and keep abreast of the swiftly changing landscape. While we are at it, we should reassess what we are doing all around, in all subjects.

It bears repeating that schools are simply not required to teach Social Science, Math, Science, English, and World Languages as separate entities. They may be combined in innumerable ways, including, to name but a few, Humanities, American Studies, Latin American Studies, Nutrition, Entrepreneurship, and of course, research and projects in infinite forms. My purpose is to provoke

---

[194] Evans, Robert. "Getting To No: Building True Collegiality in Schools." *NAIS*. Winter 2012. Web. 7 Feb. 2015.

consideration and deliberation over what should be studied and, above all, above all, *why*.

Conceding or endowing subject area experts with the power to determine curricular content in their respective fields of expertise is akin to putting the fox in charge of the hen house. They are likely to enthusiastically confect elaborate lists of elements that they deem to be essential knowledge. By maintaining the understanding that the emphasis in learning must be shifted away from the mere conveyance of facts characterizing previous eras, we reveal that the disciplines are not silos but are truly connected by their shared emphasis on critical thinking and reasoning. I propose that a learning program should encourage students to do the following:

◄ To think mathematically to recognize patterns and apply rules to deduce, analyze, calculate, and solve problems.

◄ To apply the scientific method: to develop a hypothesis, test it by gathering data, then synthesize, extrapolate, and draw conclusions in order to comprehend natural processes.

◄ To use social scientific analysis to understand the cyclical nature of time, how people and societies behave, how we came to be and where we might be heading, and to assess evidence and evaluate conflicting interpretations.

◄ To communicate effectively and to write, speak, listen, and present one's ideas clearly in diverse creative and expository formats.

◄ To express themselves through the arts: to develop the imagination, to persevere, to embrace beauty and originality, to enrich life and to nourish the body, mind, and soul.

◄ To demonstrate respect for their bodies and acquire habits consistent with the maintenance of health.

◄ To engage fully with their communities in a variety of ways.

Let us explore and flesh out this proposed framework more fully.

115

> **To think mathematically to recognize patterns and apply rules to deduce, analyze, calculate, and solve problems.**

Mathematics assists us to understand the forces that govern the universe. It is particularly helpful to students' appreciation for the relevance of math to integrate into the curriculum **mathematical modeling**, which entails the process of choosing and using appropriate mathematics and statistics to analyze real-world situations to understand them better and to cultivate rational decision-making. Statistics, visual representation of data, and computer science are the most logical triad for focus on the secondary level.

Arguably, technology has revolutionized mathematics education earlier and more extensively than the other subjects. The National Council of Teachers of Mathematics articulated the evolution eloquently:

> Technology is essential in teaching and learning mathematics; it influences the mathematics that is taught and enhances student learning....Students can learn more mathematics more deeply with the appropriate use of technology....In mathematics-instruction programs, technology should be used widely and responsibly, with the goal of enriching students' learning of mathematics. The existence, versatility and power of technology make it possible and necessary to re-examine what mathematics students should learn as well as how best they can learn it.[195]

Math educators realized the potential as well as the need to reevaluate what and how students should learn. There remains deep disagreement over which skills students should master and which may be reliant on technology. Some would point to the comparatively low scores in math on international tests of skills as evidence of the failure of current methodologies.

It appears that US students perform well until the fourth grade, after which there is a decline. In the effort to discover why, a team of researchers gathered data regarding international textbook-based curricula and found that in comparison with others that performed better on the Third International Math and Science Study, the US math and science curricula differed in four ways. First, there is a lack of focus

---

[195] National Council of Teachers of Mathematics. *Principles and standards for school mathematics*. NCTM. 2000. Pp 24-25.

in the US, where teachers "cover" far more topics in a year (even three times as many) as other countries. The content tends to be presented as individual topics rather than as a coherent whole, is repeated and reviewed year after year and "very little depth is added each time the topic is addressed." Lastly, the content is "not very demanding by international standards," particularly in middle school "when the rest of the world shifts its attention from the basics of arithmetic and elementary science to beginning concepts in algebra, geometry, chemistry, and physics."[196] Others question why the TIMMS, PISA, and other tests should matter at all, since they merely measure content determined to be of significance to subject and education experts, our foxes in the hen house. Instead, we need to reassess completely.

Financial literacy is an essential skill and teaching it lends itself to project-based learning. A public school system in California created an exciting program that combines internships with life skills, a segment of which is called "The Harsh Reality Project." Students create a simulation of life as an adult and juggle income with expenses, etc.

> First, we find our supervisor's salary and title, and then we extrapolate what our estimated salary and expenses will be. We calculated our benefits, including insurance and retirement plan. With our calculated budget in hand, we flesh out the costs of living (rental vs. home-owning) and go through the house-hunting process. We find roommates, search for houses on craigslist, and even go to an onsite open house. Students learn what to look for when buying a home and how to be realistic....
>
> Second, we gauge our transportation costs. We look for cars and compute the expenses for gas and our commute to and from our internship. Third, we figure out our health care and monthly expenses. And finally, we put it all together in an oral presentation for our peers at the end of the semester....We show the class our expenses and the life we have built for ourselves.[197]

Students will immediately appreciate the relevance of this exercise in helping them

[196] Schmidt, W., R. Houang, R. and L. Cogan, L. A coherent curriculum: The case of mathematics. *American Educator*. 26.2 (2002): 10-26, 47-48.
[197] Boyar, Lily. "High School Students Develop Life Skills and Financial Literacy in "Harsh Reality" Program." *Edutopia*. 25 Mar. 2011. Web. 21 Dec. 2014.

understand and prepare for realities they are likely to encounter. As an ongoing project with perhaps a journal component as well as the final presentation, the math and rational decision making involved are inarguably more likely to be applied in their adult lives than Multivariable Calculus.

Andrew Hacker, an emeritus professor and co-author of *"Higher Education? How Colleges Are Wasting Our Money and Failing Our Kids — and What We Can Do About It"* (2010), asserts the necessity for basic arithmetic, but questions any attempt at a "rational justification" for the higher math curriculum beyond that, citing data from the Georgetown Center on Education and the Workforce that "forecasts that in the decade ahead a mere 5 percent of entry-level workers will need to be proficient in algebra or above." Instead, Hacker insists that knowledge of **statistics** is imperative.

> ....Ours is fast becoming a statistical age, which raises the bar for informed citizenship. What is needed is not textbook formulas but greater understanding of where various numbers come from, and what they actually convey....Thus mathematics teachers at every level could create exciting courses in what I call 'citizen statistics'...[to] familiarize students with the kinds of numbers that describe and delineate our personal and public lives. It could, for example, teach students how the Consumer Price Index is computed, what is included and how each item in the index is weighted — and include discussion about which items should be included and what weights they should be given. [198]

Amusingly, to those who assert that math is important because it teaches students to think, Hacker counters that "there's no evidence that being able to prove $(x^2 + y^2)^2 = (x^2 - y^2)^2 + (2xy)^2$ leads to more credible political opinions or social analysis."

Coupled with this is the imperative for students to comprehend and represent data visually. Tables, graphs, and infographics are ubiquitous and notoriously both misleading and misunderstood.[199] Steven Salzberger, Director of Johns Hopkins'

---

[198] Hacker, Andrew. "Is Algebra Necessary?" *The New York Times.* 28 July 2012. Web. 02 Dec. 2014.
[199] See especially the work of Edward Tufte (especially *The Visual Display of Quantitative Information, Envisioning Information,* etc.) and Nathan Yau (see *Data Points* and *Visualize This* and his *Flowing Data* blog).

Center for Computational Biology, similarly agrees that comprehension of statistics is key and adds **computer science**.

> With data science emerging as one of the hottest new scientific areas, a basic understanding of statistics will provide the foundation for a wide range of 21st century career paths. Not to mention that a grasp of statistics is essential for navigating the often-dubious claims of health benefits offered by various "alternative" medicine providers[200]

When I graduated from a public high school in 1986, computer programming in BASIC was a course required for graduation. It is bizarre that this has become less rather than more common, since it certainly teaches how computers work, provides excellent training in logical thinking, and enables students to be creators, not just consumers of the technology we all use on a daily basis, which should be the primary emphasis for universal applicability. Additionally, while the recent campaign launched by Bill Gates and other leaders in the technology field regarding our country's desperate need for computer programmers and increased computer science education has elicited considerable controversy, it should prompt educators to consider introducing students to coding as early as possible. Students are unlikely to study computer science in college if they haven't had prior substantive experience in the field. Finally, a "growing share of jobs in developed countries require 'computational thinking': the ability to formulate problems in such a way that they can be tackled by computers."[201]

To apply the scientific method: to develop a hypothesis, test it by gathering data, then synthesize, extrapolate, and draw conclusions in order to comprehend natural processes.

Closer analysis of most independent schools' STEM programs reveals that most amount to little more than hype: a so-called "engineering" program here, "design thinking" and a "maker space" there, perhaps a project or two. Students are still largely passive listeners, not active researchers. Schools do their students the greatest disservice imaginable when they focus on "covering content" and reduce

---

[200] Salzberger, Steven. "Should We Stop Teaching Calculus In High School?" *Forbes.* 17 July 2014. Web. 02 Dec. 2014.
[201] "A Is for Algorithm." *The Economist.* 26 Apr. 2014. Web. 02 Dec. 2014

or even eliminate labs, like the teacher who states "he can teach more quickly and neatly by demonstrating instead of having students spend time clearing their desks, doing the lab and cleaning up."[202] That is teacher-centered thinking. Science is about the process of discovery, not merely transmitting knowledge. This chapter has featured numerous examples of students engaged in the **scientific method, original research and expeditionary learning**. Direct contact with the natural world further provides opportunities for awe, for discovery, and for the realization of one's inseparable unity with all that is.

Getting students into the lab is just the first step in the direction of lifelong learning. The next is motivating students to observe and analyze immediately relevant aspects of their environment: household chemicals, cosmetics, "broscience" (ideas that sound credible but are based on misunderstanding of science) from the gym, their household drinking water, school drinking fountains, the watershed, the local flora and fauna habitat. Then, they hypothesize, test, collect meaningful data, reflect on the results, and, if applicable, develop an action plan.

Many independent school missions emphasize the importance of fostering a sense of students' responsibilities to the larger community, and nature is a part of that. It is not enough that children be outside for regimented team sports. Richard Louv's book *Last Child in the Woods* (2008) describes the pernicious consequences of the lure of the computer screen coupled with the sensationalist media-fueled fear of being outdoors unattended and involved in unstructured self-directed imaginative play. Termed "Nature Deficit Disorder," the alienation from the natural interconnected web of which we are all part can exacerbate attention deficit, anxiety, depression, obesity, and a lack of reflection. It is with good reason that so many admissions viewbooks show classes held outside, but students need opportunities to engage with nature, not just sit immobile on the grass.

To use social scientific analysis to understand the cyclical nature of time, how people and societies behave, how we came to be and where we might be heading, and to assess evidence and evaluate conflicting interpretations.

---

[202] Ross, Allison. "Science Teachers at Loxahatchee Middle School Strike Back against Hands-on Labs." *Palm Beach Post*. 16 Oct. 2011. Web.

Edmund Burke's famous line "Those who don't know history are destined to repeat it" is often cited as the reason to study history, but knowing history does not inoculate against repeating the errors—look no further than the continuation of genocide and environmental degradation, humans' continued oppression and misuse of power by those who are quite familiar with previous patterns.

> What history actually shows is that nothing works out as planned, and that everything has unintentional consequences....the results are entirely uncontrollable, and that we are far more likely to be made by history than to make it. History is past, and singular, and the same year never comes round twice.[203]

The way that History and/or Social Science continue to be taught in the Information Age is too often a "grand, nationalistic, and moralistic master story,"[204] about Great Men [for it is almost exclusively males] Wielding Power in the Past, written of course by the victors. This is maddening for the way it perpetuates colonialist and patriarchal thought and obsolete behaviorist pedagogy when there is such enormous potential to engage students through inquiry. During what has come to be appreciated as the golden age of social studies education, the 1970s and 1980s, considerable discussion and research were distilled to define a **set of skills**:

❖ Drawing inferences from sources (any traces of the past which remain), understanding the varying status of sources, and that sources are often incomplete and so 'probabalistic thinking' is required, which is valid if it is in line with what is known of the period and there is no contradictory evidence.

❖ Making suggestions based on evidence of how people in societies with different knowledge bases and belief systems from our own may have thought and felt.

❖ Selecting and combining inferences in order to construct accounts of changes over time, causes and effects, similarities and differences, continuity, and change.

---

[203] Gopnik, Adam. "Does It Help to Know History?" Editorial. *New Yorker* 28 Aug. 2014. Web. 30 Nov. 2014.
[204] Cooper, Hilary. "International Perspectives on History Education." *Education* 3-13 38.3 (2010): 219-23. 30 Nov. 2014.

❖ Understanding why accounts may be equally valid but different, depending on the time in which they are written, the evidence available, the perspectives and interests of the historian, in groups or individuals, in gender or ethnicity, in political or social history.

❖ And that therefore history is dynamic; there is no single permanent view of the past.[205]

These competencies are applicable to all of the Social Sciences, of which History is but one, which study social phenomena and the ways that they influence people's lives. By focusing on the development of the skills, students learn critical thinking and reasoning, empathy and insight into the human condition.

To communicate effectively and to write, speak, listen, and present one's ideas clearly in diverse creative and expository formats.

There is a vital imperative for students to become effective writers and **"writing across the curriculum"** is a popular initiative in many independent schools. The centrality of writing in the Common Core State Standards in public schools is expected to have considerable impact on students' skills. The Standards mandate that students be able "to write for multiple purposes (e.g. to persuade, to inform, and to narrate)" and "use writing...to analyze, interpret and build knowledge...across discipline-specific subjects."[206] Students' writing should not be limited, however, to mere papers. Multimedia literacy is soaring in its importance on all levels and increasingly included as a core competency in universities.[207]

The CCSS expects students to "Use technology, including the Internet, to produce, publish, and update individual or shared writing products in response to ongoing feedback, including new arguments or information."[208] For well over a

---

[205] Ibid.

[206] Graham, Steve, Charles A. MacArthur, and Jill Fitzgerald. *Best Practices in Writing Instruction.* Guilford, 2007. Print. p. 4

[207] Young, Jeffrey R. "Across More Classes, Videos Make the Grade; In some science and writing courses, final papers are giving way to multimedia." *The Chronicle of Higher Education* 8 May 2011. Web. 9 Dec. 2014.

[208] CCSS.ELA-LITERACY.W.11-12.6

decade, many teachers have assigned writing blogs, websites, or posts on social media, reviews of books, local restaurants or attractions, etc. This is a suitable means of teaching students to write for the media they are likely to utilize.

There is one caveat for academic purposes. So-called "digital immigrants" are almost as likely as "digital natives" to be seduced by the bells and whistles of new technologies at the expense of competencies. Educators are surely familiar with PowerPoint presentations and two-minute digital wonderments that yield less than a few sentences' worth of content when they are closely examined. Video essays, YouTube videos and documentary films permit students to respond to the ineluctable appeal of the postmodern "pictorial turn" and develop their skills for collaboration, communication, and multimedia literacy by incorporating images with fictional or analytical writing. Of course, it is highly motivating to students to **write with a real-world purpose and present publicly**, like composing opinion essays for newspapers and news websites, and video-based public service and fundraising pieces for local non-profits.

For many years, I had a corollary to this proposition that read: "To communicate in languages or cultures other than one's own is to see the world through other lenses and to broaden one's own worldview," but I have since revised my perspective. World languages are an intriguing example of both the response of educational institutions to the wants of the age and the disruption of technology.

Language instruction is in decline in higher education. Since 2000, "the number of British universities offering degrees in modern foreign languages had declined by 40%"[209] and domestic programs are being eliminated or reduced. In fact, Spanish is the only European language available as a major to the 400,000 student in the SUNY system. Most independent schools still require the study of a language other than English, however. Not surprisingly, most students (70%) select Spanish, with far fewer enrolled in French (15%), and German (4%).[210] Once ubiquitous, the study of Latin and Greek has declined dramatically since the 1958 National Defense Education Act (which granted funding for *modern* foreign languages only), with periodic up-tics, so that now only 2% of all those studying a

---

[209] Gordin, Michael D. "Tongue-Tied Nation." *The Chronicle of Higher Education.* 27 Mar. 2015. Print. 07 Apr. 2015.
[210] http://www.actfl.org/sites/default/files/pdfs/ReportSummary2011.pdf

language other than English on the K-12 level are enrolled in Latin; Greek isn't even counted as a separate category as its numbers are so inconsequential.[211] [212]

Other languages studied have changed dramatically over time depending upon the vagaries of global economics and politics. During the Cold War, Russian was *de rigueur*, now Choate Rosemary Hall (CT) has an Arabic and Middle Eastern Studies program. In 2011, Florida State legislators introduced of a bill proposing free tuition and fees for Mandarin and Portuguese classes at state universities, underscoring the need for speakers of those languages to increase opportunities with the state's two largest trade partners, China and Brazil.

At this point, in the interest of full disclosure, I reveal a personal investment in language learning as a degreed and certified teacher of Spanish who taught it for several years on the high school level. I enjoyed studying and mastering its grammar, its literature, and the diversity of cultures that use the language as their medium of communication. I have spent a great deal of formative time in Chile, Colombia, Mexico, and Spanish-speaking communities in the US. Like most every other language teacher, and in contrast to the technology-embracing math teachers, I penalized students for using digital translation programs, the bane of every language teacher, largely because they would impede learning and they were wildly imperfect.

Then I experienced a lightning bolt. I needed to translate a two-page business contract in Spanish for a client. I am perfectly capable of performing the task, but in the spirit of inquiry, I thought I'd see what would happen if I fed the document to Google Translate. I was astonished. Google Translate served me two flawless pages in the appropriate tone.

On top of this, Microsoft has a translation tool that maintains the speaker's voice and accent, and Skype is in beta for simultaneous translation for face-to-face communication.[213] Since the twenty most popular languages are spoken by 53% of the world, the task of digitally facilitating communication among large numbers of people is possible. Computer-assisted technology for translation is already commonplace and will become even more so. It is time to rethink our purposes and methods for teaching world languages and perhaps shift the emphasis to teaching

---

[211] http://education.stateuniversity.com/pages/2160/Latin-in-Schools-Teaching.html

[212] http://www.actfl.org/sites/default/files/pdfs/ReportSummary2011.pdf

[213] "Microsoft Unveils Real-Time Skype Universal Translator - Communications on Top Tech News." *Top Tech News RSS*. n.d. Web. 28 Dec. 2014.

about cultures as experientially as possible. Intercultural competencies might represent a useful direction. Students can learn appropriate greetings, farewells, compliments, apologies, communication styles, and other cultural norms through direct instruction and contact with natives, movies, television, and of course, living in other cultures.

> **To express themselves through the arts: to develop the imagination, to persevere, to embrace beauty and originality, to enrich life and to nourish the body, mind, and soul.**

Exposure to cultural products including literature, philosophy, world religions, music, dance, paintings, and more that have touched the hearts and minds of generations help us to construct meaningful lives and live more deeply. For millennia, artistic formation was considered the purview of the privileged, so how could this have been discarded in the course of a century? In the public schools, arts education experienced radical fluctuations in support and funding throughout the 20th century. The rise of testing for purposes of intellectual measurement and prediction contributed to the demise of art, as "art abilities didn't appear to correlate with general intelligence" and artistic ability was seen as a "special gift," less subject to training and beyond the scope of essential preparation for life.[214] Art found little support in those proponents of education as practical preparation for a workaday world. As college admission became a more common outcome of independent schools, the importance of the study of art further waned in order to focus on "academic subjects."

The fall of the arts from its hallowed position in independent schools finds a telling example in Vassar.

> In the late 19th century, Vassar students at the Schools of Art and Music "received a different degree than the regular B.A. candidates, and the courses were listed separately in the catalogue" before the schools were abolished entirely and students were able to receive credit only for "history and theory of art and music." Then, in the effort to form a more academically rigorous student body, admissions requirements were changed to demand "more language, math, and

---

[214] Efland, Arthur. *A History of Art Education: Intellectual and Social Currents in Teaching the Visual Arts.* Columbia Teachers College, 1990.

science…as well as sustained sequential study in certain areas" and students were exempted from required courses in the arts if they had taken them during high school.[215]

The practice of the arts as a form of cultural capital was clearly relegated to the realm of delightful avocation rather than serious intellectual pursuit. This excerpt also serves to underscore the impact of college admissions requirements as the primary driver of curriculum. Shifts in educators' understanding of child development, learning theory, and other cultural phenomena have had significant consequences on the other subjects that survive (or haven't) in independent schools. Graduation requirements for the arts usually range from two to four semesters. Studio art, music, photography, theater, and dance are common offerings, but more likely as extra-curricular pursuits rather than as the requisite segment of the curriculum they had been, particularly for girls.

Two recent developments have occurred to bolster the arts in independent schools. First, Daniel Pink's *A Whole New Mind* (2005) made an enormous splash and was featured in scores of summer reading lists and continues to be constantly cited by speakers at professional development conferences alongside others (like Malcolm Gladwell) who present anecdotal evidence and arguments rife with fallacious logic to mass appeal. Pink appealed to widespread anxiety about the dismal economic horizon with a simplistic and specious argument that the future belongs to the "right-brained" (a notion we shall deconstruct in Chapter 6) creatives, the designers, artists, and meaning makers since virtually everything else can be automated or outsourced.[216]

Second, in 2007, Georgette Yakman started a movement to add an A for Arts to STEM to create the acronym STEAM, ostensibly to ensure that creativity be included, though it is difficult to image that an engaging science and technology program might not foster creativity. The latest initiative is to add an R for Reading, which pretty much brings us back to the original curriculum with the exception of world languages. In any case, STEM/STEAM initiatives often integrate the principles of design thinking as well as project-based learning described earlier. It seems rather tragic to have to defend the promotion and inclusion of the arts with a

---

[215] "A History of the Curriculum 1865-1970s." *Vassar College Encyclopedia.* 2005. Web. 19 Dec. 2014.

[216] Pink's assertion that "the MFA is the new MBA" is contradicted by the return on college investment lists that invariably cite art schools among the worst financial investments, though their graduates are undoubtedly satiated in other non-material ways. See also Yagoda, Ben. "'Culture Crash,' by Scott Timberg." *The New York Times.* 21 Mar. 2015. Web. 31 Mar. 2015.

rationale beyond aesthetic pleasure and beauty, but it merely reflects the utilitarian *Zeitgeist*.

> **To reflect on their values, gifts and possible paths in adulthood, demonstrate respect for their bodies and acquire habits consistent with the maintenance of wellbeing.**

Independent schools have long prided themselves on nurturing the whole child in body, mind, and spirit, but the emphasis is often squarely on the first two. For some students, participation in athletics is undeniably one of the most cherished experiences of their school years. Working as part of a team toward a common goal, constantly striving to improve skills and seeing results, experiencing success, inspiration, and encouragement, developing sportive conduct (the gender-neutral term for "sportsmanship") and grace after win or loss, and even wearing a uniform and riding the bus with other team members have a powerful positive impact. As part of schools' profiles for colleges and for prospective parents, the percentage of students who participate in athletics is a matter of pride, often exceeding 80% of the student body. In the age of sedentary habits and obesity, this is a laudable accomplishment.

Athletics has long been compulsory, particularly in boarding schools, rooted philosophically in two aphorisms: the Latin *mens sana in corpore sano* based on the much earlier saying from the pre-Socratic Greek philosopher Thales, and the British "the battle of Waterloo was won in the playing-fields of Eton." Alas, traditional wisdom has its limits. The notion that the scholar-athlete was revered in antiquity is utter nonsense, ably debunked by classicist David Young; intellectuals were just that and were not expected to be athletically inclined or able.[217] Most delicious is the following morsel. In 1881, Matthew Arnold (son of Dr. Arnold of Rugby School who declared the purpose of the English public school "to make gentlemen of savages") wrote in an essay "An Eton Boy":

> The aged Barbarian (ie: a member of the English upper classes) will, …mumble to us his story how the battle of Waterloo was won in the playing-fields of Eton. Alas! disasters have been prepared in those

---

[217] Young, David C. "Mens Sana in Corpore Sano? Body and Mind in Ancient Greece." *The International Journal of the History of Sport*. 22.1 (January 2005): 22 – 41. Web. 4 Dec 2014.

playing-fields as well as victories; disasters due to inadequate mental training— to want of application, knowledge, intelligence, lucidity.[218]

And there's the rub. Schools on all levels, whether public or private, are often held in thrall by athletics, despite the cost and, in many cases, its lack of relevance to mission. In search of the reason for this, I turned to Michael Mandelbaum's *The Meaning of Sports* (2005), in which he elucidates the reasons for the irrational power that sport wields in society: diversion, nostalgia for childhood, catharsis, predictable structure in a chaotic time, etc. It provided greater intellectual understanding, but not a satisfactorily logical justification for the way that sport dominates so many of our schools.

There are other motivations for athletic participation, of course. Parents harbor pipe dreams of college scholarships, but the reality is this:

> There are more than seven million high school athletes, but there are college roster spots for just two percent of them. Getting to the NCAA Division I level is even tougher. Just one percent of those seven million student-athletes get a full ride to a Division I program.[219]

There is no question that a skilled athlete has improved admissions prospects, though that may not translate into cash. Athletics also feeds students' hunger for glory and the joy in participation and camaraderie, and administrators' aspirations for state championships.

Unfortunately, athletics has taken precedence in many schools, with outrageous recruiting tactics, full scholarships for athletes who do not come close to meeting admissions standards, separate academic tracks and/or requirements for athletes, and profligate funding to support expensive programs and coaching staff lured from university Division 1 programs. Parents' and fans' behavior can be so offensive that many schools have created guides detailing expectations for parents' behavior.[220] What is going on here? Isn't the core of sportive conduct ethics and grace, attitude, respect, and character formation? Instead, students learn that adults cut corners and violate rules in order to win; the end justifies the means. Students

---

[218] "Misquotation: "The Battle of Waterloo Was Won on the Playing Fields of Eton""
Misquotation: "The Battle of Waterloo Was Won On... Oxford Academic, 8 Aug. 2013. Web. 19 Dec. 2014.
[219] National Collegiate Scouting Association. "Athletic Scholarship Statistics." n.d. 10 Oct 2014.
[220] A fine example is from Minnesota State High School League. *Sportsmanship: A Parents Guide.* N.d. Web. 10 Feb 2015. www.mshsl.org/mshsl/teamup/sms_guide_parentpledge.pdf

learn that athletics takes precedence over academics when they know it shouldn't be so. Young people see their parents (and occasionally coaches) behave abominably. School leaders cannot afford to let these be the lessons that students learn.

It is not my intention to propose the elimination of athletics, but rather to urge that administrators assess its proper role, particularly if we avow holistic attention to our students. Many day school students participate in community and travel teams as well, which makes for an awful lot of sport. The increase in specialized one-sport athletes in particular can lead to injuries, especially in the well-documented cases of the frequency of torn ACLs in female soccer players and concussions. Then there is the emotional stress due to the encroachment on study time, since it is not unusual for students to play or practice with the school team for several hours after school, followed by several more hours with their club team. Travel clubs can consume entire weekends.

What we do need to account for and accept is the tremendous emphasis placed upon athletics to the diminishment of intellectual development. It raises the question as to what our essential goals are for our athletics programs. If we are seriously committed to incorporating team sports for the lessons they teach about teamwork and behaving with grace and sportive conduct, we need to be more explicit in their articulation and assessment. If the main goal is lifelong fitness, we should ensure that students know what constitutes that. Fitness is not likely to consist of team sports in adulthood, but rather working out at a gym, perhaps taking classes like Pilates, Zumba and CrossFit. Realizing this, Spelman College left the NCAA in 2012, and reallocated the $1M for varsity sports to a wellness program that includes nutritional counseling, intramurals, and exercise classes for physical and emotional wellbeing.

Our students often trudge from class to class to extra-curricular activity or athletics to sleep. There is little **time for reflection** on what kind of person the student aspires to be, whether he or she is making the right choices about courses, activities, and relationships, what the responsibility is of the individual to the community, what defines the successful human being, and how he or she wishes to shape her life. In Chapter 2, I discussed the importance of vocational counseling to help young people reflect on those things they do well and enjoy and how these might take shape as a path (or a segment of one) to adulthood. Students must have guidance and time to reflect as part of their wellbeing.

This is part of **health education**, which has not always been a priority in schools, independent or public. This subject should encompass ways of developing lifelong habits for the development of physical and emotional health: balance, self-regulation, stress management, the operation and interrelation of the various systems of the body, maintenance of healthy weight, the effects of exercise, nutrition, and drugs (which should include a wide range from over the counter and prescription pharmaceuticals to herbal supplements and substances, illicit drugs and alcohol), and the cultivation of healthy relationships and sex.

The school meal program is a stupendous opportunity that is often ignored. Led by Chef Robert "Chef Bobo" Surles, The Calhoun School's (NY) culinary program is an impressive model.

> Chef Bobo's program fosters numerous opportunities for Calhoun students to learn about food and its relation to their physical and mental well-being. The Chef frequently goes into classrooms, offering cooking demonstrations that focus on health, science-oriented lessons about herbs and chemistry, and social studies and linguistic lessons that expose children to diversity in cultures and foods. There are also a number of after-school cooking classes for students, at every age level, that reinforce the importance of high quality ingredients, recipe variety and well-seasoned food. Ultimately, the integration of the food program into the life of the school creates an environment that promotes healthier attitudes about food and eating behaviors.[221]

The culinary team also provides sample sizes of foods with which they are unlikely to be familiar and takes the time to explain to students the cultural history of the foods they serve. At mealtimes, students are served controlled portions, which teaches students about serving size and reduces waste. The school also promotes Community Supported Agriculture and a Green Roof that supplies the lunch program as it teaches students about gardening. With the rise of foodie culture, the Food Channel and cooking competitions like Master Chef Junior, cooking classes are extremely popular. With the portable safe stoves (i.e. NuWave precision cooktops), students can be taught to create a complete healthy meal from appetizer to entrée with side and dessert. [222]

---

[221] http://www.calhoun.org/eatrightnow

[222] Another opportunity that a school's culinary program provides is surprisingly popular among students and one that universities are offering with increasing frequency: meal etiquette. Students learn to set a table, use the appropriate silverware in a formal or semi-formal setting, and behave with gracious table manners.

Students should be guided to explore the effects of nutrition on their bodies. While some independent schools have admirable food service programs and farm to table, bioregional, and organic initiatives, private schools were found in at least one national study to offer *less* healthy food environments than public, presumably due to the federal regulations that govern public schools' meal programs.[223] Students can analyze the food environment, from snack bar offerings to vending machines and the dining facilities. This can be a collaborative project that affords students the ability to have a positive evidence-based impact on their environment, with the assistance of a variety of food environment assessment tools available.[224] In view of the abundance of peer-reviewed scientific literature available on the effects of nutrition on adolescents, there is no excuse for vending machines stocked with caffeinated and sugary beverages and highly processed snacks. The medium is the message; the school environment teaches in everything that happens there. Be sure that the lessons are desirable ones.

Most vital is that students understand the imperative of seeking and using peer-reviewed evidence-based data to make decisions about their health, not "bro-science," random unsubstantiated articles on the Internet, or other media outlets. Recently, the British Medical Journal published an article analyzing the claims on two popular TV shows that dispense medical advice watched by millions of viewers daily. The researchers found, "Believable or somewhat believable evidence supported 33% of the recommendations on *The Dr. Oz Show* and 53% on *The Doctors*."[225] The Pew Research Center found that "72% of internet users say they looked online for health information within the past year."[226] Clearly it is a worthwhile endeavor to train students in how to locate reliable information on health, from side effects of medications to *peer-reviewed* treatment options for various syndromes and diseases.

---

[223] Turner L and F.J. Chaloupka. Slow progress in changing the school food environment: nationally representative results from public and private elementary schools. *Journal of the Academy of Nutrition and Diet.* 112.9 (Sep. 2012):1380-9.

[224] See the extensive resources available for schools in *Measures of the Food Environment*. National Cancer Institute. 21 July 2014. Web. 19 Dec. 2014.

[225] Korownyk, Christina et al. "Televised medical talk shows—what they recommend and the evidence to support their recommendations: a prospective observational study." *BMJ* 349:g7346 (17 Dec 2014). Accessed 27 Dec 2014.

[226] "Health Fact Sheet." *Pew Research Centers Internet American Life Project RSS.* 16 Dec. 2013. Web. 27 Dec. 2014.

While thirty-three states require that public schools instruct students about HIV/AIDS and twenty-two require sex education, independent schools lag behind. Faith-based schools often treat the subject through their specific lens. Others apply methodologies that run the gamut from the traditional, employing lectures, readings, tests and quizzes to convey information taught by science or physical education teachers, to discussion and information sharing in peer advisory groups led by seniors who are trained facilitators to homegrown curricula facilitated or taught by professional health educators. Schools considering the development of such a program could benefit enormously from the guidelines and research-based resources established by the Sexuality Information Education Council of the United States.[227] The most successful curricula will address a "wide spectrum of subject matter, including sexual orientation, gender identity and gender expression, relationships, human anatomy and reproduction, sexual behavior, sexual pleasure, disease and pregnancy prevention, media stereotypes, peer pressure, and more."[228]

Values clarification and ethical decision-making are essential components of sex education. Skits and situational case studies are particularly effective methods that afford students the opportunity to work through potential scenarios and be skillfully guided to reflect on the potential consequences and various dimensions of the situations that they encounter, in the effort to "clarify their values, build interpersonal skills, and understand the spiritual, emotional, and social aspects of sexuality."[229]

Fostering **critical thinking and ethical character** is a professed imperative in virtually every educational institution yet an effective means of inculcating this, its efficacy proven throughout millennia, is curiously absent except as an occasional elective course for seniors: Philosophy. Admittedly, discussing Plato's dialogues, Bacon, Lao Tzu or Confucius around the Harkness table isn't as immediately and personally relevant as it could be. Through their work with the John Carroll University Carroll Cleveland Philosophers' Program for at-risk youth, Professors Sharon Kaye and Paul Thomson have had excellent results from their method of engaging students in the timeless themes of philosophy (Truth, Beauty, Justice, Freedom, the Meaning of Life, etc) through writing and performing skits "to formulate philosophical positions using examples drawn from their own lives."[230] This encourages emotional growth and the sort of reflection on one's

---

[227] See http://www.siecus.org/_data/global/images/guidelines.pdf

[228] Corngold, Josh. "Introduction: The Ethics of Sex Education." *Educational Theory* 63.5 (2013): 439-42.

[229] http://www.uua.org/re/owl/

[230] For a sample, see a) Kaye, Sharon. "Dress Rehearsal for Life: Using Drama to Teach

purpose, values and notions of success that faith-based schools promote, but that is so often absent in independent schools, except perhaps during advisory, depending on how that is structured and conceived.[231] Do we perceive this to be unimportant navel-gazing? Do we think that students consider these themes on their own without guidance? Do we presume that we all share the same concept of success and the purpose of our lives?

Medical, law and business schools have ethics as part of their curricula, books on leadership and effective management practices frequently encourage reflection on purpose, values, and mission, yet instead of guiding our students on that path, we place them like gerbils on the wheel, in constant motion with little time for reflection. We fulfill our mission of helping to shape young people of character if we guide them to reflect, to strive for reflective equilibrium, that state of having our "set of beliefs about principles and our beliefs about individual cases achieve a state of balance or coherence,"[233] and internal logical consistency—their actions congruent with their beliefs.

On a related theme, public education follows science, as the "ruling epistemology of the day" and scientists and health practitioners are intrigued with the health benefits of **mindfulness** or meditation. Education and science publications as well as popular media frequently tout meditation programs' effectiveness with groups as diverse as at-risk youth and Silicon Valley entrepreneurs.

> While there is a clear emphasis in public school on 'bottom-lines' and 'performance', there is a growing acknowledgement of the affective domain and social emotional learning (SEL) as 'crucial to [students'] well-being.' Health (attention, memory, stress reduction, and self-regulation) was the trigger for the mindfulness revolution.[234]

Well in advance of implementing any of the curricula available, such as MindUP and ".b" [dot b], school staff should deliberate over and carefully present their

---

Philosophy to Inner-City High School Students." *Analytic Teaching*. 26.1 (2006).
b) Kaye's and *Thomas' Philosophy for Teens: Questioning Life's Big Ideas*, 2006, and *More Philosophy for Teens*, 2007.

[231] For further resources, also see Center for Spiritual and Ethical Education csee.org

[233] Edmonds, David. *Would You Kill the Fat Man?: The Trolley Problem and What Your Answer Tells Us about Right and Wrong.* Princeton University Press. 2013.

[234] Ergas, Oren. "Mindfulness in Education at the Intersection of Science, Religion, and Healing." *Critical Studies in Education* 55.1 (2014): 58. Accessed 3 Dec 14.

goals to the community and be sensitive to and prepared for pushback due to the history of mindfulness in religions, particularly Buddhism, though it has certainly had a role in monotheistic traditions and others. Beyond that, educators can "play" at implementing mindfulness for SEL purposes, but should be advised that for millennia, mindfulness has led practitioners beyond mere stress reduction to glimpsing something far deeper: the illusory nature of reality. An awareness of the interconnectedness of all things can put in its place the ego as but a small fraction of the gestalt. From that perspective comes the realization that the drive for achievement can narrow the viewpoint and lose sight of the journey.

Summary

Subjects and pedagogical methodologies will change, but there are certain elements that will retain their significance: the skills of critical thinking, collaboration, communication, creativity, the value of character, and responsibility to the larger community. School leadership must keep abreast of best practices and trends in higher education and the workplace and should examine the ways that the school might integrate them to better prepare students for college and for life. There are a number of fascinating trends with sufficient traction in higher education and certain imaginative secondary schools both public and independent to warrant serious consideration. We will next turn our attention to some of those.

Chapter 6

Let's Try This! Creating A Culture of
Professionalism, Collaboration and Innovation

Those people who develop the ability to continuously acquire new and better forms of knowledge that they can apply to their work and to their lives will be the movers and shakers in our society for the indefinite future. — Brian Tracy

Hundreds of worthy peer-reviewed articles are published each year in the field of education, but little of it is actually implemented in classrooms. Who is reading the research at your school, if anyone? Is your Head of School? Are Division Directors? Department Chairs? Teachers? How is the information disseminated? If the thought-leaders in your school are not reading, sharing, discussing, and implementing evidence-based practices, they are derelict in their duty. I reiterate: teachers teach as they were taught. Educators who reflect on their professional practice are quite willing to add tools to their toolboxes, but stand-alone professional development workshops yield notoriously poor harvests. For maximum results, teachers must be shown and have the opportunity to model and try out the practical application and comparative advantage of a new practice, procedure, technique, etc. by someone with classroom experience.

The Professional Landscape

Imagine a school culture that is a true learning organization, characterized by a rich and stimulating exchange of ideas among professional educators committed to mission, their craft, and to student engagement and achievement. Imagine an environment in which staff members review educational research and share pedagogical insights and articles in a rich online forum. They feel free to try out promising and imaginative ideas, methods, and projects in their classrooms. Teachers observe and analyze each other's lesson plans, inputs (what the teacher does) and outputs (what students do, how they react, and what they produce) in a way that is not threatening, ego-driven or competitive, as they seek ways to improve their own practice and provide insight to others regarding theirs. Imagine that teachers collaborate to construct action research projects to test their hypotheses about how best to achieve a pedagogical objective.[235] All staff are

---

[235] See Sagor, Richard. *Guiding School Improvement With Action Research*. ACSD, 2000.

engaged with their subject matter; they read the salient journals and/or blogs, attend national conferences, publish on the web, in open source journals, or peer-reviewed ones. Staff members demonstrate leadership and initiative and collaborate to create new programs and methods. They celebrate students' and each other's successes.

Performance evaluation takes place collaboratively. Teachers welcome visitors in their classrooms unannounced, confident in their expertise. Assessors are frequently in classrooms and are intimately aware of learning objectives, teaching styles, projects, opportunities, and challenges. Imagine that teachers establish annual goals and engage in continual targeted professional development and reflection on their practice. Teachers view parents and students as collaborators, partners on the journey toward realizing potential. Teachers feel valued as professionals, sustained in their goals for professional growth, and supported by a community of similarly committed individuals.

Now ask whether this is your school. If it is, congratulations! Be sure to do everything in your power to keep up the good work and keep taking the temperature of the professional climate. If it isn't your school, ask yourself and the staff why not and what can be done to work toward it.

Knowledge Workers

> *Knowledge workers don't believe they are paid to work 9 to 5; they believe they're paid to be effective. Organizations that understand this—and strip away everything that gets in their knowledge workers' way—will be able to attract, hold, and motivate the best performers.—* *Peter Drucker* [236]

On one end of the spectrum is the boarding environment, where teachers in particular are more or less on call 24/7. On the other is the open campus environment in which teachers are expected to be on campus only when they have a scheduled class. The majority of independent schools fall in the middle with varying degrees of an "8 to 4 and out the door" culture. One school administrator explained that teachers' course loads were reduced to four in order to enable teachers to spend more time one on one with students, yet it was clear that teachers felt entitled to leave when their classes were done for the day. Obviously, the

---

[236] Drucker, Peter F. "Managing Knowledge Means Managing Oneself." *Leader to Leader.* Peter F. Drucker Foundation. Spring 2000.

established objective was not being met and instead, the results were an excellent perquisite, a greater sense of entitlement on the part of the teachers, and an alarming increase by thousands of dollars in the cost of educating each student. Responsible oversight to ensure that objectives are being met is a fiduciary mandate.

It is further galling to hear teachers complain about not having time to collaborate. Such an attitude reflects a misguided sense of entitlement and erodes the public image and the core values of the profession. The traditional summer vacation is prime time for collaboration, and in many schools (including the one I led), teachers are required to return to work several weeks prior to the commencement of classes precisely for the purpose of collaborative planning. Depending on their schedule, secondary school teachers will generally teach five classes of eight. In a block schedule, that can mean *teaching every other day* or teaching one class every other day. In a straight schedule, that means teaching five approximately 42-minute periods a day. If the teacher has two separate classes to teach, it means *repeating* virtually the exact content several times a day.

That is an inefficient system indisputably ripe for disruption. In most schools, the part of the day not dedicated to teaching is open for lesson planning, correcting work, and collaborating. It has traditionally been the case that the creation and compilation of lesson content is most time intensive in the first two years of teaching, after which teachers continue to adapt and adopt, borrow and share most of their lessons greatly facilitated by the Internet. In some project-based environments, the teacher's role shifts to guide and facilitator, with far less time dedicated to correcting, grading, and lesson preparation on the part of the teacher.

Those in the teaching profession need to see themselves as knowledge workers for whom the curtain doesn't close at the stage direction exeunt students. Knowledge workers in other sectors collaborate a great deal, often long after teachers are back at home, often until 9 or 10 PM, over dinner, weekends, whatever works. The teaching force is likely to decrease precipitously due to the scalability and exponentially lower cost of online learning; educators had better demonstrate themselves to be creative innovators and figure out how to make themselves indispensable since smashing the computers like the Luddites the looms simply won't be effective.

The notion of the classroom as a "castle inviolate," as one teacher described her own, is pervasive and is extremely counterproductive. At highly effective and collaborative schools, the work of teaching is deprivatized and teachers may be in each others' classrooms constantly. In the school I led, teachers frequently team-taught, observed each other, and collaborated. Admissions and administrators escorted visitors in and out of classrooms virtually on a daily basis without advance notice. Teachers were proud that their methods were so appreciated that visitors wanted to observe them and the practice was another part of the culture of transparency, trust, and creativity. Teachers in collaborative schools "report dramatically higher satisfaction with day to day work."[237]

Collaboration can take many forms. Grade level teams and subject-specific teams can support and enrich one another in a variety of ways to share best practices and information on how best to reach individual students, especially those who may be struggling. Team teaching is a broad term that comprises many practices including a guest from outside the school teaching a class on a regularly scheduled basis, merely sharing lab/lecture responsibilities, or a History specialist and a Literature specialist co-teaching in some schedule permutation a class in American Studies. Team teaching can be a fulfilling experience for teachers and students because it enables teachers to leverage their expertise and interests to provide a rich and stimulating environment for students. Partnerships with community organizations, businesses, and universities can yield mentoring relationships for students on their projects, staff collaboration in subject areas, and more. Universities in particular may provide teaching interns, programming, equipment, and so on. Various foundations are eager to provide grants for innovative and promising university/K-12 partnerships.

In order for any of this to occur, of course, educators need to broaden and reinvigorate their understanding of their professional roles and responsibilities to include networking and cultivating relationships with other educators, prospective partners, and experts in the field. They must actively participate in events and organizations in the larger community. Other knowledge workers in for-profit and social sectors do this as a matter of course; for educators to limit their professional activities to the school grounds reflects an obsolete paradigm. This shift does require training, of course, as well as administrative support and financial backing, but the rewards are vast.

---

[237] Boston Consulting Group. "Teachers Know Best Teachers' Views on Professional Development." *College Ready*. Gates Foundation, 2014. Web. 14 Jan. 2015, p. 8

Hiring for Optimal Performance

Every January, heads of school everywhere plead with staff to advise them if they plan to vacate their position and to recommend friends who are seeking positions to fill any openings that may arise. Many claim this to be their most effective way of filling vacancies. It is lazy and the path of least resistance. Unquestionably cost-effective on the short term, it saves the school from the pricey proposition of sending school representatives to the hiring conferences as well as paying the percentage of the new hires' salaries to the recruiting firms. It also perpetuates the good ol' boy network by bringing in cronies who may "fit" with the school because, after all, Tom vouches for him. *It does not, however, bring the best candidates to the school.*

We tend to believe that the people we like are good at their jobs without any hard evidence to support that. The fact is that in most schools collaboration is rare and teachers may be aware of a project or two that another teacher is leading and may overhear a few students' comments about the colleague, but teachers rarely observe other teachers *teaching*. In response to principals' and teachers' hearty recommendations, I have invited candidates to teach a sample class only to be horrified by the presentation. Teachers routinely use their connections to find alternate employment for friends without any inkling of their performance shortcomings because their positive regard leads them to assume the best.

Similarly, letters of recommendation vary in their usefulness. When employees request a recommendation, it is an unfortunately increasingly common practice for administrators to encourage candidates to write the letter and merely submit it for their signature. Some schools do not permit administrators to write letters for staff for legal reasons and some administrators will not state anything negative in writing or orally for the same reason. On the other hand, some letters reveal red or at least subtle pink flags for the perceptive prospective employers. A cursory read simply isn't sufficient, but is too common. I have read the same letters as a dozen other people at a hiring conference and none noticed the magnitude of the writer's oblique comment about a candidate's tendency to be an uncooperative loose cannon.

Resumés and letters of recommendation should be read with an exceedingly critical eye. If an applicant has spent over ten years at a school, it's a safe bet that her pedagogical style will likely be in sync with the school's ethos, unless she reveals that she is seeking alternative employment in order to grow and express a different methodology or philosophy. Resumés can reveal a breadth of experience (or lack thereof), a propensity for collaboration (or not) or taking healthy (or not) risks, assuming responsibility, etc. The more the hiring staff know about the different schools, the better able they will be to make determinations about potential candidates. The same may be stated regarding the programmatic, technical and philosophical emphases of colleges or graduate schools when considering recent graduates. Various "data-driven hiring" programs that claim to use advanced analytics able to crunch all of this data without human bias are currently being marketed to schools, but their efficacy remains to be seen.

Hiring is not to be delegated to the uninformed; it is a complex process. For that reason, it is of limited utility to rely too heavily on current teaching staff in the hiring process. Too many teachers discard resumés and cover letters due to unreasonable prejudice: perceived errors in grammar (often stylistic, but still correct) or formatting issues, perceptions of quality of an institution of which the applicant was an alumnus or alumna or where he or she taught. In order to participate effectively, teachers need training in order to be discerning but not judgmental, to avoid falling prey to impressive pedigrees, and to really understand what it might mean for someone to have been at a series of schools for three years each—not necessarily a negative indicator. Most of all, they need to be able to bracket their own experience and values out of the equation. A varied career trajectory quite different from their own might be an enormous asset rather than, as teachers often opine, a demonstration that one is not really committed to or talented at teaching. In project-based settings, experience in the real world tends to yield the best results in students' projects.

An independent school veteran and I reviewed the hundreds of resumés that came our way with entirely disparate visions. He was looking for pedigree in experience; stints in any of the Founders League schools placed a candidate in the Second Look pile. At his insistence, I did invite several of these folks to teach sample classes; we concurred that the results were disastrous. One used twenty-two minutes of a forty-five minute demonstration class to discuss her children and her dog. I asked her afterward how she thought it went and she replied, "Really well!" I told her what I thought and she replied, "Well, I had to establish rapport." Despite abundantly clear directives issued at the time of invitation regarding our pedagogical expectations, dozens of candidates lectured at students for the entire period. Elite provenance of teaching experience did in fact affect the teaching quality, though not for the better. It may have watered the fertile soil to give rise to a strong sense of entitlement. The pure lecture or lecture and discussion format promoted by many schools and accepted and expected by the students of those schools may have benefitted them for preparing them for the poor pedagogy in many universities, but I remain firmly unconvinced that they reaped any reward from hearing daily tales of teachers' personal lives.

For project and inquiry based learning, it is helpful to hire staff with experience in publishing in peer-reviewed journals and who are professionally involved in their fields. It is also crucial that they have a commitment to and passion for helping students to engage in the research process, know how to connect with colleagues in universities and encourage students to connect with subject area mentors. Finding folks to meet these criteria is far less challenging than it might appear. With a sharp decline in full-time faculty positions in universities, there is an extraordinary glut of unemployed PhDs on the market in a wide variety of fields (only 62.7% reported a firm commitment for a job in 2013).[238] Graduate schools are an excellent place to search.

Interviewing for Insight

Interviewing is an art that one develops with practice and reading the methods of experts. First, however, reading resumés and letters of recommendation with critical attention is imperative and should lead to specific questions about various experiences, especially *why* the candidate chose a certain position or activity and what she learned from reflecting on it. Remember that interviewing is not the best way of selecting candidates, as dozens of studies have demonstrated, largely because of the interviewers' biases. They subconsciously seek people like themselves, project qualities onto them, and confirm initial impressions, which causes them to overlook information that provides greater insight. The weekly *Corner Office* feature in *The New York Times* consistently provides helpful suggestions for interviewing questions and insight into what business leaders look for in candidates, but a better method is suggested by Sheena Iyengar of Columbia Business School:

> More structured approaches, like obtaining samples of candidates' work or asking how he would respond to difficult hypothetical situations, are dramatically better at assessing future success, with a nearly threefold advantage over traditional interviews.[239]

Candidates should be able to discuss how they structure a typical class and why.

---

[238] June, Audrey Williams. "Doctoral Degrees Increased Last Year, but Career Opportunities Remained Bleak." *The Chronicle of Higher Education.* 19 Dec. 2014. Web. 14 Feb. 2015.
[239] Iyengar, Sheena. *The Art of Choosing.* Twelve, 2010, p. 125.

They should be able to provide written samples of lesson plans and students' work and discuss examples of students who have presented challenges, students who have had an impact upon them (and upon whom they have had an impact), times they have collaborated with others. Superb insight can come from asking candidates to respond to scenarios of various types:

Class management: A student says she cannot understand the reading and there is too much to read at home; how would you deal with this situation?
A student's parent complains that his son isn't being challenged in your class; how do you respond?

Collegiality: Describe a time that you collaborated with a colleague, how it was initiated, what the results were and how the results were assessed.
Several students in your class tell you in front of the class that another teacher "doesn't do anything in class;" how do you react?

Pedagogy: We value project-based learning. Tell me about how you might organize a PBL unit on [in the candidate's field: Ancient Greece, the cell, Shakespeare, etc.]. Describe what a student experiences in a typical class. Walk me through it from beginning to end.

Again, any staff participating in the hiring process must be trained. They need to know what questions they can and cannot legally ask and should be provided with consistent sets of questions, but with the freedom to pursue intriguing threads in the conversation as they appear. The major pitfall I have found in enlisting aid of teachers in the hiring process relates to the potential threat that the incumbents may perceive from the candidate, i.e. will this person replace me as the teacher for the senior Honors course? Will this person be a better fit than I? Concerns like these can sabotage the process. Fear is a powerful motivator and, as an emotion, is inherently irrational, but it may be well founded. It may well be the case that the newcomer will be a superstar at the school, displacing the long-tenured incumbent from her pedestal. That is why administrators need to take care in selecting those who will serve in this role and should carefully consider whether delegation is even desirable.

Project- and inquiry-based education displaces the teacher from the center stage and not every teacher is willing to yield the floor. In the interview, it is important to ascertain what specific projects teachers have led, but it is crucial to uncover the *students'* roles in those projects. It is quite common for teachers to do the equivalent of providing a Lego set and instructions and proudly present the resulting students' work as project-based learning, which it is not. The teacher's role is to guide the student to development and determine the feasibility of a project of the student's own creation.

Observing for Engagement: What to look for in a sample class

It is indispensable to observe a prospective teacher in action. If the budget precludes bringing a highly promising candidate to the school, substitute Skype observation of the candidate conducting class in his or her current placement. No candidate, regardless of awards, education background, or others' assertions of their skills, should be hired without being observed in action.

Project-based teaching presents additional challenges in the hiring process. It is difficult to deliver a sample class that evinces the deep engagement and research essential to project-based learning since PBL generally takes place over time, but it can be done. School staff must issue clear expectations. For Modern Language candidates, for example, I issued the following:

Welcome! We are delighted to invite you to teach our students a sample class.

While our students normally learn through projects and inquiry, we realize that in the 45 minutes you will have for your demonstration lesson it will be difficult to engage in the kind of depth our students expect, but please present at least an indication or a segment of a project you would facilitate.

The topics for the day will be:
Grammar: Imperfect; Literature: "La muñeca menor," by Rosario Ferré (text attached); Culture: Puerto Rico

Other expectations:
We expect that the entire class will be conducted in the target language (L2). If necessary, students may translate for each other into their native language, but the teacher should not. We want to see our students engaged in higher order thinking, constructing meaning. In keeping with best practices, before you begin, write on the board the topic of the day, the activities the students should expect, and the work to be completed prior to the next class (if any).

For example:
I.   **Check-in**
II.   **Review the progress on projects and/or homework** (if any)
III.   **Grammar: The Imperfect**

A. Oral exercise in pairs

B. Oral exercise in quartets

IV. **Project incorporating imperfect, vocabulary, and culture**

V. **Wrap-up**

VI. **Homework** (if any)

Drawing from best practices in language teaching pedagogy, the expected structure of the class is generally expected to resemble the following:

I. **WARM UP:** Call on each student with a question relevant to the lesson i.e. "What was your favorite toy when you were 8 years old?"

II. **LINK**: connect the lesson with something already learned and assimilated

III. **PRESENT**: Present a lesson (unless flipped and presented previously) and give examples or present examples and ask students to derive the rule

IV. **PRACTICE/REINFORCE**: Students should be involved in discrete brief (7-10 minutes each), varied (pairs, group, individual, written, oral, etc.), and engaging exercises and/or a project (or at least a segment of a project) to practice or reinforce the grammatical, literary, and regional lesson. Students should communicate exclusively in L2.

V. **STUDENTS SUMMARIZE**: In the final minutes of class, ask the students to orally summarize in L2 what they learned in class

VI. **HOMEWORK:** Clearly indicate the homework to be completed to practice the current and previous lessons

---

Hiring staff might additionally issue a scoring rubric to candidates so that expectations are crystal clear. Despite the above, which was intended to set the candidate up for success, astonishingly few candidates actually complied. Most often ignored was the essential requirement of conducting the class in the target language, which was emphasized in this sheet, in at least two emails, and by phone, and which every candidate claimed as his or her practice. That response was valuable in itself, since it is obviously indicative of the way the candidate might fit with the school culture.

The observers were hoping to see (a) well-designed, creative and rigorous lessons that (b) built upon previous knowledge and (c) inspired and excited students to engage with the material and construct meaning within (d) an environment characterized by warm rapport. This proved to be a tall order for the vast majority, but for a few, the magic was evident, pixie dust was in the air, and a contract followed.

We should exceed state standards for excellence, not fall short. In any subject, adjudicators for teacher certification in many states look for varied formats (individual, pair, group, whole class) and modalities (reading, writing, oral, manipulative, board work, use of technology), as well as engagement with each and every student. A teacher who uses the Harkness method of discussion for the entire class would never pass state muster, so why would a school encourage that methodology all day every day? Novelty matters. Discussion everyday wears thin in October; by April, it's drudgery.

Additional input is helpful to a point and within limits, for instance having one or two teachers observe and confer after the candidate's departure. It should be made clear from the outset, however, that while their input is welcome and appreciated, the administrator has the big picture view and is vested with the responsibility for hiring. Naturally, when there is positive consensus, it can bolster teacher morale, but when there is disagreement, the teachers' expectations can be difficult to manage, particularly since the candidates may become colleagues.

The students in the classroom should receive index cards prior to the start of sample class or at the end and should be carefully directed (possibly during the previous class and reiterated at the end of the sample class) to write on the card the reasons why they would or would not like to have this candidate as a teacher. Students tend to err on the generous side and are occasionally taken in by gimmicks, but they also offer impressive insight regarding elements of the class or pedagogy and, of course, the invaluable perspective of students, which can be quite different from that of adults.

How to Avoid Making a Wrong Turn on the Road to Innovation

We all know that there are marvelous innovations that lead to more effective learning, that engage students' and teachers' interest and curiosity, that inspire students to achieve more than they dreamed possible. We know, too, that some innovations are initiated with high hopes to great acclaim, but never deliver.

Perhaps they may require a great deal of training and other costly resources to execute. Perhaps they are simply ill-conceived, "all sizzle no steak." Perhaps the foundational research didn't take into account enough variables, was too optimistic regarding the scalability of the study, or failed to appreciate the complexity of the ecosystem.

With more doctorates awarded each year in Education than professional fields and Humanities combined, there is an abundance of educational research, and too much of it reaches publications without the methodological details, such as how many subjects were involved, the presence or absence of a control group, the specific circumstances of the environment, etc. There are a number of trends and initiatives in education today that are captivating administrators of public, charter, and independent schools alike, as well as the public. One of the most significant is the promise of neuroscience and its far-reaching implications for education and society at large.

Neuroscience and Learning: Whole-brain, Half-brain, Hare-brained—What Do We Really Know?

The Enlightenment has left a wonderful legacy in the scientific method, but scientists do a grave disservice when they overreach their boundaries, as they have for centuries, and neuroscience is a prime example, as psychiatrist Satel and psychologist Lilienfeld demonstrate in their book, *Brainwashed: The Seductive Appeal of Mindless Neuroscience* (2003). Lacking humility before the mystery, we have neuroscientists engaging in a "21st century phrenology," a reductionist and dogmatic aspiration to a "brain-based philosophy of life" as a panacea that will eliminate "suffering, war, and conflict." Brain science is being applied inappropriately for all sorts of purposes, to name but a few: in law, to determine guilt or innocence in crime; in business, to discern emotional preferences to market to consumers more effectively; and in education, to create educational environments that improve students' learning.[241]

We need to proceed skeptically and understand that there is an astonishing complexity to the function of genes, the brain, and so much in our world, and that premature assertions of "decoding" merely reveal human hubris and certainly should not induce us to apply them in such far-reaching ways. It is unwise to dismiss the ineffable quality to human nature and behavior, as well as spiritual, psychological, and social dimensions.

---

[241] From my review of the book published on Amazon.com. 13 Dec 13.

Some of the supporters and "experts" in educational neuroscience claim that scientists have unlocked the secrets of how the brain learns and they tend to speak of the brain in mechanistic or computer-related terms like "wiring" and "circuits." They promote various analogs of Brain Based Learning (BBL) and Whole Brain Teaching purported to integrate the functions of the right-brain and left-brain. They espouse Learning Styles and Multiple Intelligences to teach to children's strengths and preferences. Some of these techniques are entertaining and engaging pedagogy; some are gimmicky; some are both, like Whole Brain Teaching Founder Chris Biffle's *clap clap "TEACH!"* command which is the classroom prompt for students to teach the lesson fragment to their partner. Neuroscientific backing aside, peer teaching is an effective means of fostering greater retention of material (for the student doing the teaching).

Alarmingly, researchers discovered that any mention of "even irrelevant neuroscience information in an explanation of a psychological phenomenon" interfered with ordinary people's ability to think critically about the underlying logic of a claim.[243] The assertions *sound* logical and based in science, but they encroach on essentially philosophical territory. This is nothing new, and we have already seen the pernicious results in earlier eras—recall that Samuel Morton's "scientific" studies of cranial capacity as a measure of intelligence were widely accepted in the 19th century, just as Edward Thorndike's "scientific" foundation for eugenics was in the 20th. This is an opportune moment to point out that there is a profound connection between Thorndike as eugenicist and Thorndike as the father of standardized testing. There is no shortage of researchers who judge his field, psychometrics, to be a pseudoscience since it, like eugenics and cranial capacity, advantages the ruling elite.[244] In order to avoid the errors of our educational forebears, we need to assess these claims critically. Much of the educational neuroscience that informs countless professional development sessions and sells innumerable books reflects a simplistic understanding of how the brain works based on faulty methodology, correlation equated with causation, and leaps from

---

[243] Weisberg, Deena Skolnick, et al. "The Seductive Allure of Neuroscience Explanations." *Journal of cognitive neuroscience.* 20.3 (2008): 470-7.
[244] See a) Blum, Jeffrey M. *Pseudoscience and Mental Ability: The Origins and Fallacies of the IQ Controversy.* Monthly Review Press, 1978.
b) Graves, Joseph L Jr; and Amanda Johnson. "The Pseudoscience of Psychometry and The Bell Curve." *The Journal of Negro Education,* 64.3 (Jul. 1995).
c) Buckhalt, Joseph. "A short history of g: Psychometrics' most enduring and controversial construct." *Learning and Individual Differences.* 13.2 (2001).

data to application.[245] Apply a critical eye or ear to science reports in the media and track how many studies conclude causation where there is merely correlation.

The bio-mechanical camp of neuroscientists asserts that with more money (already in the billions largely due to its potential military applications) and time, they will be able to tell us why certain individuals do x and how creativity originates, the implication being that we will then be able to affect areas of the brain to achieve certain results. In contrast, neurologist Donald Stein states unequivocally that "The search for a road map of stable, neural pathways that can represent brain functions is futile."[246] Brains do not work like a computer, nor does mapping a genome reveal the infinite ways that genes interact with one another. There is constant flux, constant synergistic activity, but that complexity is reduced to the most simplistic for public consumption and we believe what we are told based on the other wonders that the scientific community has wrought.[247]

The peer-reviewed literature produced by neuroscientists contrasts so sharply with the neuro-pseudo-science in popular iterations that one wonders whether the latter group has actually read the former. The neuroscientists admit that they don't really know what specific parts of the brain *do*, yet the popularizers express utter certainty. The brain is remarkably dynamic in its ability to compensate and "often has many routes to solving any one problem."[248] The Psychology 101 information about the parts of the brain responsible for different functions, like language or vision, are too simplistic since the removal of those areas does not always result in the loss of those functions in the subject.

The facts reveal an organic and irrational system that is a far more complex system than the computer, which [it seems we need to remind ourselves] is human-created. The hemispheres of the brain operate holistically, not independently; hence, no "left-brained/right-brained" twaddle. The ability to grow dendrites does not translate into better learning. MRIs that seem to so clearly demonstrate one thing or another to the amateur are inconclusive to the expert. As science writer John Horgan explains:

---

[245] Larry A. Alferink and Valeri Farmer-Dougan ."Brain-(not) Based Education: Dangers of Misunderstanding and Misapplication of Neuroscience Research." *Exceptionality: A Special Education Journal* 18:1 (2010): 42-52. Web. 7 Nov. 2014.

[246] Horgan, John. "Do Big, New Brain Projects Make Sense When We Don't Even Know the 'Neural Code'?" *Scientific American.* 23 Mar. 2013. Web. 19 Dec. 2014.

[247] From my review of the book published on Amazon.com 17 August 2014.

[248] Marcus, Gary, Adam Marblestone and Jeremy Freeman. "Brain Theory: The Future of Neuroscience." *The Chronicle of Higher Education.* 12 Nov. 2014.

The neural code is often likened to the machine code that underpins the operating system of a digital computer. According to this analogy, neurons serve as switches, or transistors, absorbing and emitting electrochemical pulses, called action potentials or "spikes," which resemble the basic units of information in digital computers. But the brain is radically unlike and more complex than any existing computer. A typical brain contains 100 billion cells, and each cell is linked via synapses to as many as 100,000 others. Synapses are awash in neurotransmitters, hormones, neural-growth factors and other chemicals that affect the transmission of signals, and synapses constantly form and dissolve, weaken and strengthen, in response to new experiences. Researchers have recently established that not only do old brain cells die, new ones can form via neurogenesis. Far from being stamped from a common mold, like transistors, neurons display a dizzying variety of forms and functions. Researchers have discovered scores of distinct types of neuron just in the visual system. And let's not forget all the genes that are constantly turning on and off and thereby further altering the brain's operation.[249]

Humans will always search for an answer to why people do what they do, are the way that they are, and how they can improve. It is comforting to some to cling to what appears to be a certainty, but it would be wiser to embrace the mystery, for there is an ineffable dimension to life. Don't be fooled by neuro-pseudo-science just because it is couched in sophisticated language and backed by resources to rival those of Croesus; its proponents makes the same false panacean promises as snake oil salesmen. My recommendation is for staff to be aware of the media coverage that families and other staff are likely to be exposed to and be prepared to explain and counter. Educators have the responsibility of promoting healthy skepticism and reason and instructing others in how to evaluate the quality of research studies, which will be addressed later in this chapter.

Change Management and Decision Making

Change management matters. In *Leading by Change,* John P. Kotter "identifies the first step in creating lasting change as establishing a sense of urgency. This requires examining market and competitive realities and identifying

---

[249] Horgan, John. "Do Big, New Brain Projects Make Sense When We Don't Even Know the 'Neural Code'?" *Scientific American.* 23 Mar. 2013. Web. 19 Dec. 2014.

and discussing crisis, potential crisis or major opportunities."[250] In this new era for independent schools, how school stakeholders perceive the realities of the environment, manage change, make decisions, and innovate can determine whether they thrive or fail.

There is always much discussion about the imperative of getting staff buy-in, but Robert Evans states that this is the not the beginning point, but rather the endgame, at which one arrives through "a combination of support and pressure."

> Teachers deserve a chance to consider and grapple with any proposal for change, and this can help build their readiness to try something new. But to become convinced that a change has value, people often have to try it first...For those leading the effort, then, the key is to balance a willingness to listen with a readiness to insist — to be clear about what is negotiable and what isn't.[251]

This is precisely the delicate equilibrium that administrators must achieve within the broad array of structural means that schools have of dealing with the implementation of change. Each has strengths and weaknesses, advantages and disadvantages.

- Top-down and/or hierarchical, with decrees issued by a senior administrator or a designated group of them. Compliance is delegated to department chairs, student government, advisors or residence heads. The lack of buy-in can lead to resentment, resistance and a wall between administration and everyone else, but it can lead rapid change and efficient delegation.
- Democracy, with majority rule and voting on new measures introduced by some individual or group. Structural elements encourage individuals to comply with the vote. The desire to maintain the status quo can lead to stagnation. The measure can be diminished by lobbying efforts or trying to appease a majority. Those in the minority can feel unheard and remain disengaged, but a majority feels empowered. Responsibility and timelines for implementation don't necessarily follow the decision.

---

[250] Crickette, Grace. "It's Not Risk Management, It's Change Management - Risk & Insurance." *Risk & Insurance*. 04 June 2014. Web. 19 Dec. 2014.

[251] Evans, Robert. "Getting To No Building True Collegiality in Schools." *NAIS*. Winter 2012. Web. 7 Feb. 2015.

- Consensus, general agreement. Staff and students police themselves for observance. It can be difficult to gauge consensus and the structure can be too loose to enable effective implementation of a plan.
- Committees, often myriad and *ad hoc,* discuss [*ad nauseam*] and mull over decisions and trust that their outcomes will bind. Those not on the committee can feel unrepresented in the process; the time needed to arrive at decisions can protract. Committee reports may not be sufficiently thorough or binding, but they can be efficient in presenting a plan, which may then be subject to one of the other methods.
- Appreciative Inquiry, in which the whole school or subsets convene to "Discover: look for the best of what is, Dream: imagine the best we can become, Design: create an action strategy and plan to achieve the vision, and Deliver: co-create the future" in different ways.[252] AI generates a great deal of dialogue that can be productive, but it can be difficult to determine consensus or generate enthusiasm for the process.

The methods used may vary and may be implemented in diverse ways depending upon the school culture, the nature, magnitude and/or urgency of the decision, the group(s) likely to be affected by the result, and the impact of the outcome.

All of us have sat in committee or all-school meetings or participated in rousing virtual discussions of what should be done about issue x that are characterized by opinion and emotion. A case study in effective rhetoric, it is often the most articulate speaker who convincingly persuades others to adopt her perspective based on little more than charisma, opinion, and anecdotes, nary a solid research study in sight. Democracy has its limits; mathematicians do not vote on the validity of a theorem. The adoption of evidence-based best practices in education should not be a decision subject to a majority vote, especially by those with a vested interest in maintaining the status quo.

Imagine that the administration screens the film *Race To Nowhere* for the school community, prompting a group of students, parents, and staff gathered together to discuss the amount of homework that students should have. Students would be likely to decry "busy work" and worksheets and complain about how much more [or in rare cases, less] homework they have than peers at another school. Parents might complain about their students not getting enough sleep due to homework on top of their extra-curricular activities and cite the film as evidence

---

[252] See Henry, Rich. "Leadership at Every Level: Appreciative Inquiry in Education." *New Horizons for Learning.* Johns Hopkins School of Education. August 2013. Web. 7 Dec 2014.

for no homework. Teachers might emphasize the need for repetition and practice or promote the flipped classroom homework as enlightened pedagogy. They all have competing truths and in a discussion of this kind are not likely to come to any real agreement. This is where authoritative research—and educators as authoritative (not authoritarian) experts—should come into play.

Research-Based Best Practices

We routinely require our students to cite five peer-reviewed sources...and then require no such support with evidence-based best practices data in the decision-making that affects some significant aspects of our school life. That must change. Hundreds of worthy peer-reviewed articles are published each year in the field of education, but how much of the research is actually implemented in classrooms? Find out who is reading the salient *peer-reviewed* research at your school and how the information is disseminated, shared, and implemented. If they are not reading it, find out why and fix it. Educators cannot dismiss keeping up with the research any more than a professional in any other field. It is an exigency of the position. Educators who reflect on their professional practice are quite willing to expand their knowledge base; how do they go about doing that? Professional development through workshops or seminars is insufficient, often passive, and sporadic, rather than continuous, engaging, practical, and reflective. Staff enrolled in graduate programs in the field of education can and should be encouraged and offered means by which to stimulate discussion and implement best practices in the school. Unfortunately, even teacher preparation programs tend to perpetuate the ways things have always been done and label the slightest alterations in practice as innovations.

Educational research acquires a particular imperative in independent schools because, unlike public schools, our staff has largely not experienced systematic academic and practical formation in pedagogy and educational best practices. As a rule, we do not require that our teachers be state certified or study in a teacher preparation program--or that they have any training in teaching whatsoever. We have the opportunity to turn this potential liability into an enormous strength at this volatile time because paradigm shifts are led by outsiders, people who are not committed to or invested in doing things the way they have always been done. However, true outsiders can be hard to find since it has been well documented that teachers teach as they were taught, which can perpetuate nostalgic and obsolete practices. This is untenable and unhelpful in view of the rapidly changing conditions.

One of the most urgent exigencies of the Information Revolution in which we live is that staff and students be trained to engage in and recognize quality research. Mass media articles intend to titillate, escalate anxiety, or generate some other emotion in order to appeal to the market. *Education Week* can be helpful as it points to important studies that can be perused in detail, but its articles are most often authored by non-educator journalists who are charged with creating appealing headlines rather than reporting serious research. *Education Week* commonly cites anecdotal evidence garnered from the study of a single school or district. Some of the research that educators need may be collected from Google Scholar, but more likely will come from the electronic database of a nearby university, which often offer educators access for an annual fee.

Knowing how to evaluate a study is key. Librarians are professional researchers and can provide considerable assistance in this respect. They are a good place to start. A few points to consider:

- **Consider the intention of the study.** If you are seeking information about various aspects of homework on the secondary school level, a study about the effects of homework on the primary or tertiary level is not necessarily applicable. Similarly, a study about the effects of a new homework strategy on low-income Asian-American inner-city K-12 students is not necessarily applicable to suburban elite high school students. What keywords might you use in an advanced search to focus the results?

- **Consider the authorship.** Search the credentials of the authors. Are they qualified? Sometimes the biography will reveal a corporate, political, or ideological bias.

- **Consider the currency.** Is the data sufficiently current? What date delimiters make sense to use in an advanced search?

- **Consider the sponsor.** Search for any sponsorship or funding details, bias, or commercial affiliation. Is the study funded by an entity (or an organization with ties to an entity) that stands to gain in any way from the results?

- **Consider the size and selection of the sample**. In general, randomized studies are stronger than those that are not. A sample size of 45,000 is certainly more reliable than one involving 100 students. What is the composition of the cohort? Is it a sufficiently random (or targeted) sample, cohort or cross-section to be useful? In what ways does the sample affect the data? While a study based on a single school or district is not authoritative, it can provide an idea of how one might structure a similar experiment or study in one's own school.

- **Consider the methodology.** In general, stronger data is yielded when
  a) An intervention is conducted on one group while a similar group, a control group, has no such intervention;
  b) A study is conducted on a group and the data is analyzed, rather than examining the effects of an intervention already performed (*post hoc*);
  c) A study compares contemporaneous groups, rather than a current group with a historical one.

Is the method logical? Is there a control group? In a time series, are the baseline, interval, and outcome reliable measures of the efficacy of the intervention? How was the data collected? Did they collect the right data? How did they reduce bias? What modeling strategy was used to analyze the data? What variables are the researchers taking into account? What were they unable to consider or what did they fail to consider? Are there rival explanations? Are the results generalizable? Have the results been replicated? In what ways does that affect the integrity of the outcomes?

- **Correlation is not causation**. This is a common error (political parties make it frequently regarding the economy during one candidate's tenure). Just because two events are connected does not mean that one gave rise to the other. Do the researchers presume causation? Is there enough evidence and were enough variables considered and controlled to make this claim?

- **Seek confirmation or refutation.** Examine related studies and compare the samples, intentions, methodologies, and outcomes. Cherry-picking the research to share without providing contrary views is the surest way to lose the trust of the community.

Professional Development

It is not enough that some senior administrator peruse *Education Week* and be aware of a trend or two. It is not enough that she occasionally share an article of interest from *The Atlantic Monthly* or a précis of the latest education-related bestseller, though it is appropriate and important that staff discuss, perhaps with students and parents, the issues that appear in the media since those issues might be drawing their attention (and producing anxiety). Staff should be reading *Independent School* and the media specific to their subject and pedagogical strategies and discussing them in online fora both in-house and in a broader context. This is part of being a professional.

However, existing research is all well and good, but just as we are teaching our students to execute their own original research, teachers should be encouraged to engage in action research projects of their own, form and test hypotheses, and share their work at least in-house and with the broader community of educators. In one school where I worked, I wanted to set up an experiment comparing performance metrics of a control group with a group that participated in the curriculum I had developed to help students create research projects from finding a workable idea through final redaction. The head of school rejected my plan because she wanted all students to benefit from the program. But how do we *know* whether there is, in fact, any advantage to the program unless we test it with a control group?

Teachers consistently cite professional development as a strong motivator and contributor to job satisfaction, but they also express a high level of dissatisfaction with its execution, relevance, and effectiveness. In 2014, the Gates Foundation sponsored a study of over 1000 teachers and their attitudes relating to the topic.[253] Teachers identified specific characteristics of their ideal experience:

- Choice regarding what they wanted to learn and relevance to each teacher's individual context
- Interactive with hands-on practice and participation, rather than passive lectures or presentations
- Delivered by someone with extensive classroom experience and who has actually had great success implementing the target method
- Sustained and practiced over time
- Treats teachers like professionals and respects their expertise and experience

These, of course, are the same elements that students want from their classroom experience. The report revealed an enormous disconnect between what

---

[253] Boston Consulting Group. "Teachers Know Best Teachers' Views on Professional Development." *College Ready*. Gates Foundation, 2014. Web. 14 Jan. 2015.

administrators and districts seek to implement and what teachers found most useful, with the lowest levels of teacher satisfaction centered on professional learning communities, workshops, self-guided methods, and the highest on courses. Teachers were also dissatisfied with the way that lesson study and coaching were implemented, which is unfortunate since these can be productive and meaningful when structured well and with extensive training. As further affirmation of the positive impact of control and autonomy, teachers who chose their own development experience had a much higher level of satisfaction than those compelled to participate to comply with guidelines. Overwhelmingly, teachers favored practical, hands-on opportunities to improve the effectiveness of their classroom teaching through planning and reflecting on instructional methods. These are important considerations to bear in mind when constructing a professional development plan.

An endowed fund earmarked for professional development is certainly a worthwhile objective since money is often the key factor in the extent and quality of support of staff participation. Schools can tie the grant to a specified number of semesters of service (e.g. for each semester of graduate work that the school funds, the staff member must teach a semester beyond it or reimburse the school), require that the participant regularly share what he or she is learning and applying at the school and present the means of gauging effectiveness. School-wide initiatives such as online platforms can go a long way to providing a venue for staff collaboration on projects, lesson planning and more, share helpful resources for improving pedagogy, meeting students' needs, data analysis, etc. Still, the model that staff present to the community when they engage in their own action research is invaluable, as is the site-specific data they collect. A culture of expectation for continuous learning, growth, improvement, innovation, and exploration and the holistic attention to staff wellbeing are fundamental to a vibrant school.

Staff Structure for Engagement

Schools vary widely in terms of organizational structure, but what can be done to ensure the highest levels of student engagement and organizational vitality? Remember that schools are learning organizations (see Peter Senge's classic, *The Fifth Discipline Fieldbook: Strategies and Tools for Building a Learning Organization*, 1994) and in order to constantly construct, not merely gather, and apply new information and pivot accordingly, they need to be lean and flat, have self-regulating and cross-functional teams, and avoid silos and rigid hierarchies. Facilitation and coaching replace top-down control. In my research, one of the most disheartening aspects of independent schools has been the presence of extensive and convoluted bureaucracy. One small struggling school of just 200 students had over 20 full-time administrators, with several additional part-time. This is grossly excessive. Now is no time for such profligacy. Work can expand to fit the hours in a week. Administrative staff need to work smarter and the corps needs to be lean. It is high time that productivity audits be introduced to independent school culture to assess effectiveness and efficiency.

It must be emphasized that, first and foremost, all school employees share the responsibility

- To embody, manifest, and advocate the mission of the school
- To articulate the vision for the school and its future
- To monitor school climate and culture
- To respond to communication from stakeholders within one full business day
- To attend the major events (performances, guest speakers, etc.) in the life of the school

Beyond that, of course, the organization needs to attend to its various domains: academics, student services and support, community life and culture, viability and sustainability. Cross-functional teams should replace hierarchies and silos. Some functions may be best outsourced, like business management or educational testing or shared with other schools, like certain teaching staff. The key is to evaluate existing and emergent structures to strive for and attain excellence, characterized by high levels of engagement, innovation, generative learning, and creativity.

Below are several models for how team structures can work with brief descriptions of the responsibilities in the domains of Community Life, Student Services, Academics, and Curriculum Coordination. (Detailed position descriptions appear in Appendix Section I). Position descriptions are often lacking in independent schools and dismissed as "not part of the culture," and this is a mistake. At worst, it puts the school at risk for litigation in the event of termination for not outlining the expectations for the position, but the failure to meet amorphous, inchoate or unspoken expectations can lead to frustration on the part of employee and employer. Position descriptions outline responsibilities and greatly assist with performance reviews, another facet of good management often absent in independent schools.

The retention of teaching duties was deliberate. Chief executives teach in many schools and even universities, notably Colorado College under President Jill

157

Tiefenthaler, New York University under John Sexton, and Georgetown University under John J. DeGioia. In fact, at Shenandoah University, all senior administrators are required to teach, as long as they have the proper qualifications. University of Richmond President Ed Ayers has taught a freshmen history class ever since arriving in 2007.[255] These chief executives underscore teaching and learning as comprising the core mission of the school. They connect better with the institution and mission, build esprit de corps and experience empathy, since they have a better sense of what the faculty experience in terms of scheduling, assignments, use of the learning management system, etc. Working with students inside and outside of the classroom context establishes rich multidimensional relationships with them. If these university presidents can find the time to prioritize teaching, why wouldn't administrators in our schools?

Work can expand to fit the time allotted. It should be noted that the many administrative duties were intentionally part-time. It can be argued that it is preferable to have two people fully integrated as teaching staff sharing a full-time administrative job, *particularly one that has cyclical ebbs and flows in workload*, than to hire a full-time person who may stand as a silo with considerable downtime. It also allows for those staff to experience serving in a leadership capacity, spread their wings and explore other dimensions that energize them. *Depending upon the position*, an effort might be made to reduce the course load, sufficient attention is dedicated to both sets of responsibilities. Where it is impossible to reduce the course load, the extra duties might be construed as service to the school, which should be part of the annual evaluation (more on that in Chapter 8 and Appendix Section II), but a stipend really ought to be offered to demonstrate an appreciation for quality work.

---

[255] Johnson, Jenna. "University Presidents Pitch in as Professors." *Washington Post*. 19 Jan.2012. Web. 21 Dec. 2014.

Community Life Team: _How We Are Together_

The Community Life Team assists with shaping the culture of the school as a caring and learning community, committed to intellectual inquiry and social justice. It integrates and links experiences in and out of school with learning from academic programs. It inspires and provides opportunities for **_all_** members of the school community to participate together in intellectual, spiritual, social, cultural, athletic, and service activities. It develops and supports programs that foster diversity and inclusion among all school community members. It communicates a set of expectations that support and infuse the school's core values, help students mature, and become responsible and productive members of the community. It creates and sustains an environment that promotes personal growth and discovery, the pursuit of healthy minds and bodies, and responsibility for self, community, and public service.

These positions contribute to the development of school culture. Further, these positions are considered equivalent to school service and as such do not generally permit the release from the typical five course teaching responsibilities.

The Community Life Team takes the lead in shaping the culture of the school by engaging in the following:
- Develops, communicates, implements, assesses, and invests students, employees, and families in a plan to foster core values of empathy, integrity, honor, respect, and responsibility to community
- In collaboration with others, develops, refines, communicates, implements, and assesses plan for school culture and invests students, teachers, and families

159

- In collaboration with others, supports the planning and execution of regular community meetings
- In collaboration with others, develops and takes the lead in facilitating a participatory and engaging introduction to school culture during the summer orientation for new teachers, students, and parents
- In collaboration with others, conducts monthly seminars for parents that deal with other topics pertaining to parenting adolescents
- In collaboration with other staff and students, develops, refines, and communicates weekly advisory curriculum
- Teaches a course load to be determined

Coordinator of Service Learning/Activism/Community Engagement

Creates and implements curriculum comprised of action, reflection, and assessment, focused on addressing the systemic political and socio-economic issues of injustice, with the purpose of realizing authentic and lasting change for the better.

Coordinator of Community Peace and Justice:

In collaboration with others, develops programs to promote positive student behavior as well as intervention strategies, consequences for behavior, and restorative justice.

Class Curators:

Class Curators are assigned to a class during the freshman year and stay with that class through graduation to curate the school experience for students. They get to know students on a deeper level and closely monitor their progress throughout their time at school. Class Curators work closely with other employees and students to develop events and activities that are relevant to the respective class year. Class Curators must be skilled collaborators to work as a unified group with each other, with students, with the Grade Coordinators, and with the school administration to provide and communicate a uniform set of expectations that will help students mature and become responsible and productive members of the community.

Student Services Team: How We Help Each Other

The Student Services Team assists with providing students, their families, and their teachers with the tools they need to enhance personal, intellectual, and social development at the school and beyond. As mentors and guides, the Student Services Team develops, delivers, and advocates a broad range of programs and services to seek solutions to persistent issues, to encourage students to be proactive and to advocate for themselves and their needs, and to assist students in the pursuit of programs during and after their time at school that will enable them to explore their world, capitalize on their strengths and minimize their challenges.

These services can be outsourced, provided in-house for a fee at market rate, or provided at no cost to users, as determined by market and stakeholders' interests and the mission of the school. It is only recently that non-specialized schools are beginning to attend to the learning support needs of students, finally realizing that they do indeed have students in their midst who experience considerable impediments to processing, executive function, reading, math, etc. In part, this can be construed as an issue of equity of access, since students of means have always been able to pay the exorbitant fees for testing, tutoring, and therapy, while others have suffered in silence. Offering such services on site can be life changing and affirming. These are full-time positions and it is expected that the employees will find additional ways to contribute to student life beyond the school day.

Director of Learning Support:

Ensures that all students receive the support they need to become effective and enthusiastic learners. Sets policy, develops initiatives and strategic goals for learning support, supervises the Learning Specialist and Center Coordinators, and shares responsibility for the advisory/mentoring program with the Counseling Office. Works intensively with staff, students, and families to ensure that they understand students' learning strengths and challenges and the accommodations, interventions, and methods that will help the students to succeed.

Learning Specialist:

Supervises the day-to-day functions of the academic center that assists students and their families by training them in executive function and other skills for success, and by helping them understand challenging content or complete an assignment. The incumbent should be skilled with assistive technology (Kurzweil, Livescribe, dictation software, etc.), which will be offered in the academic center. Responsible for **extensive training of tutors** and scheduling tutors needed for students with diagnosed learning differences as well as those for occasional assistance. Also works with the study hall proctors to supervise students in academic distress and ensure that they remain on task and focused on the intended work.

School Psychologist:

Identifies at-risk students, performs cognitive testing, psycho-social evaluations of referred students, and monitors student progress. Educates students in the identification of their strengths and challenges, and how best to work with them to maximize success. Serves as a resource and/or consultant to administrators and other school personnel on best practices for meeting the needs of students.

Coordinator of Life Planning and Guidance:

Guides the members of each year's graduating class through post-secondary planning. In collaboration with Counselor, develops, evaluates, oversees and makes continual improvements to a comprehensive four-year program that guides students individually and in advisory groups to reflect on their values, strengths, and interests and formulate a post-secondary plan and/or select a gap year program, college, or university that will help them to find fulfillment in relationships and meaningful work and be engaged with their community. Markets the school effectively to secondary institutions and to prospective students and parents. Advises the faculty, administration, and trustees regarding the college admissions process and trends. Excellent administrator and communicator with various stakeholders.

Subject Support Staff:
    Provide targeted support in Writing and Math. Writing and math assistance is available during the day, especially lunch period and during tutorial with possible extended hours on some weekdays and weekends by appointment.

b) *Writing Center Coordinator*: A full-time teacher with a reduced load who has expertise in *teaching writing* assists students on all grade levels to become better writers through one-on-one consultation in all stages of the writing process, from note-taking and pre-writing to revision strategies and proofreading techniques.

b) Math Center Coordinator: This position may be staffed by a full-time teacher with a reduced load *who has a credential and specific training in teaching mathematics*[256] at least through the pre-calculus level or by current Math teachers on a scheduled basis for half their planning period. Students will also have access to engaging software for personalized learning and adaptive assessments, such as ALEKS or some analog, to develop a strong foundation of skills in computation, geometric and algebraic reasoning, and higher math.

Tutors:
    Tutors should be positive, proactive, patient and persistent and have a positive attitude toward students and learning. Tutors should be trained in executing their various roles:
- Pedagogical: To support the learning process itself by providing instructions, stimulating questions, examples, feedback, and motivation etc. to the learners
- Managerial: To help the student organize work, establish benchmarks and track deadlines; to track student progress and data etc.
- Social: To establish a friendly and comfortable environment that stimulates learning

---

[256] In a longitudinal 10-year study of students statewide, researchers discovered that teacher credential, experience, and test scores contributed to student achievement in math more than other subjects. Clotfelter, Ladd and Vigdor. *How and Why Do Teacher Credentials Matter for Student Achievement?* National Center for Longitudinal Data in Education Research. March, 2007.

163

Academic Team: How and What We Learn

The Academic Team is responsible for inspiring, coordinating, overseeing, and evaluating the academic mission of the school. The Academic Team is committed to conducting ongoing research to find, assess, and implement evidence-based best practices that promote academic rigor and integrity, excellence in instruction, intellectual accomplishment, skills in information literacy and research, critical thinking, effective communication, and service to communities. The Academic Team acts in the best interest of students to foster their ability to be compassionate, empathetic, and creative innovators, leaders, entrepreneurs, critical thinkers, effective communicators and collaborators who contribute to the betterment of society and the realization of their own potential.

The teaching load of each of these positions varies in accordance with the level of responsibility.

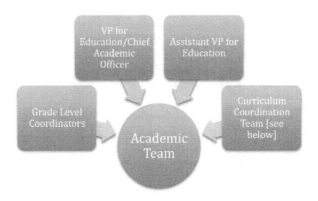

Vice President for Education/Chief Academic Officer:
The academic servant-leader of the school is responsible for developing, guiding, implementing, communicating, and assessing the philosophy, mission, vision, and curriculum, the wellbeing of students, and the school's day-to-day operation. Conceives and directs initiatives, provides leadership in the identification of annual and long-term goals of the school, and serves as a consultant to staff.

164

Assistant Vice President for Education:

Serves as a consultant to instructional staff, particularly in academic matters including individualized and differentiated instruction; modifications and accommodations; layered curriculum and learning contracts; pre-, formative, and summative assessments; respectful interaction with students, parents, and colleagues; and the sustainment of a rigorous but not overwhelming learning environment. Ensures compliance with legal requirements of government regulations and agencies. Establishes programs for the orientation and mentoring of new instructional staff and for in-service training and evaluation of all instructional staff.

Grade Level Coordinator:

Each Grade Level Coordinator is assigned permanently to one grade. The function of the GLC is more academic, while the Class Curator function is more social. The GLC works collaboratively with the Class Curator for that year, the grade level staff, and the administration in the development of plans and procedures that support instruction for the upcoming school year in scheduling, student placement, and ensuring opportunities for interdisciplinarity in the curriculum. The GLC is the "point person" to ensure that grade level curricular goals and student outcomes are clearly communicated and that support is in place to implement the curriculum. Provides leadership regarding staff development and curriculum development needs. The 9th Grade Coordinator will assist extensively with Orientation, while the 11th Grade Coordinator will assist the College Counseling Office with College Tours, and the 12th Grade Coordinator will help with the college application process and transitioning to the world beyond.

Curriculum Coordination Team

The Curriculum Coordination team meets regularly twice each month as a grade level to discuss curriculum, to collaborate on instruction, to strategize for differentiation, accommodation, and modification, and to ensure that opportunities for the integration of technology, research, and artistic expression are explored and applied. Quarterly, the team will reflect upon and discuss expectations for student learning and curriculum alignment across grade levels. The team will review the curriculum map periodically and make recommendations, and will ensure that there are updated written curriculum guides and support materials that serve as a basis for implementing the curriculum. The team revises goals and objectives for each course and provides a forum for ongoing review of current practice and curricula. The teaching responsibilities vary.

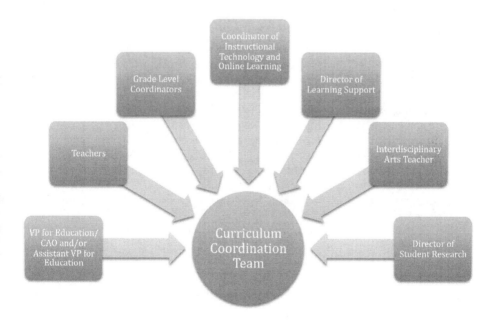

Coordinator of Instructional Technology and Online Learning:
Integrates technology in academics, provides for technical support, and coordinates online learning initiatives. This position assists students and employees

with the integration of technology in the classroom and provides professional development to groups of employees and students as well as individualized assistance as requested. Keeps abreast of developments in instructional technology, assesses their relevance to the school context, recommends trial and adoption when appropriate, instructs stakeholders in their usage, and evaluates. Assists with student registration in online courses and serves as liaison with virtual/online providers in case of difficulty. Identifies, investigates, and proposes additional online learning providers and provides documentation and recommendation to VP for Education regarding accreditation and quality.

Director of Student Research:

Inspires a love of learning through collaborating with staff and students to develop projects that ignite students' curiosity and passion. Enthusiastically seeks out fora promoting student research (i.e. science fairs, history day, and similar venues) on local through international levels. Teaches the research process, assists classes and individuals in research strategy, source gathering, organization, extrapolation, synthesis, and presentation of final product. Helps students to identify prospective mentors and collaborators in their subject area locally and globally.

Interdisciplinary Arts Coordinator:

Integrates creative expression with other academic coursework. In collaboration with classroom teachers, actively seeks out opportunities for the integration of drama, music, dance, and visual art to be utilized as learning vehicles, taking care to ensure that creativity supports rather than diminishes academic rigor and that the highest standards are upheld in the evaluation of artistic merit. Cultivates relationships with arts organizations, area universities, and the community, including non-profit and commercial sectors. Encourages student participation in the arts and art education, both in the school and in the community.

Teachers:

Teachers are the most direct contact between students and the school. They foster a lifelong love of learning, spark curiosity, encourage students to make good choices, and serve as role models. They provide excellent classroom experiences that engage and inspire students, and ensure that all students have rigorous and inclusive access to the curriculum and instruction every day to meet their learning goals.

Teachers nurture strong bonds between and among employees and students, and are actively engaged in the life of the school. They are expected to support

167

students by attending important events in their students' and/or advisees' lives, such as performances, occasional athletic events, and/or others. Advisors are required to meet their advisory group outside of school for a meal, a movie, or some other event.

Teachers routinely substitute for each other, team teach and collaborate, and *seek out other means to contribute to the good of the school* beyond the classroom, from directing a program or coaching a sport to escorting tours at Open Houses. When asked to serve in an additional capacity, it is expected that the teacher will gladly welcome the opportunity and does it to the best of his or her ability.

In Curriculum Coordination Teams, teachers meet at least twice a month to work collaboratively on such areas as creating and revising curriculum, review student work, selecting and developing instructional resources, planning and coordinating portfolio and exhibition activities, meeting with specialists, and preparing common assessments.

Summary

Independent schools can improve their effectiveness in serving their stakeholders by being lean and nimble, adhering to best practices and fostering a strong sense of professionalism. Educators have a responsibility to keep apprised of quality research, share it, perhaps conduct their own action research, and, should it prove fruitful, implement it. Hiring must be executed purposefully and deliberately and not merely result from perception and personal affinities. These challenging times call us to transcend ol' boy (and girl) networks and impressionistic assessments of our schools' quality and attain higher standards of excellence and efficiency.

Chapter 7

Part I: How Do We Support One Another?
Forming and Maintaining a Caring Community

Your most lasting legacy, the only one that really matters, is how your children treat their fellow creatures and the world you're leaving them.—Wendy Mogel[257]

The More We Get Together

When asked what they value most about the independent school(s) with which they are associated, by far the most common response that parents, students and staff give is "We love the strong sense of community. It feels like a family." Any time a relatively small group of people (the average number of students of a private secondary school is 282)[258] spends a considerable amount of time and experiences daily life together, there will be a certain amount of bonding that occurs as a matter of course, independently of any organizational effort.

In our schools, we generally aspire to have a close-knit community, one in which the members support one another, treat each other with respect and compassion, celebrate each others' successes, contribute to each others' understanding and development, and help shoulder each other's burdens. In reality, this is accomplished with varying degrees of success, asseverations notwithstanding. Moreover, interestingly, "strong sense of community" is not often mentioned in our mission statements, yet it is inextricably connected to mission because a school that has a strong sense of community can influence students' achievement, attitudes, and persistence. [259] We are intensely aware that learning in our schools occurs in the classroom and outside of it.

Scholar of Educational Leadership Thomas Sergiovanni draws upon Hackman and Oldham's essential work on organizational development and motivation in stating that staff and students must

---

[257] Wendy Mogel's books, *The Blessing Of A Skinned Knee: Using Jewish Teachings to Raise Self-Reliant Children* (2008) and *The Blessings of a B Minus: Using Jewish Teaching to Raise Resilient Teenagers* (2011) offer valuable insight and practical methods for fostering holistic growth and caring communities.

[258] NCES, Table 7.

[259] Sergiovanni, Thomas J. *Building Community in Schools*. Jossey-Bass, 1994.

"1. Find their work and personal lives meaningful, purposeful, sensible, and significant."

This is why we must ensure that we have a living and inspiring mission worthy of being served. What we do in our school communities must provide meaning, affirm relationships and shared values, and above all, give individuals a sense of larger purpose.

"2. Have some reasonable control over their work activities and affairs and to be able to exert reasonable influence over work events and circumstances."

This is where the importance of autonomy discussed in Chapter 3 enters into the equation.

"3. Experience success, think of themselves as winners, and receive recognition for their success. People are willing to make a significant investment of time, talent and energy in exchange for enhancement and fulfillment of these three needs."[260]

Of course they are! They have a meaning system and values they share with others in a community. They see the results of their work in the wonderful achievements and progress of students and staff and they are celebrated for their contributions. This is at the core of what we do—or should be doing.

How do we know if we are genuinely doing a good job of fostering a caring community? One of the premises of this book is that we need to do a better job of integrating analysis and evidence and acting with greater precision, rather than relying on the ways we have always done things and/or amorphous impressions that all is well. Do we complacently rely on positive affirmations? Stakeholders simply don't often have enough experience of other communities to serve as points of comparison. A tour guide in almost any school or university will extol the virtues of his or her institution. Someone who has only had butter on toast will pronounce it sublime because she has never tried raspberry preserves. We don't know what we don't know and thus we are satisfied too easily.

It is challenging to develop reliable survey items without considerable training (and testing them on a small population first). Fortunately, there are survey instruments available that have been tested for validity and widely applied.

---

[260] Sergiovanni, Thomas J. "Leadership and Excellence in Schooling." *Educational Leadership* (1984): 4-13. *ASCD*. Web. 28 Feb. 2015.

Administrators can feel confident in applying them in their own schools to help them ascertain how well they are accomplishing their goals. A general Parent Satisfaction Survey may be found in Appendix Section VII and others are available through NAIS. The Sense of Community Index (SCI) may be used to specifically ascertain the health of the community.

> The Sense of Community Index (SCI) is the most frequently used quantitative measure of sense of community in the social sciences. The SCI is based on a theory of sense of community presented by McMillan and Chavis (1986) that stated that a sense of community was a perception with four elements: membership, influence, meeting needs, and a shared emotional connection.[261]

Available free of charge, the 24-item Likert scale survey addresses those four elements as it seeks responses to prompts such as these:

> Members of this community care about each other.
> I expect to be a part of this community for a long time.
> If there is a problem in this community, members can get it solved.
> I am with other community members a lot and enjoy being with them.

The SCI is applicable to the whole-school environment. The point is to test the hypothesis that the sense of community at the school is as functional in reality as the perception and to take appropriate measures to address areas that need attention.

An alternative to the SCI and more focused on schools, the Comprehensive School Climate Inventory (CSCI) is available through the National School Climate Center. Administered to multiple segments of the community, this survey yields the attitudes of students, staff, and parents toward school performance in ten dimensions, including "sense of social emotional security," "school connectedness/ engagement," and "social and civic learning." The final report analyzing the data examines strengths and weaknesses and, significantly, provides "targeted action plans for sustained improvement."[262]

---

[261] Chavis, D.M., Lee, K.S., & Acosta J.D. (2008). *The Sense of Community (SCI) Revised: The Reliability and Validity of the SCI-2.* Paper presented at the 2nd International Community Psychology Conference, Lisboa, Portugal. Available at www.communityscience.com

[262] See National School Climate Center www.schoolclimate.org

Some schools can be justifiably proud of their achievements in the realm of community because they attend to it assiduously and demonstrate a kind of genius in terms of the way they foster cohesion in the present with the past and future. The difference between these schools and others that are less successful is the degree of attention and intention that is applied. This is not to say that every school needs yet another administrative position, most popularly called Director of Community [or Student] Life, to attend to the matter, but rather that stakeholders must pay attention and direct their efforts there.

Each school culture assigns a different weight to the rights and responsibilities of the individual on the one side of the scale and the community or the common good on the other, just as each school culture promulgates a different way of regarding the present moment as part of a history and future. In some schools, it is clear to students that they are participating in a brief but not insignificant segment of an extended timeline proudly featuring so many who have gone before and they will be expected to actively preserve and revere their association long after graduation. In others, the students' connection to the school is far more ephemeral, tangential and tenuous. The school is viewed mainly as a temporary provider of a service, namely preparation for college; a community of teachers and learners and certain opportunities are supplied for that purpose.

There is an axiom in sociology that states that the greater the demands placed upon members of the group, the more cohesive the group. Group cohesion also tends to increase with prestige and homogeneity and decrease with size. This matters because members of highly cohesive groups are less anxious, participate more and have greater satisfaction with their groups than others. Success, agreement, and external threats or pressures buttress cohesion, while competition within the group, cliques, and domination by a few members erode it. In schools with strong cohesion,

> ...a sense of purpose rallies people to a common cause; work has meaning and life is significant; teachers and students work together and with spirit; and accomplishments are readily recognized. To say excellent schools have high morale or have students who achieve high test scores or are schools that send more students to college misses the point. Excellence is all of these and more.[263]

---

[263] Sergiovanni, op. cit.

This chapter will examine what a healthy cohesive independent school community looks like and ways to construct it. It starts with the leadership attending to the mission, vision and culture as its most important function. Beyond that, building culture takes place through:

- Cultivating and maintaining healthy relationships
- Establishing, reinforcing, and redirecting positive standards for behavior
- Balancing the tension between the rights of the individual and the responsibility of that individual to the collective or community; this balance is a prime determinant of the kind of culture a school will have
- Creating caring classrooms
- Attending to rituals and traditions
- Maintaining ties with those who have gone before
- Building relationships with the community beyond the school

Cultivating and maintaining healthy relationships:

Perhaps the most important promise that independent school staff make to parents is that we will *know* their children. Relationship is at the core of the experience we offer, inside and outside of the classroom. The primary role of advisory groups is often identified as ensuring that every student has at least one adult who knows him or her well. It may come as a surprise that the importance of this relationship is increasingly recognized on the tertiary level as well.

> While conducting research for our book, *How College Works*, we saw how a single meeting with a professor to work through a paper could have a decisive effect on a student's writing, and how just a single visit to a faculty member's home could significantly shift a student's entire vision of the college experience. Time and again, finding the right person, at the right moment, seemed to have an outsize impact on a student's success—in return for relatively little effort on the part of the college.[264]

We must never underestimate the positive impact that one caring adult can have on a student to foster a lifelong love of a single field of inquiry or endeavor or even learning in general, to guide to appropriate post-secondary plans, to mentor through personal crisis, and any number of other effects. Conversely, of course, a

[264] Chambliss, Daniel F. "The Power of the Personal." *The Chronicle of Higher Education*. 15 Sept. 2014. Web. 09 Jan. 2015.

single adult can have a devastating effect. At the beginning of every year, amidst the many positive and inspirational messages I issue to staff is this caveat by CUNY Professor of Philosophy of Education Steven M. Cahn:

> Instructors should be constantly mindful that they have been entrusted with their students' intellectual and personal growth—and that it is always possible for teachers to do damage. 'People often think that education works either to improve you or to leave you as you were,' Cahn says. 'But that's not right. An unsuccessful education can ruin you. It can kill your interest in a topic. It can make you a less-good thinker. It can leave you less open to rational argument. So we do good and bad as teachers—it's not just good or nothing.'[265]

We hold fragile egos and malleable minds in our hands. We must be careful to use our force for good, for its power is mighty.

The establishment of a culture of respect for students and their autonomy, as discussed in Chapter 3, and the elimination of the educationally indefensible practice of inflexible policies that establish an authoritarian and punitive dynamic with students are important steps toward creating a community in which students know that adults care about them. It means so much to students and their families when staff attend students' extra-curricular events and events not associated with the school but which are significant to them. Sending a personal note afterward indicating appreciation for the student's hard work takes little effort but can be received as a significant expression of caring.

School Culture Manifesto: Live the Southwest Way

The model of staff effectiveness, engagement, and motivation provided by Southwest Airlines is featured in many MBA programs. Southwest's performance metrics are superb. Southwest has a singular culture. Elements of its manifesto are woven through all that employees do and are explicitly voiced daily. The culture page on the company's website describes it this way:

Warrior Spirit

Work Hard	Desire to be the best	Be courageous
Display urgency	Persevere	Innovate

---

[265] Glen, David. "Course Reminds Budding Ph.D.'s of the Damage They Can Do." *The Chronicle of Higher Education.* October 25, 2009. 12/13/14

Servant's Heart

Follow the Golden Rule   Adhere to the Principles   Treat others with respect
Put others first   Be egalitarian   Embrace SWA Family
Demonstrate proactive Customer Service

Fun LUVing Attitude

Have FUN   Don't take yourself too seriously   Maintain perspective
Celebrate successes   Enjoy your work   Be a passionate team player

Work the Southwest Way

Safety and Reliability   Friendly Customer Service   Low Cost

What would your school's cultural manifesto look like if your stakeholders were to draft a description like this one? It is an instructive exercise and the results can be helpful to new families and staff, as well as a reinforcement of values and vision for those of long standing.

Community standards

Community standards are the accepted norms and guidelines for behavior and how members treat one another. They include written honor codes, dress codes, and the rules contained in student and staff handbooks. Those can become stultified and were often crafted long ago, perhaps even by consultants, attorneys, or other people outside of the community. Far more revelatory of a school's culture are the implicit conventions, like whether students greet adults in the hallways or avoid their gaze, how students and staff treat guests on campus, whether students and staff clean their tables after eating, and whether profanity is tolerated. Standards matter as they set the tone for the school.

The community needs to be deliberate about deep observation and discernment of what the behaviors are and where their contribution falls on the spectrum from positive to neutral to negative and determine whether they need revision, because standards can become lax and rules can lose their relevance. It is imperative that students actively participate in this process, for adults often see only the most superficial level of behavior, while students experience life in the trenches.

In this process, it is helpful to consider the degree to which community values are woven through the school culture, supported by staff, students, and parents. For example:

175

If there an honor code, do students and staff value it, observe it, and make it an inextricable part of daily life or is it merely for show?

How do stakeholders demonstrate respect for one another?

How is truth telling valued? How is lying confronted?

How pervasive are cheating and plagiarism? How is it addressed?

How do parents support the school's standards of behavior?

How is bullying or teasing regarded?

How do students learn to stand up rather than stand by when they observe an unkind act?

How is profane language treated?

How do community members speak to one another? Are biting sarcasm, personal attacks, and angry language acceptable?

How is personal property treated? Will a backpack or laptop be left outside? Will it be there the next day or will someone have taken it?

How is the school property (i.e. books, desks, supplies, grounds) cared for by all stakeholders?

How are guests to the school, either prospective students shadowing or adults treated?

How do staff and students treat each other in the hallways? In the lunch line? Do staff members wait in line or cut in front of students?

How are visiting teams treated by the home team and fans?

These are just a few of the aspects of school life that might be subject to discussion and deliberation in the effort to improve daily life for students and staff and shape the kinds of behaviors that we want our alumni to demonstrate.

Gossip

Gossip is endemic to organizations of all kinds. It wields extraordinary potential for the erosion of morale and community and can destroy self worth, reputation, and identity. The media spotlights student suicides resulting ostensibly from online rumors and harassment. Its toxicity must be contained. An excellent community standard to put firmly in place is to refuse to listen to gossip, which is defined by the impact of what is being expressed.

- Does it cast negative aspersions?
- Does it create rifts?
- Does it exult in the misfortune of others?
- Does it have a negative emotional charge?
- Does it serve to perpetuate conflict or negativity?
- Is it hurtful or damaging?

- Is it something you would say in front of that person?[266]

Consenting to listen to gossip supports and promotes it; refusing to do so stops it. This is a principle that can serve our school communities well and inculcates an important aspect of strong moral character.

On an institutional rather than personal level, mutual support, trust, and transparency, especially regarding decisions that affect departments or staff or students, can go a long way to assuaging the anxiety that leads people to imagine and disseminate information to fill the interstices. As the old saw often misattributed to Mark Twain (though it predates him by centuries) goes, a lie gets halfway around the world before the truth can get its boots on. Gossip among staff should be dealt with as soon as it emerges by confirming or denying rumors immediately and by speaking directly with those who are spreading it, especially those who originate it. Staff need to understand the power they wield to edify or erode the community and if they choose the latter, it becomes time to put restorative practices in place or resort to disciplinary measures.

One of my favorite community standards is the Third-Time Rule, from Robert Evans. If John asks Mary for advice about how to deal with Alan's negative behavior, after two times, Mary "must invoke the Third-Time Rule and insist" that John take the issue to Alan. Mary may insist that the other two speak with each other or offer to mediate, but to persist in listening and/or advising implicates her as "part of the problem, even if she didn't create it, and is reinforcing a culture of avoidance, of talking about one another instead of to one another."[267] This works equally well with students and staff, of course, and can be instilled as part of school culture.

Social media, for all its usefulness, has a horrific downside. Perpetrators of bullying and abuse on Facebook can often be identified and dealt with. In contrast, applications like Yik Yak that facilitate anonymity are wreaking havoc in schools and universities. In fact, the failure of universities to protect professors from offensive comments made by students on Yik Yak is a subject of a labor dispute citing hostile environment.[268] As large universities have been dealing with this

[266] Abbajay, Mary. "The Danger of Workplace Gossip." N.d. *Careerstone Group.* Web. 15 Mar. 2015.

[267] Evans, op cit.

[268] Schmidt, Peter. "A New Faculty Challenge: Fending Off Abuse on Yik Yak." *The Chronicle of Higher Education.* 29 Jan. 2015. Web. 15 Mar. 2015. See also Fabris, Casey. "Anonymous

situation for some time and have far more sophisticated technological infrastructures and resources than independent schools, it is instructive to note that they have not identified any realistic means by which to confront the issue. Some create their own platforms to offer an alternative to Yik Yak; others merely assert the importance of civility and "owning one's ideas," rather than expressing them anonymously. Phillips Exeter (NH) had the company geo-fence the campus to render it inaccessible in several buildings and the Dean of Residential Life pleaded with students to stop using the app in the name of preserving community.[269] Alas, none of this helps in any substantive way and the appeal of anonymous fora is unlikely to disappear anytime soon.

Honor Codes

In a community with strong cohesion, there will be shared values that will assist in the maintenance of the social contract. "When the community is intact, there will be little need for government of any kind."[270] Many independent schools and colleges profess to have honor codes, but in some, the code is woven through the very fabric of the school, while in others it has little to no impact. (In fact, academic integrity experts McCabe and Treviño found that schools with no honor code can still have strong cultural commitments to academic honesty). Honor codes need not be limited to issues of specifically academic dishonesty and, depending on the culture of the school, can extend far into the behavior of students off-campus (i.e. shoplifting, drug offenses, etc.), but the emphasis on the academic is more common. A culture of integrity is not achieved by a quick fix implementation of an honor code and takes years and deliberate and continuous work. "Academic dishonesty is a complex behavior influenced by multiple variables beyond the mere existence of an honor code." [271]

Using large random samples of undergraduates across the country, McCabe and Treviño have demonstrated repeatedly that tertiary institutions with honor codes have higher rates of academic integrity than those without. The efficacy of

---

Feedback, Fine. Insults? Not on These Platforms." *The Chronicle of Higher Education*. 5 Feb. 2015. Web. 15 Mar. 2015.

[269] Mahler, Jonathan. "Who Spewed That Abuse? Anonymous Yik Yak App Isn't Telling." *The New York Times*. 8 Mar. 2015. Web. 10 Mar. 2015.

[270] Quoting Amitai Etzioni in McCabe, Donald L., and Linda Klebe Treviño. "Academic Dishonesty: Honor Codes and Other Contextual Influences." *The Journal of Higher Education*. 64.5 (1993): 522-38.

[271] Ibid. Also see Center for Spiritual and Ethical Education's *Creating a Culture of Academic Integrity*, 2011.

honor codes in the reduction of academic dishonesty correlates strongly with "understanding/acceptance of academic integrity policies," "certainty of being reported" and severe penalties. There are mitigating factors, however, particularly the perception of peers' academic dishonesty, which is most influential.[272] Dishonesty needs to be abhorred as socially unacceptable and a possible source of embarrassment.

Honor codes have a far greater likelihood of success when stakeholders can "develop a shared understanding and acceptance of its academic integrity policies." Schools can do this in various ways that have proven effective:

- Signing an honor pledge, perhaps within the context of an Honor Ceremony (the plan for one appears in Appendix Section IX)
- Signing each assignment and assessment with "On my honor" or some appropriate analogue
- Communicating the issue often, especially during orientation for new students
- "Reminders about the seriousness and consequences of academic dishonesty, statements in course syllabi about academic misconduct."[273]

Clarifying to students and their parents the deleterious impact that academic dishonesty has on college admissions will also doubtless leave an impression, for reports of such offenses, particularly when repeated or part of other behavior demonstrating questionable integrity, red flag an application. And, finally, such offenses should be dealt with in a timely way that underscores that the community takes such issues seriously. Honor Councils comprised of students, staff, and administrators can be effective in dealing with offenses as well as the creation and maintenance of cultural norms.[274] As always, "hate the sin, love the sinner," and keep the focus on repairing the rupture in trust.

Parent Pledge

It must be communicated to parents that the enrollment of a child in an independent school is an active affirmation of the school community's educational principles and behavioral expectations including the honor code, and that they are counted on to uphold the standards. Many schools require that parents sign a

---

[272] Ibid.

[273] Ibid.

[274] For a fascinating article regarding the role of the Honor Council in reinforcing integrity at the University of Texas, see Melgoza, Pauline, and Jane Smith. "Revitalizing an Existing Honor Code Program." *Innovative Higher Education*. 32.4 (2008): 209-19.

pledge along when they submit their deposit each year. A sample pledge might read something like this:

We believe that our students will benefit from a unified statement from families regarding our standards and values. In particular, we reject the increasing acceptance in our society of adolescent use of alcohol and drugs as a normal part of growing up, and we want to take every possible measure to ensure safe passage of our students to adulthood without the interference of alcohol and other drug-related problems. While some parents believe that students are going to drink alcohol and it is safer for them to do this at home under the parents' watchful eye, in addition to being illegal, this practice is not supported by the research. The National Institute of Health study of 43,000 adults reveals that

47% of individuals who began drinking before the age of 14 developed a dependence on alcohol and are more likely to develop alcoholism within 10 years of when they first started to drink. They are also at an increased risk during any year of adulthood.[275]

As a condition of the acceptance of your son or daughter, we ask that you sign the following pledge:

We have read the student handbook [*add other codified treatments*] and pledge to uphold the school's rules, principles, and honor code and the decisions made by the Honor Council.
We pledge to support the academic standards of the curriculum and treat the staff as professionals who are working for the best interests of the students.
We will encourage our children to do their best work and their own work.
We will not offer or approve or provide unauthorized assistance with assignments.
We will not endorse the sharing of homework without permission.
We will not allow the discussion of a test that some have taken and others have not.
We will teach our children to treat others the way that they would be treated.
We take the responsibility to ensure that all social events in my home for teenagers will be chaperoned by a parent and free of alcohol and other drugs.

Signed_____

---

[275] "Early Drinking Linked to Higher Lifetime Alcoholism Risk, July 3, 2006 News Release - National Institutes of Health (NIH)." *U.S National Library of Medicine*. 3 July 2006. Web. 17 Mar. 2015. The same finding is reported by the WHO, see Jernigan, David H. *Global Status Report: Alcohol and Young People*. World Health Organization, 2001.

When Things Go Wrong, Making Them Right

Like so many other practices in our schools, the way we treat students who fall short of community expectations for behavior hasn't changed much over time. The options generally range from restrictions on privileges and liberty to expulsion from the community. The implicit message of some of these practices should prompt reconsideration. For example, many schools, especially boarding schools, assign students to "work crew" as punishment, which often means students working in the dining hall, cleaning off other students' plates and wiping the tables, or else on the grounds, emptying recycling bins and trash, etc.

First, it should be noted, it is a laudable part of some educational philosophies, notably Waldorf, that students perform these activities daily as part of their personal responsibility and contribution to the community, in which students take pride. This is as it should be. By construing this sort of service as punishment, we deride the dignity of manual work and disparage those hired to perform these actions. This is especially troublesome if those employees belong to some marginalized group that is underrepresented in the school, for it speaks volumes about the community's attitude toward diversity (and social justice), despite any professed initiatives. Staff and students need to be more creative in inventing a more appropriate course of action.

The U.S. Department of Education research revealed that Black students are suspended and expelled at a rate three times greater than White students,[276] prompting public school district staff to realize that the way punishment and corrective action were handled needed to change. Increasingly, they are looking toward restorative practices that endeavor (a) to ensure that those harmed receive some reparation and recuperate the control and power that they lost and (b) that offenders take responsibility and experience consequences for their action and repair the rupture they caused with individuals and/or the community and regain lost trust.[277]

---

[276] U.S. Department Of Education Office For Civil Rights. "Data Snapshot: School Discipline." *Civil Rights Data Collection.* U.S. Department of Education. Mar. 2014. Web. 15 Mar. 2015.
[277] This guide is comprehensive and indispensable for anyone considering this transformative philosophy: Ashley, Jessica, and Kimberley Burke. *Implementing Restorative Justice: A Guide for Schools.* Illinois Criminal Justice Authority, 2009. Web. 15 Mar. 2015.
See a) Various options for training and professional development are offered by the International Institute for Restorative Practices. www.iirp.edu.
b) Wachtel, Ted, and Paul McCold. "In Pursuit of Paradigm: A Theory of Restorative Justice." Proc. of XIII World Congress of Criminology, Rio de Janeiro. 12 Aug. 2003. Web. 15 Mar. 2015

When integrated systematically into the way that the entire school community functions, restorative practices can transform the way that members interact on a daily basis. Students learn to actively participate in the process, rather than rely on administrators to solve problems for them. The attention is shifted from rules to *relationship*. Training in the methodology is, of course, essential for staff as well as peer mediators and mentors. Major benefits of this practice include:

- Accepting ambiguity. Fault and responsibility may be unclear.
- Separating the deed from the doer, recognize students' worth and disapprove of their wrongdoing.
- Seeing every instance of wrongdoing and conflict as an opportunity for learning. Turn negative incidents into constructive ones by building empathy and a sense of community.
- Developing trusting and caring relationships between adults and students.
- Fostering skills to resolve conflict, such as listening, empathy, critical thinking, and self-control.
- Determining what has happened and why by asking questions and listening to the answers.
- Resolving problems with open-ended questions, exploring different responses, reflecting on motives, and allowing for disagreement.
- Assisting students in considering ways to make amends for misbehavior, such as replacing, repairing, cleaning, or apologizing.
- Following up to determine whether the problem was solved and or more work needs to be done.
- Encouraging reflection.
- Allowing flexibility for different students, needs, and situations.
- Minimizing the punitive impact when control is necessary to repair the relationship and address underlying issues.[278]

Certainly these are far superior outcomes than those that proceed from demerits, loss of privileges, detention, suspension, or expulsion, which yield only negative results and do nothing to repair any interpersonal rift. They also foster the holistic development of our students and the cohesion of our communities.

---

c) Davis, Matt. "Restorative Justice: Resources for Schools." *Edutopia*. 4 Oct. 2013. Web. 13 Mar. 2015.

[278] Ashley and Burke, op cit.

Balancing the Individual With the Collective

The tension between the rights of the individual and the responsibility of that individual to the collective or community is part of every group, from the family to the corporation, the nation and the world. Educational institutions as well as religious organizations and parents have fundamental roles in the shaping of young people's attitudes toward participation in the communities of which they are a part. Many of our schools have mission statements that affirm the promotion of citizenship and character in our students; the way that we teach them to behave vis-à-vis the school community fertilizes the soil for those qualities to blossom.

The competing trends of increasing customization and standardization present public schools with serious challenges and independent schools with glorious opportunity. Independent schools have historically been marketed as providing extraordinary individualized attention for students who desired it or who required it due to cognitive or behavioral challenges or considerable time away from classes due to professional, athletic, or familial commitments. Several renowned independent schools in Florida were founded to accommodate families wintering there with a program of study that mirrored their curricula at home in the frozen North. The consumer culture further encourages the assumption that when one pays for a service, one is entitled to receive it in precisely the way desired, perhaps generating alternatives and options that suit and picking and choosing among them.

Independent school parents have a significant and expanding range of educational and operational expectations for modifications and adjustments: for learning styles, individual interests, familial moral imperatives, emotional turmoil (both chronic and acute, however insignificant it may seem to staff), and dietary needs and preferences, to name but a few. School staff can become resentful of the perceived special treatment they are asked or required to provide. Too often, I have heard teachers relay to students and parents that students need to get used to deadlines and rigid rules because college instructors will not be so flexible, when in reality, this depends on the college; selective institutions are far more accommodating than non-selective ones.

Similarly, parents in some of our schools demand alternate assignments to avoid an offending text. Such requests are by all accounts becoming increasingly frequent and administrators have to make thorny decisions regarding when to heed the ancient proverb, "Bend like a reed or break like an oak" and when to stand firm. A willingness to meet individual needs has been at the core of independent education and certainly needs to continue, albeit with reservations. The school provides a general framework and must be flexible to accommodate the vagaries of circumstance but not frivolity, and not when the modification is too onerous or costly in terms of school resources.

For example, a parent requests a different book for her daughter, a junior, to read in lieu of Upton Sinclair's *The Jungle* on the grounds that it appears on the list of books her Church urged avoiding. However, *The Jungle* was selected by the English and U.S. History teachers as a group for its ability to illustrate various themes in planned interdisciplinary units and projects to take place over the course of three weeks. They consider it integral to the program of study. Identifying an alternate selection that could serve as well would require many resources in terms of time and effort and would be unlikely to yield equivalent educational benefits. How a school administrator handles this situation reveals the relationship he or she has with parents, staff, and students, and how he or she navigates the dangerous straits between individual and community.

That relationship is affected by the mounting tendency in both K-12 and tertiary educational institutions to regard the students and/or parents as customers. The customer is always right, but the student isn't. There are necessarily errors to be made in the path to learning and educators have expertise that merits respect.

> "The corporate model treats students like customers, and as customers they expect services and products for their tuition fees. The services include high grades in return for little effort. The products include guaranteed credentials with a guaranteed value. With this sense of entitlement, most will not prepare for classes, and expect all material to be told to them in simple terms in entertaining classes."[279]

Moreover, despite our assertions to parents that we do not "get" students into the most selective universities possible, for some that persists as the endgame for enrolling their students in our schools, and we play into this through questionable college counseling practices, the publication of our list of college acceptances as proof of our quality, and speaking with prospective parents as if college admission were our ultimate product. If that is the expectation, any grade of less than A can

---

[279] Quoted from an interview with the authors of *Lowering Higher Education: The Rise of Corporate Universities and the Fall of Liberal Education,* James E. Côté and Anton L. Allahar by Bell, Steven J. "Antidote for Entitled 'Customers'" *Inside Higher Ed.* 29 July 2011. Web. 07 Mar. 2015.

be perceived as obstructing admission to desired colleges. This conceptualization devalues our mission, undermines faculty, and contributes to a sense of entitlement on the part of both students and parents. From the outset, we need to be clear about the rights and responsibilities in the relationship between family and school. The family buys *access* to a caring community and skilled staff who use expert techniques and a well-structured program of studies in safe facilities to carry out the school's mission and vision. What students do with that opportunity is ultimately up to them.

Creating caring classrooms

Naturally, the classroom and the relationships one forges there with staff and peers are central to students' experience of the school. Other parts of this book have dealt with the pedagogical aspects; here the focus is on the affective dimension. When staff are intentional about involving the students in a community, rather than merely a place where students receive the instructor's knowledge, the classroom becomes far more cohesive, motivating, stimulating, challenging, and positive.

Kathleen Gould Lundy and Larry Swartz have authored a wonderful book, *Creating Caring Classrooms: How to encourage students to communicate, create, and be compassionate of others*, replete with suggestions. Among the many ways they identify for teachers to create a classroom as a community are greeting students by name at the door, determining rituals to begin and end each class, and publishing a book of class work.[280] Getting-to-know-you ice breakers should not be limited to the first day of school, but should take place periodically throughout the year in order for all members of the class, including the instructor, to learn and understand more about one another.

One technique that I have practiced and enthusiastically promote is for the instructor to lead the creation of a classroom constitution by soliciting ideas from students about how the class should be together, how it should not be, how the class will know if it is succeeding in meeting the standards it sets, and what should happen if standards are violated. Each class creates a mission statement and a set of standards for class behavior, like "One person speaks at a time," "Always do our best work," "Give each other the right kind of help." One of my favorites was "Don't harsh on other people's mellows." Each class writes its mission and

---

[280] Lundy, Kathleen Gould, and Larry Swartz. *Creating Caring Classrooms: How to Encourage Students to Communicate, Create, and be Compassionate of Others*. Pembroke, 2011.

185

standards on a poster board mounted at the front of the classroom. If this is treated not merely as a first-day gimmick, but taken seriously as a code of conduct and erstwhile manifesto that is referred to frequently, students tend to buy in with aplomb and police themselves.   In conjunction with established standards, predictability and ritual are important to foster a sense of security and trust, which help students to attend to the learning task. Novelty is imperative to get students' attention on occasion, but the established framework is paramount.

Absences, especially due to illness or challenge, are opportunities to demonstrate caring on a classroom or school level. Technology permits students who cannot attend school for a time but who are healthy enough to participate virtually. Beyond that, the class may find some way to determine responsibility for reaching out to a classmate and working together virtually, which is often facilitated by the Learning Management System and other technology. Extended absences require more effort on the part of the class to determine how they want to show care.

Communication with parents is vital. The beginning of the term presents an excellent opportunity for staff, particularly classroom teachers, to introduce themselves, their enthusiasm for students and for teaching, and the goals, objectives, methodology, and principal projects of the course to parents and students. It establishes a positive and enthusiastic impression and affords teachers the platform for explaining why this course matters and what students can expect to take away from it. It can also impart important information that establishes the educator as a professional who keeps abreast of the research and forges a partnership with parents in the formation of their children. One key study from the Organization for Economic Cooperation and Development I like to share emphasizes the magnitude of what happens at home in students' formation:

> Students who discuss complex topics – like social or political issues – with their parents are better readers, enjoy reading more and are better able to identify successful strategies to summarise complex information.[281]

We must remember that parents are students' first and most important educators and role models. Instruct them as to how to help their children succeed, and strive to enlist their cooperation whenever possible.

---

[281] Borgonovi, Francesca and Guillermo Montt. "Parental Involvement in Selected PISA Countries and Economies." OECD Education Working Papers, No. 73, 2012, sec. 173.

As a matter of course and standard procedure in our schools, it is imperative for teachers to have multiple positive contacts with parents. When a student makes a particularly fine contribution to the class in some way, that should not merely be noted for mention in the summative narrative assessments as discussed in Chapter 3. Rather, the moment that it takes to place a call (with time, date, and content logged for future reference) or draft and send such an email is an unparalleled investment and presents the teacher with the impetus for a positive contact with parents that demonstrates the teacher's support of and positive regard for the student. (And, should any challenge present later in the term, it has already been established that the teacher is not "out to get" the student). Learning Management Systems (LMS) that permit parents to monitor the daily performance of their son or daughter are no substitute for this personal contact, nor should it be presumed that parents are actually using the LMS. The positive impact of home visits on students, staff, and parents has been well-documented and implemented in public school systems large and small. This practice meshes particularly well with the independent school ethos of parents and teachers as co-educators and is worth exploring with any day student population.[282]

In alignment with the survey instrument for determining the sense of community in the school as a whole, there is a separate inventory for application within specific classroom settings.[283] Items include statements such as these:

> I feel reluctant to speak openly
> I feel uneasy exposing gaps in my understanding
> I feel that members of this course depend on me

These surveys can also serve as a rubric for the instructor because they render explicit the specific objectives to achieve as well as an assessment of progress toward them. Such instruments are best issued at logical intervals to give the staff and students time to redress any shortcomings that might be revealed. These surveys often dispel complacency. Nevertheless, classroom dynamics may vary widely; one class gels nicely while another does not, sometimes despite the teacher's best intentions and actions. For that reason, the results of these

---

[282] See a) "Parent/Teacher Home Visits: Creating A Bridge Between Parents And Teachers As Co-Educators in Springfield, MA and Seattle, WA." *NEA Foundation Issue Brief.* NEA Foundation. Mar. 2012. Web. 9 Mar. 2015.
b) Parent Teacher Home Visit Project (pthvp.org) and teacherhomevisit.org
[283] Rovai, Alfred P., Mervyn J. Wighting, and Robert Lucking. "The Classroom and School Community Inventory: Development, Refinement, and Validation of a Self-Report Measure for Educational Research." *The Internet and Higher Education.* 7.4 (2004): 263-80.

inventories are best applied by the teacher in the classroom; great care must be taken by an administrator using them for purposes of teacher evaluation.

Together on the Journey Throughout the Year

Participating together in rituals to mark the passage of time serves to bond us to one another. The school day and year are characterized by repeated behaviors, from morning bell to weekly assembly, but these aren't what we mean by ritual. When we craft rituals intentionally, they have enormous potential to create and reflect change, to heal, to celebrate joyful events and transitions, to express shared beliefs and identity, to affirm relationships, and more. Rituals use symbols and sensory elements that may be visual, olfactory, auditory, kinesthetic, and/or tactile to work on a subconscious level to affect change. They cause us to leave ordinary time and enter special or sacred time to remember our unique place and community. In order to retain their power, rituals should not become stagnant and should incorporate dynamic elements that relate to the present.

Religious schools have the advantage of convening the entire school community, including parents, for holidays in the liturgical calendar, but there are many rituals that secular schools can use to foster greater cohesion. Several humanistic groups including the Society for Ethical Culture and religious traditions with similar inclinations like Unitarian Universalism and Humanistic Judaism that offer many examples of rituals that schools can adapt for their purposes. There are various resources for secular and humanistic expressions and affirmations that can replace theistic prayers at such events.[284] The following is a list of events throughout the school year that stakeholders can imbue with specific significance over time.

Forgiveness Day may be held at the beginning of the year to start the new academic year fresh and repeated during the year to periodically press the reset button on relationships. The way it is structured can vary each time. A period of guided reflection on how we may have injured others might be a first step. One practice is to place platters of sliced apples with honey or something sweet and small plates or napkins around the room or school and those who realize they have injured someone may offer that person an apple slice with honey as they ask forgiveness. Or everyone who wishes to might write a grievance on a paper and

---

[284] See a) Brownstein, Ted. *Interfaith Prayer Book*. Lake Worth Interfaith Network, 2014,
b) Foerster, L. Annie. *For Praying Out Loud: Interfaith Prayers for Public Occasions*. Skinner House, 2003.
c) Goular, Frances Sheridan. *God Has No Religion: Blending Traditions for Prayer*. Sorin, 2005.

place it in a bonfire to release it. Or people might hold pebbles representing injury committed or suffered and cast them into a running body of water.

If *assembly* is merely a time for announcements and the results of the most recent athletic events, it fails to take advantage of a wonderful regular occasion to share joys and concerns. This is the time to celebrate individual and collective achievements with jubilation, not just an announcement. It may also serve as a community forum to address problematic issues. Birthdays may be observed by creating a custom of permitting a few people to say something affirming the person's life or ways that they were touched or influenced by him or her. Care should be taken to ensure that this doesn't just favor the social stars, however. There may be a weekly inspirational quote or performance and a communal recitation of the school affirmation. There are many secular affirmations that a school may use that all present may speak together. Here is an example of one that I composed:

> *May all who study here, who work here, who contribute to this school community continue to be blessed,*
> *May each of us grow to become the unique person we are meant to be,*
> *May we treat one another with kindness and compassion and be a positive influence on those we meet,*
> *May our learning help us to better understand ourselves, understand others and understand the world around us.*
> *May we act with integrity and truth in all things, and give the very best of ourselves in all we do,*
> *We are grateful to [founders] for creating this school.*
> *We are grateful for blessings yet to come.*

August/September: *Gathering In*. In this first ritual of the school year, all students, staff and other stakeholders bring a stone or water from a place that represents some place they visited over the summer break. These are commingled in a public place as a symbol of unity.

September: *Honor Ceremony*. Stakeholders commit to values such as civility, respect, and trust. The community demonstrates through an outward sign such as signing a book, poster or banner, or older students bestowing pins on younger students, that it takes seriously the policies and guidelines regarding cheating and academic integrity and promotes mutual respect between staff and students. (See Appendix for sample Honor Ceremony).

189

October/November: *Remembering Ancestors*. Revering and remembering our ancestors is part of the human experience. Students and staff may be invited to contribute to a special communal place of reverence for a certain period with photographs or objects and a short description of the one(s) they choose to honor. This is also a time to remember founders, alumni, and others who have contributed to the community and who are now deceased. A brief ceremony may mark the beginning and end of the period of remembrance.

November: *Thanksgiving*. This is an opportunity for the community members to engage in reflection and gratitude for special people, events, and other blessings. They may create a representation or write words on paper or perform some similar action and place these on a communal table during a brief ceremony and share a special potluck.

January: *New Year*. The new calendar year is an appropriate time to reflect on goals and other elements that one wants to either manifest or eliminate in the coming year. Elements to manifest may be drawn, constructed, cut from magazines or printed and ensconced in a visible place as a reminder. Elements to eliminate may be written on paper and placed in a bonfire.

January: *Recent Alumni Lunch*. Those who have graduated within the past five or six years are invited to visit and dine as honored guests while still home for winter break.

February: *Heartfest*. Valentine's Day brings thoughts of romantic love, but school communities can invite and honor grandparents, siblings, other members of the extended family or "family of choice," alumni, and other supporters.

March: *International Women's Day*. Schools may host a speaker or dedicate a full day to workshops and speakers whose work and interests center around a theme, perhaps chosen by the students who make up the International Women's Day Committee.

May: *Celebration of the Year*. The end of the year is a great time to recall and rejoice in all that a community has accomplished together and the gratitude it feels for the bounty it has received. This is not just the typical end of year awards ceremony that often bestows certain awards to a small number of students with academic, athletic, or artistic achievements. This is a time to bring the community together and really consider and display some representation of all of the wonderful research, learning, and service that students and other stakeholders have done throughout the year. It is also a suitable time to acknowledge donors with all stakeholders present.

June: *Graduation.* The transition of seniors to alumni is an opportunity to recognize and celebrate their uniqueness and contributions to the community and nurture and emphasize the expectation of their continued relationship with the school. Senior trips, dinners, service projects, etc. are wonderful bonding experiences. Younger students also look up to these students and observe the festivities with anticipation.

Other days of significance:

Founders' Day: Stakeholders express appreciation for the vision and work of the founder and/or important figures in the life of the community or people the community chooses to recognize for their contributions. This includes donor recognition events in which students and staff might present their accomplishments that result from donors' generosity.

Celebration of Seniors Day: Seniors may display some sign (like an article of clothing) featuring their post-secondary plan: college, gap year, work. In some schools, there is a venue for students to vent about colleges that did not accept them. Staff may choose to wear a shirt from their colleges too.

Art Auction: Students (and other stakeholders) donate their artwork to the school-wide auction with the profits reverting to the school. This is a great way to foster the desire and responsibility to give back to the school. Students should be treated the same as adult donors would be treated, with appropriate expression of thanks.

Maintaining Ties With Those Who Have Gone Before

Some schools are brilliantly effective at inculcating in students the sense that they are part of a legacy, a long line of those who have graduated in years past and those who have yet to come. In some schools (especially girls' single sex schools), alumni(ae) remain very much a part of the life of the school. It bears repeating: the more demands placed on a group's members, the more cohesive the group.

It is crucial to connect alumni with current students, whether virtually or on campus, and treat them as honored guests. Various venues afford meaningful interaction.

191

- Alumni may provide some special treat during exams, for example, or tailgate festivities, especially related to a significant tournament.
- Teaching students to network is invaluable, so an expert might instruct students how to work a room and then alumni participate in periodic mocktail parties to give students practice.
- Many colleges are now teaching students business dinner etiquette; consider instructing students followed by hosting such an event with alumni.
- Invite alumni to participate in service days, holidays, and traditions and celebrate successes (tell those stories!) and artistic, athletic, and other events. Hold special performances just for alumni.
- Invite them to lectures, workshops, or trips led by staff or invited experts. Make the sessions available online for those who cannot attend.
- Recent alumni can speak about what they learned from their first year(s) at college. (They *must* be surveyed regarding how well-served they were by the school; NAIS provides such an instrument, described in Chapter 1). Those who have graduated within some period, say six years, can attend a special lunch or dinner while they are home from college in January. Recent college graduates can speak about getting their first job.

Social media can help locate and track alumni. Evertrue and Graduway are two new companies that parse social media to offer specialized alumni information and networking sites for colleges that may apply to secondary schools as well.[285] Survey alumni, but also pay close attention to what they post or like on social media. Separate from fundraising purposes, maintain records of any special interests, expertise, careers and where alumni attended college and ask to make connections with students with similar affinities or considering those schools. Request that they share their expertise or experience with students beyond career day (on which their participation is essential) or that they facilitate a meeting with someone in their social or professional network. Draw upon alumni for mentoring, internships, and opportunities for current students or graduates. Ask them for advice. Determine special interest groups that might connect alumni to other alumni (e.g. alumni whose children have attended or currently attend the school) or alumni to current students (e.g. Athletics or Arts Hall of Fame).

Use affinity groups and any other relevant data to target the information that alumni receive via email, social media, and/or newsletter. The message that resonates with a millennial is unlikely to do so with a Baby Boomer. Requests for

---

[285] Singer, Natasha. "Your College May Be Banking on Your Facebook Likes." *The New York Times*. 24 Jan. 2015. Web. 16 Mar. 2015.

donations should not appear every time—Fundraising 101 dictates that there are categories of donor preferences in terms of being asked; it is imperative that those be tracked. Messages should be interesting, inspiring, and very much in keeping with the brand. Alumni should be able to contribute joys and concerns and any other content of interest. It goes without saying that alumni lifecycle events and accolades and alumni visits and gatherings, however impromptu, should be featured in all of the usual media. Display a Google Map on the website and social media of where alumni are living. Alumni should be integrated with the present life of the community as much as possible to provide a sense of cohesion and continuity. The connection that they perceive will determine their willingness to contribute in other ways such as volunteering, advocating for the school, referring students, and donating.

Relations With the Community Beyond the School

Day schools tend to be far better than boarding schools at weaving the school into the tapestry of the larger community, but this certainly need not be the case. In addition to the partnerships and internships discussed in Chapter 4, many schools, both boarding and day are developing extraordinarily ingenious means to both contribute to and draw upon the resources in their environs to create a synergy that enriches both.

The Hill School (PA) Student Philanthropy Council is one such program. The Council members are selected on the basis of a rigorous application and spend the fall term studying the processes of philanthropy. They send Requests for Proposals to area nonprofits, visit the sites, speak with representatives, and make decisions about how to award the funds allotted from an endowment specifically created for this purpose. This is exceptional experience for the students, serves to inform them about the needs of the larger community, and establishes a favorable connection between the organizations and the school.

Various schools hold annual symposia, a series of workshops, interactive seminars, and participatory projects on a given theme. At Stevenson School (CA), the Symposium on the theme of Ocean featured keynote speaker Donovan Hohn, author of *Moby-Duck, the true story of 28,800 bath toys lost at sea and the beachcombers, oceanographers, environmentalists and fools, including the author, who went in search of them* (2011); Spector Dance's NEA funded piece *Ocean*; tidal pooling; touring Monterey Bay Aquarium, the Oceanography labs at the Naval Postgraduate School, NOAA's research vessel; and workshops with various experts, including alumni, involved in marine research and conservation. In

193

addition to providing an unforgettable and stimulating highlight to the year, this is a superlative means to initiate connections and acquaint academics, entrepreneurs, social sector leaders and staff, and other professionals with the school.

Another way of connecting the school with the social sector pertains to boarding schools. Many colleges are adopting environmentally- and budget-friendly ways of dealing with the end-of-year detritis beyond adding to landfills (and paying thousands of dollars in removal fees). Students bring items to collection centers around campus or a central location like the gym and teams of volunteers sort the items and price and sell them, hold auctions, glean items (like half-full laundry detergent) for institutional use, donate food and housewares, store housewares (futons, lamps, televisions, mini-fridges, etc.) in good condition for sale to students the following fall. Staff might allow direct providers of social services to take what they can use or haul items away for sale. Alternately, in advance of studying for final exams, students and other vendors pay for tables at a school-wide rummage sale. Various universities across the country have been doing this for years and donate tens of thousands of dollars to charity.[286] In the case of schools that rent out their facilities immediately following students' departure, the massive scale of goods and the time and space constraints require a team of volunteers that is energetic and discerning and the cooperation of the departing students in bringing their items to the designated areas.

Service Learning

Service is one of the most common ways for schools to make a positive impact on their communities. At its most basic level, community service is performed by students to fulfill a certain number of required hours for graduation. It tends to be limited in scope, duration and impact on both the community and participants. Community service encompasses an enormous array of activities: walking in American Cancer Society's Relay for Life, painting walls in a Habitat for Humanity house, working in soup kitchens, mission trips, etc.

Compare these experiences with those of one school in which, during the course of just one year, students engaged in projects to study feline, simian, and human behavior at the city zoo; analyzed the presence of pharmaceuticals in the area groundwater; surveyed residents of an area with a cancer cluster to learn their practices surrounding the care of their water wells; and researched the campaigns

---

[286] See Huber, Bridget. "Colleges Turn Students' Trash into Cash for Charity." *The Christian Science Monitor*. 26 May 2009. Web. 17 Feb. 2015.

that local veterans of World War II participated in and learned to interview and record their oral histories to assist in the development of an exhibition at the local history museum. Students rightfully perceived the relevance and practical nature of their projects. They were treated as adults and were appreciated for their important contributions to the community. Engaging experiences such as these convince many schools to implement service learning.

While community service usually refers to a one-time contribution by an individual often "ministering unto" a marginalized person or group, service learning is ideally exemplified by sustained engagement over time, reciprocity, and integration with the curriculum. It addresses some authentic need in the community and intends to have significant and lasting impact. There are clear goals for students to learn about the complex factors and systems that influence an issue, gather data, interview and work beside experts, governmental leaders, and residents, and present their findings to improve some aspect of community life. The National Youth Leadership Council is a leader in school service learning and its website contains a wealth of indispensable resources, including the foundational *K-12 Service-Learning Standards and Indicators for Quality Practice.*[287]

A service learning experience typically is selected by the student, followed by contact with relevant parties and careful project design in collaboration with others. It often involves identifying potential resources, especially funding and partners. Service learning helps students to understand target concepts and apply their knowledge. Students keep journals and reflect upon what they are learning. The concept of praxis (action and reflection) is at the core of service learning and there are specific methods to employ in the process. Service learning may also culminate in public presentation to the school or larger community of the goals, procedure, outcomes, and evaluation.

Service learning has been found to have an enormously positive impact on students. The guided application of academic skills to complex social, political, and economic issues in the community leads to the development of collaborative skills, social sensitivity, and civic responsibility. Further, the following exciting outcomes were derived from a study of over 1000 students in geographically diverse high schools:

---

[287] http://www.nylc.org/sites/nylc.org/files/files/Standards_Oct2009-web.pdf

- Service learning students had significantly higher scores on enjoyment of school overall than comparison group peers.
- Students who reported stronger engagement in service-learning were statistically significantly more likely to be academically engaged, value schooling, become attached to school and community, enjoy content courses, perceive a gain in civic knowledge, skills, and dispositions, become more civically engaged in general, and felt greater efficacy.
- Students who chose the issue for their service-learning project made greater gains on the objective questions of civic knowledge than others.
- Participating in civic or political action (i.e. circulating a petition) was positively related to civic knowledge and civic dispositions.
- Direct service activities (i.e. tutoring or visiting seniors) were associated with community attachment.
- Indirect activities (i.e. fundraising) were associated with higher post-test scores on academic engagement, valuing school, and enjoyment of specific subject matters.[288]

These outcomes respond to many mission-driven objectives established by independent schools. Certainly, service learning merits serious consideration.

Like any program, educating stakeholders regarding the features of the different paradigm is essential. The very concept of social justice needs explanation. Enlisting the aid of alumni, trustees, staff, and other stakeholders in identifying prospective partner agencies in the community is helpful to having an effective program, but a student ideally selects his or her own project based on interest. Naturally, invitations should be extended to all stakeholders and community participants to attend the presentation of student work at the end of the year. Service learning experiences can significantly influence students in both cognitive and affective domains and can serve to inspire stakeholders regarding the significant positive and lasting impact that the school has on those beyond its walls as well as students' lives.

---

[288] Billig, Shelley, Sue Root, and Dan Jesse. *The Impact of Participation in Service Learning on High Schools' Civic Engagement*. Center for Information and Research on Civic Learning and Engagement, May 2005. Web. 15 Mar. 2015.

Part II: The Other Side of Service-Learning:
Teaching Activism For Citizenship

By Diego Duran-Medina, M.A., M.Ed., LeadServe Consulting © 2015

As independent schools define their role and identity in a quickly evolving economic landscape with increasing competition and personal choice for families, they must work to define their public mission in a clear and powerful way. Beyond academics, why do they exist? Increasingly, families will begin and continue to ask difficult questions as they scrutinize schools and their programs in order to justify the cost of an independent school education. This is both a matter of competitive advantage and a matter of responsibility for independent schools, illustrated by two questions: how do we set ourselves apart beyond academics, and how do we build not just scholars, but engaged, committed citizens?

Independent schools are not just part of a market system where they serve as both non-profits and businesses, they are also part of a democratic system, at least in the U.S. As schools consider how they will remain relevant, their instinct may be to rely first on effective business practices. One already sees this trend in innovative programming around partnerships with China, increasing use of technology and offering classes online. These could be seen as programs that try to either ride or predict current future trends, and seize opportunities quickly as they arise in order to remain competitive. This approach also makes it difficult to remain grounded in a specific mission, as mission creep and the market help guide actions, as opposed to sound educational decisions that benefit both the institution and the student.

It does not have to be this way; another way is possible. It may seem counterintuitive, but independent schools should be looking backwards, to our very foundation as a country and the beginning of our nation as a new democracy to define their missions and what they want to become as institutions. Specifically, as institutions located in the United States, they should redefine themselves as places of learning designed to teach both academics and civics, or put another way: both scholarship and activism are of primary importance. Activism is a term heavy with history, partisanship and politics, but what remains true regardless of one's stance is that the very existence of our country depended on both the few and the many; selected individuals who spoke both for themselves and for an idea; and the masses which were moved by both words and actions in order to make that idea into a democracy and a new nation. Independent schools serve the few and elite, and for better or for worse, the ones which are or will be on the path to leadership positions both in the public and private sectors.

There remain two formidable challenges in how democracy is conceptualized within independent schools. The first is that schools see academics as the most important mission they serve, and they ignore or see as secondary the ethical, moral, spiritual and political development of students, which in turn, serves to erode democracy. But one can ask, academics for what purpose? Or even worse, what purpose do academics serve if they exist without values that tie a student to responsibility?

The second problem, more subtle in its inception and consequences, is that even when a school defines their public mission and attempts to develop students as political beings, they do so in two shortsighted ways: the first is by defining civics in as narrow a way as possible, usually by only focusing on learning history and voting. The problem with this approach is that it only shows a small aspect of what it means to be an engaged citizen. To focus on history is to only see what was and notice patterns, not what could be. This can be useful if those patterns are used to shape present and future actions and go beyond an intellectual exercise. In essence, what does it mean to teach for not just the past and present, but for the future?

Related to this is when institutions develop programs around service, either community service or service learning. Community service is centered on the idea of serving community needs through either direct or indirect action, often involving fundraising or charity efforts. Service learning involves service tied to the curriculum, providing a context for the community need or problem through academic inquiry. Community service is commendable, as it can help develop empathy in students and make a dent in real societal needs, especially if there is a focus not just on resources but also on relationships, but does not go far enough, as needs and students change on a constant basis. Service learning goes a bit further, as students develop a deeper understanding of needs, but academics can only take a community so far, and often the academic program stops before long-lasting, permanent change can happen.

The idea here is not to critique the noble efforts of school, but instead to ask: after community service and service-learning, then what? After a student learns empathy, and learns about a need or an issue, its history and context, then what? How do they actually do something besides writing a paper or debating an issue?

198

This is where activism can provide a way forward for moving beyond service and developing active citizens.

The nexus of knowledge with and for action is activism, where students learn about an issue along with the actual steps necessary to change and improve an issue. Activism is where one teaches the very essence of what it might mean to be a citizen beyond voting, a citizen who can understand the issues and can act on their examined beliefs and even strive for a deeper, more human purpose in this sense: we are teaching students to exercise their fundamental right to shape the world, to apply their education to go beyond the textbook to the actual application to people and places. We teach them to not only learn history, but to also create it.

Activism is not a particular stance on an issue, it is an intellectual process. One does not just learn *about* an issue on a strictly academic level, although that is important. One becomes an activist through a rigorous process of examining beliefs, actions and messaging. Activism does not belong to a particular political orientation or camp. In its most basic form, activism seeks to test democratic ideals and to speak against ignorance. It is messy, complicated and unpredictable, but it is also where students can find the tools to make sense of the complex world in which we live. Activism asks students to be both rational and creative, teaching and demanding a set of skills currently not explicitly taught in independent schools, borrowing from social studies, history, art, debate, speech, technology and language arts to create anew.

This article aims to explore how activism can help independent schools become more responsive to societal needs, a changing educational landscape and the needs of students in a rapidly changing world. To the extent that independent schools can embrace a more nuanced, deeper definition of developing civic engagement, grounded in both the past and the future, they will find that not only can they use this to stand apart, but they also can fulfill a deeper mission in helping maintain and strengthen democratic ideals for the present day.

This course was developed across three years in an urban independent school within the Washington, DC area. The class was comprised of juniors who also used the course to fulfill their 15-hours a year service requirement in the high school, and Activism was a graduation requirement.

Activism was a class largely influenced by the interests and expertise of the instructor, and was located within the Values department of the school. Values department was considered a hybrid between a program and department and was

199

led by a chair, with teachers spanning grades 6-12 participating in once a trimester meetings for planning and evaluation. Values was closely interrelated with the service-learning program at the school, present since 2000, as well as the Health and Wellness program, charged with teaching healthy choices.

The class met for roughly 8 contact hours per week in a 13-week trimester, and included both 45 and 90-minute periods. The 90-minute periods were an absolute necessity for service-learning programming, and the school was purposeful in designing a schedule with increased contact time with students in order to facilitate using the city as a living classroom.

The Activism curriculum exists as a trimester-long class with roughly 100 contact hours, but can be modified and adapted to various time and scheduling constraints, including week long intensive programs for scheduling over breaks. What must be present is a service-learning period of at least 90 minutes that allows for travel time, service performed and reflection. There must also be at least 6+ visits over time in order to avoid "one and done" service opportunities. Multiple visits help attain a deeper understanding of the social issue or need being addressed and help form a strong, long-term relationship with the service organization.

Activism consists of four main parts, all which work together to help students become aware:

1) Service-Learning: Service is tied to the curriculum through a partnership with a local organization working on homelessness. The partnership includes an orientation to the organization, visits to the shelter to provide direct service to clients, meeting with actual clients and fundraising activities (i.e. Talent Show, Clothing Drive, School Walk) organized by the students to benefit the organization.

2) Activism Curriculum: The curriculum consists of three parts: exploration of personal, school and societal values, history of activism and readings about activism from modern history. The class begins with asking students to think about what values are, what purpose they serve in both individual lives and society and what values they hold most important and why.

This is done through a series of public exercises where students are asked to defend their positions on difficult moral and ethical questions as well as private writings and reflections. Secondly, students are presented with a comprehensive history of activism, mostly focusing on social issues in the 20th century (women's suffrage, civil rights, labor rights, anti-war, etc.). Although the issues tend to be based on progressive/liberal values, there is an attempt made to present issues from various sides and to critique assumptions and beliefs held as "truths." The course is guided by the personal values and orientation of both the instructor and the school. There is no such thing as being "neutral" in this curriculum, but one can be critical.

Finally, students focus on readings from important historical leaders that attempt to move beyond the mythical hero-activist. There is an attempt to complicate "heroes" as human beings with faults, as well as moving beyond a notion of the "lone activist" to seeing activism as a series of actions by individuals working to inform, change attitudes and affect process.

3) Critical Inquiry: This is a research process involving a set of questions where students choose a topic of interest around a social issue or problem, and begin to collect data from various sources, including people in the community, to become experts on a specific idea. The Blueprint acts as a repository of stories, statistics, sources, data and people on the topic. Students become familiar with the Blueprint through using the class topic (Homelessness) as an example, as they learn more about the issue through visiting and serving at the local shelter.

4) Podcast: Students use a critical inquiry process to write, record and present a 2-3 minute podcast on their issue using the research they have completed. The podcast can be modeled after a news report, a public service announcement, a human-interest story, an interview, a song, a poem/spoken-word or a short fictional play. The point is for the students to move beyond the traditional research paper and apply the knowledge they have gained through developing voice. The key is presenting data in an engaging, creative way.

It is less important what it is called (artivism, civic engagement, service-learning) and much more important that the school deeply explore how it is actually preparing students beyond academics. This process begins with the mission and seeing where the mission is realized. What are the values of the school? What are parents and students asking for? What do they need to not only understand the present, but to also affect and change our collective future?

To ensure success, as mentioned above, the schedule must also be conducive to going beyond the classroom. As well, faculty must be given the training, encouragement, freedom and support to remain innovative and to find ways to apply taught knowledge. This is not just "progressive" teaching, but effective learning, where students can retain more of what is taught by applying it to a community need and can clearly explain ways that their knowledge can be applied for good. As mentioned above, the schedule must also be conducive to going beyond the classroom.

Finally, schools must realize there is a monumental shift in how students learn and evolve. What is education when most information is already available online? This is a challenge to help students move beyond merely being consumers of data to becoming critical co-creators.

Activism can help institutions move forward "with" and "beyond" service-learning, creating an academic space where students can explore their own values and topics of both societal and personal interest (curriculum and the critical inquiry), as well as developing ways to use their knowledge to both inform (podcast) and help (service). In creating these spaces for students, independent schools can help redefine themselves as institutions where knowledge learned is knowledge applied, so as to retain relevance and a sense of connection with the community. Activism places students at the center of their learning, helping them develop with the content and the skills necessary for not only learning about the world, but helping shape it. Students are not only an audience for the past; they are also the actors, making a future through action.

Summary

Parents, students, and staff most often name close-knit community as the element they value most about our schools. To generate greater cohesion among our stakeholders, they must have control over their work, find it meaningful and significant, and receive recognition for their success. We must be deliberate about our community standards, the ways that our members treat one another, and the systems at work beneath the surface. We must honor the symbolic dimension of the community, for its influence is subconscious and powerful. We must find ways to maintain ties with alumni so that they continue to feel inspired and driven to participate in our mission. We engage meaningfully with the larger community to find out its needs and work with others to build a more just world.

Chapter 8

Staying Above Board and in the Black:
Leading Mission, Strategy, and Stewardship

One of the great challenges of leadership is balancing hope with reality while moving an organization forward boldly, confidently, and creatively. The best way to build a culture of innovation and continuous improvement is not by fiat, but by continually questioning the status quo and changing as reality warrants, while holding true to a vision of the future. If we are too slow to change, foreseeable and preventable crises will become genuine, full-blown ones. It is our responsibility, indeed our obligation, to meet the future with the same pragmatic and pioneering spirit that has shaped our education system from its beginnings.—Scott Cowen, President of Tulane University, 1998-2014[289]

Managing Chronic Anxiety for a Healthy Community

In his brilliant work, Dr. Edwin Friedman identified chronic anxiety as the greatest challenge to both leadership and change. This certainly is relevant to secondary schools since chronic anxiety is one of the emotions that most certainly flourish in secondary schools. Much of it revolves around college admissions and life plans and goals, but it also results from pressure from various sources, the often painful process of individuation, peer relations, and negotiating relationships of all kinds. In this post 9/11 era, it often manifests as school security systems featuring front door buzzers, sex offender license scans, badges for staff, students, and visitors, locked classroom doors, and other theatrical absurdities. These assuage fears for school safety and shore up defenses, despite the realities that violence occurs most often at the hands of family members and school shootings occur with minute statistical probability: according to FactCheck.org, since the Newtown, CT, incident, thirty-four shootings have occurred amongst 134,000 educational institutions in the US. To paraphrase Kipling, the task of school leaders is precisely to keep their wits about them while all others are losing theirs.

A trio of factors often present in schools are toxic to leadership: anxiety, the tendency of educators to avoid conflict and value peace over progress as discussed

---

[289] Cowen, Scott. "You Don't Need a Hurricane to Know Which Way the Wind Blows." *The Chronicle of Higher Education.* 5 Jan. 2015. Web. 16 Mar. 2015

in Chapter 6, and the propensity of educators and school stakeholders for supporting the underdog. These are guaranteed to undermine and preclude effective leadership if the leaders

> allow the most dependent, most easily hurt members of any organization to effectively 'set the agenda'...and promote an attitude of *adaptation toward immaturity* rather than one of responsibility, effectively shifting power to the recalcitrant, the complainers, the passive-aggressive, and the most anxious members of an institution rather than the energetic, the visionary, the imaginative, and the most creatively motivated.[290]

The invasive and destructive nature of these toxic forces is like a cancer or un-self-regulating pathogen, asserts Friedman, and as such, can only be dealt with by taking a stand, i.e. limiting "a toxic agent's invasiveness" and *not* through "reasonableness, love, insight, role modeling,...and striving for consensus."

Alas, taking a stand is the least common way of dealing with such members in our schools, and when a leader does so, stakeholders, often including trustees, tend to reactively sabotage. It is easier to join with others who are similarly anxious to displace blame, seek quick fixes, gather more information (e.g. hire a consultant), escalate victimization and indulge in emotion rather than take responsibility. These "counterrevolutionary characteristics" reinforce the stagnation in our schools. School staff might add a STEM initiative, an online course, a leadership program or a trip abroad, and stakeholders might even believe these are genuine innovations, but they are the path of least resistance in an imaginatively gridlocked organization, the only solution for which is adventure.

Schools are on what Friedman describes as a treadmill, holding fast to the notion that all would be well...if we only raised more money / enrolled more students or more full-pay students / built a new facility for x. Those are quick fixes that are not serviceable for the long term. Instead, we need to ask the big questions: What does the massive disruption in higher education mean for us as college preparatory institutions? What about the shifts in the economy? Why teach for the century that was rather than the century that will be? We must leave the treadmill for an authentic journey. In this book, I have suggested as a first step that we reconsider and re-envision what and how we teach and why.

---

[290] Friedman, Edwin H. *Reinventing Leadership: Change in an Age of Anxiety. Discussion Guide.* The Guilford Press, 1996, p. 9.

We are convinced that what we do in our schools is excellent and well worth paying for, though I hope that this book has chipped away at complacency. Perhaps we believe that by adding more technology, some online options, and/or a STEM/STEAM/STREAM program, we will appear innovative and all will be well—until the next trend that parents demand or that the cross-app academy implements. Why do we stay with the pack, adhering to the same structure, the same format, same schedule, same modes of delivery? We must embrace a revolutionary shift in what the objectives of education should be and how they are delivered. There is no path to follow. There will be experimentation in the implementation and not everything will be successful. We can revel in our agility and pivot as needed to seek more fruitful directions.

However, chronically anxious stakeholders will likely resist the significant changes necessary to ensure that students are prepared for the demands of the 21st century and that the institution is renewed in its vitality and viability. They will resort to those counterrevolutionary characteristics and actively seek to sabotage the leader(s). For the hard decisions to be made in the face of stiff resistance, what is needed is differentiated leadership.

Many organizations from corporations to religious congregations have come to appreciate the relevance of family systems theory and applied it to their own contexts. In fact, it has become foundational to the fields of Leadership Studies and Organizational Behavior. Murray Bowen, the founder of the theory, described differentiated leadership in this way:

> A differentiated leader is one who attends to the work of defining the self, who is as invested in the welfare of the [group] as in self, who is neither angry nor dogmatic, whose energy goes to changing self rather that telling others what they should do, who can know and respect the multiple opinions of others, who can modify self in response to the strengths of the group, and who is not influenced by the irresponsible opinions of others....A responsible [group] leader automatically generates mature leadership qualities in other...members who are to follow. [291]

Change management is fraught with pitfalls, but an understanding of systems theory can help stakeholders to recognize the way that these systems are at work in

---

[291] Kerr, Michael E., and Murray Bowen. *Family Evaluation: An Approach Based on Bowen Theory*. Norton, 1988.

205

our communities and support the vital importance of strong and differentiated leadership for optimal organizational health.

Leader as Keeper of Culture and Vision

Thomas Sergiovanni identifies several dimensions that stakeholders have valued when selecting and evaluating heads of schools: expertise in educational practice, sound business management techniques, stakeholder relations, and fundraising, with oscillating emphases. These, he writes, are elements present in the leader of the "competent" school. In order to transcend competence and achieve excellence, however, Sergiovanni makes a convincing argument for the vital importance of two more dimensions, which he terms symbolic and cultural, that relate directly to the issue of community building. The symbolic dimension involves

> Modeling important goals and behaviors....visiting classrooms; seeking out and visibly spending time with students; downplaying management concerns in favor of educational ones; presiding over ceremonies, rituals, and other important occasions; and providing a unified vision of the school through proper use of words and actions.[292]

It is a mistake for the school leader to step down from presiding over ceremonial events and allow students to serve in his or her stead. While it may seem a democratic effort to affirm students' ability in such matters, the head of school provides a symbolic personification of the connection between the fiduciary/material interests of the school and the ideal interests of the school. Students can serve as acolytes but not as the high priest/ess. It is the school's leader who connects all the stakeholders of the school with the "deeper meaning and value" of their association with the school. The leader bestows "a sense of importance, vision and purpose about the seemingly ordinary and mundane," and in response stakeholders engage this sense of purpose with "increased work motivation and commitment."

Related to the symbolic function, but even more crucial to excellence in Sergiovanni's construct, the cultural activities of leaders include

---

[292] Sergiovanni, "Leadership and Excellence in Schooling," op. cit.

seeking to define, strengthen, and articulate those enduring values, beliefs, and cultural strands that give the school its unique identity...articulating school purposes and mission; socializing new members to the culture, telling stories and maintaining myths, traditions, and beliefs; developing and displaying a system of symbols over time; and rewarding those who reflect this culture. [293]

Leaders are the vision keepers, the chiefs, and the high priest/esses. It is precisely these transcendent roles that have the capacity to guide a school from competence to excellence. This cultural function inspires in stakeholders the sentiment of belonging to a special enterprise larger than themselves and of great importance. The leader promotes and preserves the mission, goals, ideals, and ways of relating and behaving with one another that together form a compelling ideology.

Mission Congruence

We have discussed the vital importance of staff and students finding meaning in their work and feeling that what they do is purposeful and significant. At the core of that is the mission. One of the most inspiring books on the topic of mission is surely August Turak's *Business Secrets of the Trappist Monks: One CEO's quest for meaning and authenticity* (2013), in which he urges us to realize that it is not merely possible to achieve wholeness and reconciliation of our personal spiritual lives with our what we do in the workplace; it is imperative.[294] He demonstrates the necessity of an organization having a lofty overarching mission that is worthy of being served, of being lived, for serving such a mission inspires us to sacrifice for our commitment to it and we, in turn, are transformed in service of the greater good. We must revisit our schools' missions from time to time, preferably with all stakeholders' input. Our stakeholders should be able to recite the mission statement, reference it every day and see its expression in all that we do, commit to it and be transformed by it. If this is not the case in your school, it's time to have a meeting. Everything proceeds from mission: what we want to achieve, how we treat one another, how we run the operation, and why we do what we do.

---

[293] Ibid.
[294] From my review of the book published on Amazon.com 14 Jul. 2014.

The Big Picture vs. Pixels

In my visits to schools, one of the most painful observations has been the degree of mistrust of administration by other employees. In some cases, to be sure, there was a lack of transparency, but in others, there seemed to be a willful antipathy. In one case, for example, the cost of health benefits was rising astronomically in the area, a cost that would have to be shared by the employees in order to ensure the financial viability of the institution. The Chief Financial Officer took great pains to methodically and comprehensively present the situation to the staff, step-by-step. The staff reaction was overwhelmingly negative and reflected a deliberate refusal to recognize the facts and the financial implications for the institution.

Too often, departments compete for bigger slices of the pie; staff perceive favoritism as the deciding factor in operations decisions; stakeholders dismiss school initiatives that have strategic importance as misguided. While I cannot speak to the presence of favoritism (and have seen too much of it to claim to be skeptical), I can speak to the importance of helping staff to understand the big picture. Staff should be treated and expected to behave as adults and professionals. That means that it is not acceptable to remain blissfully ignorant regarding the business side of school operations, particularly the exigencies of market realities.

Simulations can go a long way to facilitating understanding and dialogue. The Academic Leadership and Innovation Institute of the Great Lakes Colleges Association brings together faculty leaders in the interest of helping them to see the perspectives of various stakeholders:

> At the heart of the institute's schedule lies an exercise called "Design a College and Make It Work." Over the course of five hours, participants are given a quick overview of how the money comes in to a college and how it goes out. They're asked to dream up hypothetical liberal-arts institutions with distinctive missions that will appeal to students. Then they have to make their imaginary colleges work financially, with real numbers. While administrators spend decades learning how to shape a mission, serve competing constituencies, and keep a budget out of the red, professors' understanding of how their college works often does not go much farther than their own departments...the workshops seek to give professors a better grasp of the broader workings of their institutions so they can help make them

better.[295]

In this scenario, participants are presented with unanticipated contingencies, including a $20M gift from a benefactor, a 40% decrease in the endowment, various scandals, demographic shifts, an increase in energy costs, etc., and they have to make their budget numbers work. Engaging in this exercise with independent school staff can deepen their understanding of the broader context of the institution and improve their relations with and attitudes toward administration and trustees significantly.

Strategic Human Resources: Compensation and Value

The importance of strategic Human Resources is often overlooked, but should be seen as integral to any effective independent school. The cultivation of leaders and planning succession, the determination of appropriate compensation and rewards, and the creation of individual development plans and performance appraisal systems all contribute to organizational excellence, equity and sustainability.

Starting At the Top: Executive Compensation

Several years ago, a brilliant article appeared in *The Chronicle of Higher Education* regarding skyrocketing presidential salaries. In collaboration with higher education analysts, the author debunked the perceived imperative of comparisons with either peers (which gives rise to an "arms race") or corporate executives (this is a false analogue; why not use nonprofit executive salaries?), the notion of pay as determining factor of retention (in reality other factors are greater motivators), and proposed the "Campus Salary Ratio," which established a ratio of 3:1 "between the average annual salary of the president and that of full professors at the same institution."[296] A quick glance at the NAIS statistics places the median highest salary for teachers at $78K and the median head salary at $217K, which would be in keeping with the proposed ratio. However, far too many schools have executive salaries that are egregiously and indefensibly high. There certainly are independent schools in which the ratio approaches 10:1, which can put the organization at risk for IRS scrutiny as excess benefit. It also can lead to

[295] Gardner, Lee. "Faculty Leaders Try Their Hand at Running a College." *The Chronicle of Higher Education.* 15 Dec. 2014. Web. 03 Feb. 2015.
[296] Curris, Constantine. "How to Stop the Arms Race in Presidential Pay." *The Chronicle of Higher Education* 6 Dec. 2009. Web. 03 Feb. 2015.

unpleasant publicity from disgruntled stakeholders since the IRS 990 forms disclosing the salaries of the top five most highly compensated employees are publicly available and easily accessed online.

Staff Compensation

Staff compensation figures are a well-guarded secret in many independent schools—salary confidentiality agreements are built in to the process. Why? Are we perhaps aware of the inequalities and afraid to reveal or defend them? This is particularly bizarre in view of the easily accessed IRS 990. Transparency is neither undesirable nor so difficult to achieve and forces us to examine the ways that we determine compensation and value to the organization. Sacred cows need to be put out to pasture, and foremost among them is longevity.

In my undergraduate business classes in the late 1980s, my professor, who had worked as a Vice President under CEO Jack Welch at General Electric, told us not to stay in a job for more than four years without a significant promotion. When I arrived in independent schools with a resumé packed with a series of full-time positions that exceeded six years each, held concurrently with a number of part-time positions of shorter tenure, I was aghast to be told frequently and with visible disdain that I hadn't stayed anywhere very long. There was an extraordinary disconnect between the cultural expectations of independent schools and everywhere else. Add to this the comment of a wise member of the clergy, who once said to me, "Jesus' ministry was only three years; it's easy to be dazzling for just three years. I'm twenty-five years in, and it's really hard to be inspiring and fresh." Isn't it better to have six, four, or even two years of brilliant than ten or fifteen of mediocre? Today's young professionals expect to be much more mobile, so we need to adjust our expectations. Yes, the cost of acquisition of a new faculty member must be calculated, but that cost stands to be the most important investment we make in our institution. In placing such value on longevity, we cling to the obsolete paradigm emphasizing reliability and loyalty over innovation, productivity, and excellence.

The practice of tenure is rapidly dissolving in both higher education and public education, and while it is rarely explicitly present in independent schools, it is certainly present *de facto*. Decision makers in other sectors have come to realize that everyone must continue to engage professionally and prove his or her worth or find somewhere else to bloom precisely because employers are providing certain goods and have expectations in return. It must be acknowledged that teachers score higher than other professionals in valuing job security, so it is important to help them feel secure and valued, but on the other hand, we must emphasize that it is not an entitlement but earned.

Of course retention is positive because it can enhance the culture and contribute to camaraderie and collaboration and the cost of replacing an employee is high. Institutional memory, however, is overrated and often inhibits innovation when "we tried that twenty years ago and it didn't work." What has not worked in the past may have failed for a constellation of factors and it may well be time to try it or something that is similar but different in significant ways. Further, school cultures *need* to shift and adapt and the forces of conservation can serve as powerful impediments. We all know teachers who haven't done any substantive professional development in years and who teach students the same material the same way they did decades ago. For some who have found a magic formula that works to inspire students year after year, that may be adequate, but it's not necessarily great, and greatness is what we need to aspire to, since our constituents are paying tuition with that expectation.

In many other cases, we are acting out of misguided loyalty and need to do better for our schools, our stakeholders, and our staff. Working beside a stagnant colleague, especially a highly paid one and/or a disaffected disenchanted gadfly can be a powerful demotivator, particularly for newer lesser-paid yet highly productive staff. I emphasize that there are of course senior staff with Dweck's "growth mindset" who happily embrace challenge, new techniques and resources, and learn to use technology and other social media to enhance their jobs, while others remain in their stultifying routines, confident that, as one administrator proudly crowed, "They will have a job here for as long as they want." Those senior staff must continue to demonstrate their vitality and worth. To tolerate stagnation is dereliction of duty.

Weighing longevity heavily is not only antiquated, it is unhelpful to the realization of organizational objectives. Independent school end-of-year meetings typically reward employees for their ten years of service with a paperweight or twenty with the colonial chair and so on. An administrator says some kind words about the hallowed veteran, yet we say nothing of Dr. T's publication with students, Mr. M's new program or Ms. R's inaugural trip with thirty students to the sister school abroad. Aren't *these* the practices we want to reward, rather than mere dependability year after year? When we look to highly successful companies with high levels of employee satisfaction, we see that there is clarity regarding the value exchange: what is expected of employees and what the employee can expect in return. Valuing longevity over productivity maintains the greater benefit on the employee side of the equation to the detriment of the organization.

Let us take a moment to delve into the basics of organizational management. The rewards of work for employees fall into five categories:[297]

1. Affiliation. The feeling of belonging to an admirable institution that shares the employee's values
2. Compensation. The money employees receive for their work and performance
3. Benefits. Indirect compensation, including health insurance, retirement programs, and time off
4. Career. Employees' long-term opportunities for development and advancement
5. Work Content. The satisfaction employees receive from the work they perform.

Every effort must be made to offer employee benefits and base pay that are comparable to equivalent institutions public and private. Just as the "Rah! Rah!" celebration of what students and staff are achieving weekly and monthly should be inextricable to the fabric of the school, administrators must take account of all of the holistic benefits, tangible and intangible, offered to employees and make staff keenly aware of what they are actually receiving. These need to be made explicit and marketed continuously; they cannot merely appear in the annual benefit review meeting. Teachers in some schools need not prepare for more than two separate courses, while in others they may need to prepare for four. In some schools, instructors teach only four of eight periods, in others five. Amazingly, I found that the teachers with the easier loads were unaware of their extraordinary comparative benefit because it was not made explicit as such.

Then there are HR policies that are dehumanizing. In some schools, there exists a pool of flex days, for example. Employees may donate unused sick, personal, and vacation days to a fund that other employees who encounter personal hardship and use all of their sick, personal and vacation days may draw from. This contributes to employees' perception of being interchangeable cogs in a wheel. It does not help the organization in any real way when the Instructional Technologist

[297] Kochanski, Jim, and JP Elliott. "Improving Performance through the Employee Value Exchange." Sibson Consulting. (13 Oct. 2010): 109-18. Web. 4 Feb. 2015.

contributes days that are then used by the Culinary Assistant; their job functions are entirely different. This program reflects an industrial sensibility irrelevant to a school environment and the absurd notion that there is some fixed amount of time that must be paid to the organization, like a sacrifice to a blood-thirsty god. A community demonstrates compassion and care for its members, and treats staff as the precious resources they are. Such behavior can seem costly, but the benefits of doing the right thing, so long as they are equitably applied (which is key), are invaluable.

The employer's expectations of employees generally include:

1. Performance. The specific levels of discretionary efforts required and the desired objectives needed to achieve the organization's stretch goals and deliver superior performance.
2. Three Cs of Teamwork. The coordination, collaboration, and communication of organizational performance that is expected of individuals within and across units and teams.
3. Engagement. The knowledge of what the priorities are and the motivation to attend them.
4. Behavior. The acceptable/desired behaviors required of individuals to support the desired culture and achieve results.
5. Retention. The level of retention that is desired of individuals and required to support the overall strategy.[298]

How are these expectations articulated to employees? How do we evaluate whether individuals are meeting our expectations? Finally, are we compensating employees according to our expectations? We need to use more sophisticated measures to determine salaries than the NAIS medians, local and national peer institutions, etc., at least in part because each of our institutions is comprised of unique individuals and opportunities. Setting aside the fairness and effectiveness of merit pay based on student performance on standardized tests (i.e. AP or IB), the determination of pay should be correlated with employees' performance as a matter of course. "Measure what you value" is a popular saying among educators, yet we don't always heed it.

If environmental economists can quantify the value of a tree or a park to a city, and corporations can quantify the value of everything from decision x to employee y to using one brand of toilet paper over another, we can most certainly

---

[298] Ibid.

quantify the value of, say, the Director of College Counseling or the English teacher who also coordinates the trip to Cambridge, coaches tennis, and is a much beloved residence hall parent. On the most basic level, administrators can review and extrapolate from the results of surveys of prospective applicants, those who actually choose the school, current student and parent surveys (see Appendix Sections II and VII), and exit interviews of alumni upon graduation and several years out.

Beyond that, performance appraisal must be tied to compensation and organizational values such as advising, coaching, teaching, personal attention to students, and esprit de corps/organizational harmony. Teaching faculty in certain fields like science must keep apprised of rapid developments, while others may have less of an imperative to do so, but they should still be expected to attend to evolutions in pedagogical methods and the emerging trends in the field. Staff who engage in research with students and who are distinguished in their fields should be recognized and remunerated accordingly. There are certainly categories of high performing employees who should be rewarded financially and in other ways they find meaningful (ask them!) for their contributions:

Admissions magicians: The staff members to whom we present prospective students and families, perhaps teachers whose classroom magic is palpable, a charismatic admissions employee, coach, or advisor.

Innovators: The staff who bring dynamism and vibrancy to the school through innovation in practice, procedure, and programs that may even be copied by others.

Glory bringers: The staff who bring distinction to the school, through student projects and competitions as well as their own distinguished contributions to the profession and/or community.

School spirit and community builders: The staff who encourage the community members to support one another, celebrate one another's successes and share each other's burdens.

Signature program developers: The staff who create the programs unique to the school, whether research, travel, environmental science, or whatever it may be that distinguishes the school among others and provides competitive advantage.

214

Performance Appraisal

By now, we all know the pithy exhortation from Jim Collins in *Good To Great* (2001) to "get the right people on the bus, the wrong people off the bus, then figure out where to take the bus," but too many of us tolerate mediocrity (and worse) in the classroom and the school as a whole. Administrators are entrusted with the responsibility of ensuring that our staff is the best it can be, which means that we must be extremely deliberate about hiring, celebrating excellence, coaching for growth and optimal performance, and making hard decisions about those who do not serve our organization.

Unfortunately, there is a lack of consistent and systematic staff evaluation in many independent schools for a variety of interconnected reasons. First, as Michael Huberman characterized the issue in *The Lives of Teachers,* "Noninterference with the core work of others constitutes a sign of professional respect."[299] Second, the aforementioned conflict avoidance among educators means that "congeniality often stifles awkward but necessary acknowledgment and forthright discussion" needed for growth and development of professional practice.[300] Third, we tend to conceptualize our schools as communities,

> organized around relationships and the felt interdependencies that nurture them....Once established, the ties of community become substituted for formal systems of supervision, evaluation and staff development; for management and organizational schemes that seek to coordinate what teachers do and how they work together; and indeed for leadership itself.[301]

Thus, we essentially abdicate fiduciary responsibility for the sake of maintenance of social ties. Evaluation needs to be reconceived as part of professional development, not as fault finding, since all of us can improve our practice. It is an opportunity to celebrate the wizardry a staff member demonstrates in the classroom, the ball court, or the kitchen. Self and peer evaluation and lesson study are all helpful. Finally, if there is a hierarchy with those higher up in rank conducting evaluations, the presumption of a claim to greater expertise must be examined for its legitimacy. If it is lacking, a reassessment of responsibilities is in

---

[299] Huberman, Michael. *The Lives of Teachers.* Teachers College Press, 1993. p. 29.
[300] Gow, Peter. "Professional Growth? Teacher Evaluation? Caveman Simple!" *Independent School.* NAIS, Fall 2013. Print.
[301] Sergiovanni, Thomas J. "Organizations Or Communities? Changing the Metaphor Changes the Theory." *Educational Administration Quarterly* 30.2 (1994): 214-26.

order. Even if such a claim may be established, staff are often untrained in best practices and procedures, which can be remedied by the many resources available to help staff to develop standards and measures.

The work of Charlotte Danielson and Robert Marzano on teacher evaluation is popular in public schools; the Nova Scotia Teacher's Union Self-Reflection Guide is extraordinary and provides some outstanding tools. And then there is the Folio Collaborative, a consortium of over 45 independent schools that is focused on the process of professional growth, from reflection, goal setting, classroom observation, and feedback, through an end of year summary meeting and ongoing follow-up. The Folio method provides a clear process and invaluable insight and tracking in a secure online platform.[302]

In the same way that we wouldn't dream of assessing a student's annual performance on the basis of one or two observations, the widespread practice of basing a staff member's evaluation on one or two announced observations is untenable. Numerous unannounced observations with face to face feedback immediately following provide a far more complete description of performance and more effective conversations about what is going well and what opportunities for growth there might be. It also changes the school culture for the better and demonstrates a firm commitment to continual improvement.

For maximum organizational effectiveness, performance appraisal should be as objective as possible, provide meaningful distinctions regarding how well standards are being met, and avoid surprises and any appearance of capriciousness or favoritism. In independent schools, 360° evaluations of administration should certainly be considered, with vertical and horizontal lines from stakeholders. The NAIS Head of School Assessment Survey and Board Self-Assessment Survey are useful for their intended purposes, but beyond those, I used the following questions to help senior leadership team members to learn about how they were perceived by others and to identify their strengths and areas of growth:

1. Score the following attributes from 1 to 5
    1 = Disagree completely and 5 = Agree completely

    Understands and embodies school mission
    Demonstrates effective working relationships with peers
    Invites information, constructive criticism and cooperation from others

---

[302] Gow, op. cit. See foliocollaborative.org.

Exercises a positive influence on co-workers
Demonstrates personal accountability
Demonstrates attention to detail
Responds quickly and effectively to daily issues
Seeks ways to add value
Creates initiatives that enhance school culture
Exercises sound judgment
Visualizes and anticipates issues before they occur
Analyzes issues and problems accurately
Identifies what to communicate, and the right audience, vehicle and time
Interacts effectively at all levels of the school
Keeps others well informed

2. What good / outstanding attributes does this teammate have? What would you recommend about this teammate to others?

3. What are some of the weaker attributes this teammate has? What areas do you think this teammate could improve upon?

4. If you were starting a new company and choosing employees, would you pick this person to be on the team? Please list the factors that most influenced your answer.

In the semi-annual or quarterly surveys of faculty, it is prudent to use the opportunity to ask questions such as:
In what ways can the administration serve students better?
In what ways can the administration help you to serve students better?
In what ways can the administration help you to be more satisfied with your position?
How can the administration communicate more effectively with you?
In what ways would you change the school immediately?
What policies do you feel should be changed and how?

Granular Accounting and Cost-Benefit Analysis

Colleges and universities are increasingly implementing granular accounting procedures to analyze the costs and benefits of individual programs and I argue that we should be doing it in independent schools, too. To quote one consultant, school administrators "tend to look at their offices, programs, and departments as a big basket of stuff, not knowing what the individual pieces in the basket cost."[303] And program budgets are often spent gratuitously just to ensure that the budget will not be decreased the following year. When there is transparency and staff know exactly what each facet of the school contributes and costs, they will be more likely to understand how the pieces fit together. Greater precision can also contribute to better strategic planning regarding programs to scale back or eliminate.

Balancing the budget overall is one thing; examining how much each segment of the budget actually costs and contributes to the mission is another. In the analysis of one school, author of *Educational Economics* (2010) Marguerite Roza found that the expenditure on math was $328 per student and $1348 per cheerleader on cheerleading—in a district that professed math to be the primary focus.[304] Independent schools that engage in precision accounting are far better equipped to make informed decisions that support the mission and the strategic plan.

Too often, the positions and programs that schools add contribute to "function lust," the performance of tasks to a higher degree—and cost—than the institution or the mission requires. Their cost outweighs their benefit. Consider the following questions regarding policies and practices:

(1) Is this policy / practice/ program central to the accomplishment of our mission?
(2) Is it an important institutional priority?
(3) Can it be changed in view of our competition and our markets for labor and students? [305]

One way of affecting the change mentioned is à la carte services and programming, a practice with a long history in independent day schools, in which transportation, meals, tutoring, athletic participation, travel programs, extended day programs, standardized test preparation, and specialized lessons of all kinds frequently entail additional fees. This conserves the financial resources of the school and those of families without need of such services or programming.

---

[303] Carlson, Scott. "Accounting for Success." *The Chronicle of Higher Education*. 3 Feb. 2014. Web. 05 Feb. 2015.
[304] Ripley, Amanda. "The Case Against High-School Sports." *The Atlantic*. 18 Sept. 2013. Web. 11 Feb. 2015.
[305] See Paskin, Sorrel L. "Rethinking Cost Drivers in Independent Schools." *NAIS*. 11 December 2002. Web. 15 Feb. 2015.

It is my contention that it is irresponsible for us to persist in business as usual and merely accept "that's the way we have always done it" as a rationale for continuing any practice. Analysis is mandatory. Certain programs are extremely expensive and their return on investment must be calculated. Among the most costly is unquestionably interscholastic athletics: salaries and stipends for coaches, trainers, and administrative assistants, referees, insurance, equipment (acquisition and reconditioning), facilities maintenance (and keeping up with the neighbors and cross-app institutions), transportation, membership fees, etc.

Realizing this, a number of charter schools have decided not to offer these programs and redirect their district-allotted funds-per-student to academics. Most communities offer ample opportunities for athletic engagement and many independent school students take advantage of those *in addition to* the school's own. In fact, some independent schools restrict participation in outside sports not for the sake of protecting students' physical well being and stress levels but rather in order to preserve the integrity of the athletics program from "erosion" by other programs. We may continue to be steadfast and enthusiastic supporters of the great benefits that students derive from athletic participation without being the primary provider of those opportunities when they are offered by other outlets.

In some markets, an independent school without football might be unsustainable as it is an essential means to secure market share. Understandably, in some schools athletics is the core means of establishing school spirit and community and securing alumni financial support. Nevertheless, even these assumptions should be tested. If the stakeholders knew the costs of the program within the financial context of the school, they might well alter their expectations. The broad slate of athletics (and other) offerings must still be reexamined regularly in terms of service to mission and marketing/admissions objectives, accommodation to student interest, numbers of participants, time commitment and schedule, facilities, gender equity, etc.

The viability of any program should be continually up for review. Ideally this is an open process that avoids sentimentality and surprises and which stakeholders view as a means of attuning with the mission. Determinations regarding retention or elimination should be made according to a cost benefit analysis factoring in students' needs, regional and demographic concerns, uniqueness, relevance, and any others that make sense. There is no wonder, for example, that many schools (and colleges) have dropped French and Japanese programs.

Finally, we must terminate the ol' boy network practices that are entrenched in so many of our schools. The outrageous machinations that occur in auditing to occult the egregious conflicts of interest, failure to send projects out for bids for the best price, other practices that grant financial benefit to trustees, donors, or other interested parties are illegal, unethical, a gross dereliction of duty, and a flagrant violation of the trust of the other stakeholders with whom we are covenanted to wisely and justly steward the institution and its resources.

Strategic Planning

In some schools, the strategic plan is a document created by consultants, trustees, or senior administration for accrediting agencies and no one sees it, which is a tragic loss of a fine opportunity. Strategic plans can be an impetus for school-wide revitalization, a touchstone that provides direction, a constant topic of discussion, and posted on the walls and website. This is not a process to be either out-sourced or monopolized by an oligarchy (or plutocracy, come to that).

On the most basic level, participants in strategic planning should be educated about the process in advance and cautioned against allowing either consultants or a vocal minority to hijack the process and impose their own priorities. Having amorphous or overly (or insufficiently) ambitious goals can result in too little concrete action. The goals should be narrow, few (many experts suggest five) and clear enough to be achievable, with measurable outcomes, a description of process, a sequence of programs, and timelines for implementation. The process should be tied to resources and the budget cycle in order to ensure that resources are actually allocated to supporting the measures. Vendors' input matters. When they are informed of how they might fit into the process, the results can be mutually beneficial.

It is important to build enthusiasm about the plan to prod stakeholders out of complacent satisfaction with our curricular and extra-curricular programming, communications and marketing, fundraising efforts, alumni and community outreach, affordability, diversity, and any number of other issues. Scott Cowen posed the question, "How do you nudge the conversation forward when many people are passionately invested in a model that needs to be altered or discarded in the interests of future growth and innovation?"[306] Cowen, who was president of Tulane University at the time of Hurricane Katrina, advises that, short of

---

[306] Cowen, Scott S. "You Don't Need a Hurricane to Know Which Way the Wind Blows." *The Chronicle of Higher Education.* 5 Jan. 2015. Web. 16 Feb. 2015.

catastrophe (which worked wonders for his illustrious institution), and scaring stakeholders "to death about the consequences of not changing," leaders must "focus on possibilities—developing a vision of, and excitement about, the future." When orchestrated with great attention, the strategic planning process can provide that focus and be a reinvigorating experience for the institution, in which various stakeholders join together to formulate meaningful goals that provide direction for the immediate future.

The strategic plan presents a superb opportunity for best serving the students, revisiting the mission, examining both current and future directions, and transforming the school, yet too often the strategic plan suffers from fatal errors that severely restrict its utility or render it useless. Foremost among them is that strategic planning is executed too infrequently. The increased volatility in the education landscape translates to the need for more frequent strategizing and planning. Three years is now the outer limit, since too much changes in the interim and agility matters. Technology companies have found that strategic plans executed for shorter periods, even quarterly (!), mean greater momentum, stronger sense of urgency, and ability to take advantage of opportunities. While quarterly seems ludicrous for our situation, condensing the time frame is prudent.

Developing knowledge is critical. Failing to gather preparatory information from staff and other sources and share it with those directly involved in planning can result in participants being too far removed and ill-informed of realities to be effective. Organizations stagnate or even fail when they look inward more than outward, and this is all too common in independent schools. Participants in the strategic planning process must be informed about the cross-application competitors in the market and emerging trends in K-12 and higher education landscapes, not merely the immediate ecosystem of the school, though an intimate knowledge of that is also essential. As Cowen asserts, "it is impossible to develop a significant change agenda without a common understanding of reality among stakeholders and without contextualizing needed changes in your own institution." Toward that end, competitive intelligence is an essential practice for any school's sustainability.

Keeping Up With (and Differentiated from) the Neighbors: Competitive Intelligence

Competitive Intelligence (CI) is the process of collecting and analyzing information about competitors' strengths and weaknesses in

221

a legal and ethical manner to enhance business decision-making. CI activities can be basically grouped into two main types
1) Tactical, which is shorter-term and seeks to provide input into issues such as capturing market share or increasing revenues; and
2) Strategic, which focuses on longer-term issues such as key risks and opportunities facing the enterprise.[307]

If the for-profit perspective rankles, it is imperative to understand that in non-profit circles, the SWOT (strengths, weaknesses, opportunities, threats) analysis is considered to be an essential procedure and it shares many of CI's characteristics. It is critical that competitive intelligence be executed at least annually.

School staff must realize and concede that no school is right for every student and each school has certain strengths. When schools consider their ethical responsibility to help students identify their best options, they should carefully consider the needs and interests of the student and recommend the best option, even if it is another school. With that in mind, there is no reason not to share information (it may even result in pooling resources), and no excuse for leaders of independent schools not to be conversant with neighboring schools' curricula and that includes the Common Core State Standards, if the area schools are implementing them. They should review other schools' strategic plans *not to copy them* but to ensure that their own school is a leader in innovation *in its own [preferably inimitable] way*. Representatives should attend local schools' and cross application schools' open houses, websites, and any other materials to get a sense of what is offered, what is new, strengths, and weaknesses.

There are several steps to creating a useful CI analysis. First, carefully consider the desirable data points to compare. Thoroughly review the websites of a handful of schools for ideas and see the chart below for examples. Note the absence of faculty to student ratio in the sample chart—it is one of the most misleading and meaningless data points. On the university level, the ratio is considered virtually nonsensical as it counts research faculty who never teach, graduate faculty who never teach undergraduates, adjunct faculty who may only teach one class and may be difficult to access, and *undergraduate and graduate teaching assistants.*[308] On the secondary level, every potential teacher is counted,

[307] http://www.investopedia.com/terms/c/competitive-intelligence.asp
[308] Borden, V. M. H. (2011). *Suggestions for Improvements to the Student-to-Faculty Ratio in IPEDS.* U.S. Department of Education. National Postsecondary Education Cooperative. Web. 12 Nov. 2014.

even those who only teach only one class or tutor or who teach only honors level or a special education self-contained class. Class size may be similarly misleading, since honors or AP courses may have far fewer (or far more, depending on the school) students than the average presented, which can alter an individual student's experience considerably. A more revelatory detail is the number of students in the caseload of the college counselor or learning specialist, etc. Mission statements, when they reflect the true *geist* of the institution, can be useful for understanding the very real differences in the core purposes of the schools.

Sample Competitive Intelligence Chart:

School	Type	Size Cost	Honors/ AP Other	Avg Class Size	Student :Coll. Couns. Ratio	Special programs	Mission
Our Lady of Grace	Cath. Girls Day	245 $6500 plus fees	Honors	20	60:1	Global Issues Diploma Creative Arts Diploma *Dual enrollment with adjacent college *Service projects abroad **Note: "Not equipped to offer an individualized learning program...does not offer special education."** ***Rigid curriculum with little choice**	To educate and nurture a diverse student population so that each girl may achieve her full potential to excel intellectually, to live spiritually, to lead responsibly, to act justly, and to serve selflessly.
Old Field Comm HS Newsweek Top 100 schools USA	Public Co-ed Day N/A Some fees	2200	Honors AP IB AICE Biotech Comp Sci Engin-eering	29	225:1	*Certifications in Adobe, C++, etc. *Internships in area for biotech and engineering **Note: College guidance is weak; few resources available** ***Parents say, "Great for challenging academics and special ed; not so good for 'average' kids"** ***Tracks offer no electives** **Many electives outside of tracked programs**	To be a student centered community that empowers each member to engage in authentic and substantive learning, develop effective leadership, and demonstrate humane character.
Camelot Academy (Upper School)	Indep Co-ed Day $17K plus fees	408	Honors AP IB	12	100:1	Study Abroad Global Studies Certificate Center for Global Studies Center for the Common Good Center for Excellence in Teaching **Note: Avg SSAT 80th percentile** **Compulsory team athletics** **Win State and Regional tournaments often** ***Many challenging electives**	To be the best college preparatory school by cultivating young people of integrity, who honor wisdom, justice, inclusion, service and the pursuit of truth.
Arts Magnet HS Newsweek Top 100 schools USA	Public Co-ed Day N/A Some fees	2300	AP Arts Majors	29	570:1	Majors in Communications, Dance, Music, Theater, Digital Media, Visual Arts **Note: College guidance is virtually non-existent** **Admission by audition for most majors**	To provide an outstanding arts-centered education within a strong academic program, for students with exceptional ability in communication arts, dance, music, theatre, digital media or visual arts.

223

Table Summary:

Our Lady of Grace is a small Catholic girls' day school with a set curriculum offering little choice. They have honors courses, but no IB or AP. Their college counseling is not particularly strong and they have no services for learning disabled students. They do offer dual enrollment with the college next door, however, so girls can graduate with credit for up to five college courses. Their girls participate in service programs every year in disadvantaged countries.

Old Field is a large public high school that offers honors, AP, IB, and AICE Curricula as well as special rigidly programmed tracks for Biotech, Computer Science, and Engineering. Computer Science students can earn professional certifications in various computer languages and programs. Engineering and Biotech are connected with great internships in area companies. Class sizes tend to be rather large, up to 40. The college counseling program is very weak. The students who are not in those tracks or special education tend to get lost. It has been listed in the Top 100 High Schools in the US by *Newsweek* and *Washington Post*.

Camelot is a medium sized co-ed day school that offers honors and extensive AP courses. Admission to the Upper School for students not continuing from the school's own K-8 is highly competitive. Students are encouraged to be internationally-minded global citizens, and that focus motivated the adoption of the IB Diploma Program about two years ago. The number of electives is impressive and expanded through participation in a regional online consortium. A traditional emphasis, athletics is compulsory and the school is a powerhouse for football and boys' and girls' basketball and lacrosse.

Arts Magnet High School is a large public arts magnet high school. Students must audition for a spot in the highly competitive dance, music, theater, and visual arts programs. The communication and digital media are the strategic "backdoors" into the school. There are many AP courses, but many classes have nearly 40 students; the specialized classes bring down the average size. The college counseling program is just about non-existent and students must fend for themselves or hire independent counselors. It has been listed in the Top 100 High Schools in the US by *Newsweek* and *Washington Post*.

Postulates:

- Students who are highly interested in the arts (and talented enough to audition successfully) are likely to attend the Arts Magnet.
- Students who are star athletes tend to be recruited for full scholarships at Camelot.
- Students who have strong interest in global issues attend Camelot.
- Students with strong interest in Computer Science generally attend Old Field.
- Families with either strong religious inclinations, not necessarily Catholic, or confidence in the benefits of single-sex education for girls tend to send daughters to Our Lady of Grace.

Thus informed, the strategic plan for the school conducting the study comes into focus.

CAUTION:
Stakeholders will be likely to suggest expanding programming in the direction of the strong programs that other schools are offering.
That is precisely the wrong tack.

Instead of replicating, possibly inadequately, what is already being done elsewhere, the school must create unique programs difficult to duplicate. This will distinguish the school from others, position the school as a leader, rather than a follower in innovative education, and establish a niche market.

- Superlative college counseling is a clear blind spot that is not being adequately addressed in the community. The school should offer community outreach programming, such as lecture series, panel discussions featuring admissions officers, fee-based summer application "bootcamp" and standardized test prep, and could consider offering college counseling for a fee.

- The needs of average students, particularly boys not interested in the tracks offered at the other schools, are not being addressed adequately and represent an opportunity for outreach and targeting.

225

- Area companies other than those related to biotech and engineering are ripe for being tapped for partnerships, internships and career exploration.

- The immediate community is a completely open field for various types of study and service learning. The school must consider the social, civic, environmental, historical, cultural, ethical and any and all other dimensions of life in the community and exploit them insofar as possible. There are opportunities for signature programs in Environmental Science, History, Math Modeling, Creative Writing, local literary history, and much more.

- There is likely at least one staff member who has a singular talent or interest not easily replicable that will appeal to some segment of students. Capitalize on it!

- Survey the current students and parents to learn what programs *not currently offered in the community* they might wish for. If the budget permits, of course, conduct market research to determine the programming that is most relevant to the target market.

Fundraising

In this era of MBAs serving as university and school presidents, it is abundantly clear that the role of the chief executive is frequently less that of educational vision keeper than fundraiser. It is increasingly hard to imagine (and, one hopes, encounter) the attitude of one long-serving headmaster of a school in Connecticut, who declared to the board of trustees that he would not ask people for money; "That's not me; I don't feel comfortable doing that." Astonishing. Yet in school after school, there is reticence and resentment about the eleemosynary nature of the independent school even on the part of staff who should certainly know better.

Some social sector organizations do a much better job of being transparent and helping all staff to be clear about the rationale. Educators often have a kind of aversion to the business side of schools, for which administrators might feel grateful, for if that were not the case, they would likely be in another line of work. Nevertheless it is administration's job to get them on board. Educating staff can go a long way toward this objective. Resentment can build from any number of causes, from class-based animosity to perception of favoritism. Of course philanthropic parents and their progeny should not be exempt from the rules governing the behavior of others, but they should certainly have the same expectations for attentive and solicitous service.

The "Design a College and Make It Work" simulation described earlier in this chapter can help staff to understand that fundraising is a critical and inextricable part of independent schools. In particular, it is well worth the administrative time to help staff to understand the reasons for centralizing it. Otherwise, undesirable events can occur such as staff developing wish lists and distributing them to parents, which can undermine faith in the organization's ability to provide for instructional resources and other basics. At one school, the Aquatics Director was, naturally enough, the primary point of contact for parents who wanted to fund a new pool and diving platform. Fond of the parents, he was indisposed to refer those parents to the fundraising staff. He was pressed by those parents to investigate the various construction options and do initial reconnaissance, which in turn prompted the parents to commandeer the process. When the senior administration of the school found out and explained that the pool project would not be approved, the personal relationship between the Director and the parents caused the institution to lose out on what could have been a long-term positive relationship for the school, the parents, and the Aquatics program.

Transparency and staff education are imperative. At a minimum, staff should receive an annual Fundraising 101 that covers the following points:

- Fundraising is about the cultivation of relationships with the purpose of inspiring people to partner with the institution in the shared mission, enabling them to allocate resources to an exciting vision that stirs them, and creating a legacy by accomplishing more together than either could independently.

- It is wise stewardship of fundraising staff resources to spend more time cultivating relationships with donors who have greater capacity to give. It is also vital to the sustainability of the organization.

- Donors should have three deep contacts with the school in order to have meaningful roots and in order to ensure continuation of support in case one relationship fails or is eroded. Staff must understand their responsibility in serving as one of those connective relationships.

- Fundraising is about listening, not merely asking, to find out the donor's wants and needs. One donor might prefer a consolidated ask, while

227

another might prefer to fund specific programs that she or he finds compelling. There *is* something to be gained by the donor. The school should strive to provide maximum value and return on the investment.

- There is a comprehensive cohesive story to be told, and stray pages here and there can seriously undermine that story and its momentum. It is the mission rather than a specific need that is to be supported. This cohesive story is part of the reason that branding norms are so important. All contact from the school should maintain a consistent look and feel.

- The development of a database of donors is critical to the process. It involves prospect research (the resources people have available to them, giving potential and interests), networking, making and recording all contacts, checking sources, detailing their giving history and preferences, etc. Casual "asks" that are not tracked can damage the relationships that are being cultivated.

- Organizational priorities necessitate a certain order of operations.

- Gifts with strings attached are often more trouble than they at first appear.

- Expressions of appreciation should come from multiple sources— trustees, administration, and any relevant staff member or student who benefits from a particular donation. Direct communication with the benefactor and a handwritten note should occur as a matter of course.

Diversifying the funding streams

The current economic landscape presents enormous challenges, but even during flush times, it is best to plan for the lean. Social sector organizations are increasingly learning the importance of being entrepreneurial and finding multiple sources of income. Schools have long offered athletics camps, summer camps, and extended-day programs, held auctions, rented facilities, etc., but as John Farber points out,

> The problem is that the people who are writing checks for these "extras" are mostly part of our existing school families. If we keep going back to the same well over and over again, one day we are going to find that it is dry. The smart move today is to reach out to

new constituents/customers who are not already making major financial investments in our schools."[309]

There is ample opportunity to be entrepreneurial. Lectures, workshops for parents and for educators, online courses and homeschool curricula, and participation in special programs or research opportunities for students are just a few of the more common ones. In the case of boarding schools, the end of year sales of items that students leave behind mentioned in Chapter 7 can generate surprising sums (one school reported a profit exceeding $40,000). Creating a second-hand clothing shop is a related income stream and can provide students with limited experience running a business. Several schools have used their real estate holdings for various revenue-generating purposes:

- Part of King Kamehameha's (HI) extensive (365,000 acres) real estate holdings is used for agriculture and a wind farm. Less than 2% of these holdings dedicated to commercial real estate alone generates $130M in net income annually.[310]
- Georgetown Preparatory School (DC) leased three acres of school property to a developer for luxury apartments, earning $1.3M per year for the school on a 99-year lease.
- Shattuck-St. Mary's School (MN) built a golf course community on some of its property and sold lots, netting $2M in the first year.[311]

Tutoring services offered to the broader community for a fee can represent a beneficial service as well as a lucrative one—Elmwood Franklin School (NY) earns $100,000 annually from the service.[312] Outreach related to college counseling can be exceptional in its draw and yield. This fee schedule appears on the website of St. Paul's School for Girls (MD):

College Counseling:
Initial 1 hour College Consultation: $200 (If additional services are contracted, $75 of this fee will be credited towards those services.)
Comprehensive College Counseling Package: $2,000 (The Step Up college counseling package includes: compiling & narrowing a college

---

[309] Farber, John S. "The Independent School Financial Model Is Broken Here's How We Fix It." *NAIS*. Fall 2012. Web. 15 Feb. 2015.

[310] http://www.ksbe.edu/commercialrealestate/commercial_properties/

[311] "Independent Schools Turn to Unconventional Methods to Fund Operations." Dick Jones Communications. *Newswise*. 10 Nov. 2005. Web. 18 Feb. 2015.

[312] Ibid.

list; college visit preparation; guidance with applications, including essays; negotiating financial aid opportunities; and guidance with wait list and competing opportunities.)
College Application & Essay Guidance (4 hours): $500
Maximizing Your College Visits (1 hour): $125
Negotiating Financial Aid / Grants / Awards: $250
Guidance with wait list & multiple acceptances: $125 per hour.[313]

In other schools, college tours are an add-on. Schools often contract out for these tours, but those that plan them in-house can enjoy windfalls. The typical fee ranges between $160 and $225 per student per day with resource materials, breakfast, shared lodging (3-4 per room) and transportation included. One school reports an annual net profit in excess of $40,000 from college tours, a fine contribution to the budget.

Homeschoolers represent another growing market. Independent schools can enable them to enrich what they are able to offer either at home or in their cooperatives with participation in school based programs for athletics, arts, world languages, and more sophisticated and advanced laboratory or specific content experiences. All of these can be offered *à la carte*.

Taking a page from the higher education playbook, global partnerships and satellite campuses, particularly with China, are another means of increasing revenue. Wasatch Academy (UT) and Shattuck-St. Mary's (MN), among others, have partner programs that feature student and teacher exchanges and dual diplomas that they hope will eventually include campuses.

These are examples of the typical mission congruent enterprises in which schools engage, but schools can do more. John Farber relates the case of the Cleveland Zoo, which owns an 18-hole golf course, a water park, and an amusement park, which do not correlate with the mission but certainly generate funds that support it.[314] Consult with a qualified tax professional in the ideation phase to ensure that whatever enterprise the school might consider will not imperil the 501(c)3 status with unrelated business income (UBI).

---

[313] https://www.spsfg.org/page.cfm?p=1084&LockSSL=true
[314] Farber, John S. "The Independent School Financial Model Is Broken Here's How We Fix It." *NAIS*. Fall 2012. Web. 15 Feb. 2015.

Summary

Independent schools are mission-driven enterprises. The leadership has a privileged role in maintaining the vision and embodying the mission of the school. Leadership and stakeholders must collaborate to ensure that the mission reflects the authentic principles, values, and virtues that they wish the school to manifest. Serving a worthy mission inspires cohesion and commitment to the common good.

While there are significant differences between independent schools and businesses, there are many evidence-based best practices that we can certainly adopt to ensure that we are exercising faithful stewardship of the resources with which we are entrusted and that we are effectively promoting and executing our mission. We must discern our individual school's strengths and fully exploit its potential to serve its constituents. Certain practices will require a mere baby step and others great leaps and much deliberation. Managing change is especially challenging in secondary schools where chronic anxiety is the prevailing emotion. Stakeholders must consider the unconscious systems at work that strive to undermine leadership and maintain the status quo. Independent schools must counteract the gridlock of imagination and embark on adventure to explore this exciting new world.

Conclusion

Independent schools are at a critical juncture at the dawn of the 21st century. A constellation of factors presents enormous challenges: charter schools that offer many of the benefits traditionally to be found only in private schools, highly individualized and unbundled educational opportunities in a variety of formats, a dramatic shift in the very notion of what it means to be an educated person. Access to a particular social network and participating in tradition are no longer sufficient inducement for parents and students who perceive little comparative advantage—and return on investment—in our schools over no-cost or lower-cost options. The benefit to independent schools is further challenged when those other options offer the very things that the NAIS Parent Motivation Survey identifies as the decision factors in selecting a school: challenging curricula, especially "pre-professional" programs of choice that promise to offer a leg up in college admissions, teachers trained in best pedagogical practices, an environment of achievement, etc.

Further, public schools, even the worst for all their flaws, do have a state and federally mandated culture of assessment. Everything is measured. Historically, independent schools do not have such a culture. To prove our quality, we have used little more than standardized test scores (SAT, ACT, AP) just like the public schools do, along with college acceptances and perhaps the number of teachers with advanced degrees, inflated faculty-student ratios and length of teacher tenure. We rely on our impressions to support our belief that we are worth the tuition. We must do a better job of ensuring that our case is self-evident.

We cannot persist in this fashion. Let us make full use of our freedom to innovate, to experiment, and to pivot in more fruitful directions. With great freedom comes great responsibility. We can and must do everything imaginable to ensure that we engage each of our students, that we know and accentuate the unique talents and interests of each one. We should never be following others, copying others, but leading the way that others may follow us.

Independent schools need to consider the emerging trends in education at the dawn of this century. Students increasingly expect and indeed flourish with extensive autonomy. They must learn to regulate themselves and be encouraged to find their own paths and pursue their interests and natural propensities. Various schedules and platforms: face-to-face, virtual and blended should be available in order to permit students the greatest array of choices. The format of the lecturer at the front of the room with students passively receiving knowledge seated had a

232

long run (since the 12th century!), but our far more extensive knowledge about how people assimilate information mandates that we subject it to the similarly medieval fate of defenestration.

For that matter, memorizing information isn't rational when the impetus for memorization, i.e. that information is scarce and sequestered, no longer exists. We can no longer teach the way we have done for centuries when students can access on their phones more information than the greatest scholars could in a lifetime. It is entirely illogical to maintain the status quo when circumstances have shifted so spectacularly. Let us teach students to apply knowledge and to flourish in this interconnected world with a new economy that encourages sharing and entrepreneurship. We need to teach (and many faculty need to learn) to use the tools available, to discern quality research from mediocre and poor, corroborate or disprove, formulate a hypothesis, examine the opposing views, extrapolate and synthesize, and craft an original product in a logical and professional way. Beyond *how* we teach, it is crucial that we deeply consider *why* we teach and *what* we teach and how that needs to change to reflect present and future realities. The curriculum is up for rediscovery and should never have been allowed to become stagnant in the first place.

Students are capable of wondrous things that adults can't imagine but they must be guided and encouraged and expected to do them. Projects can result in extraordinary discoveries and improvements to the lives of individuals and communities, but these things will not happen if they are never attempted. Rather than follow the established paths, independent school stakeholders can wield figurative machetes to cut new ones through the overgrowth. We need to analyze the resources, in terms of location, staff, other stakeholders, etc. that are highly specific to our individual school to determine what singular program(s) we are uniquely capable of offering. To fail to do so is to leave opportunity on the table to rot.

Let us cherish our human resources, and entice and inspire them to find meaning, value, and purpose in our mission and community. Teachers must be treated and come to view themselves as knowledge workers and professionals. The time for teachers to revel in being lone wolves is past, just as the subject area silos are becoming less distinct. Let us hire with an eye toward collaboration, interdisciplinary convergence, and the new paradigm of engagement and facilitation, not for ability to ensure that students do well on AP or IB exams. Let us honor productivity as well as longevity.

Changing the paradigm, however, does not mean embracing anything and everything new that comes into focus. We need to discern solid research from that which is flawed or anecdotal. We shall have to educate stakeholders as well, for the search for truth often means countering the popular media (i.e. the current emphasis on neuro-pseudo-science). Navel-gazing rarely leads to innovation. Instead, we need to do the research and pilot programs with an open mind and curious spirit to find more effective ways of doing what we do as well as inspiration for innovation.

Let us attend to our communities consciously and deliberately. We can use tools to determine whether they are as healthy, positive, and cohesive as we lead ourselves to believe. There is so much we can do to make our community life better: crafting rituals that join us together throughout the year, creating caring classrooms, determining what our implicit and explicit community standards are and how they might be improved so that we treat one another with respect. We can examine the ways that we interact with those outside our walls so that we shape our students into responsible citizens who desire and labor for justice.

Let us strive for transparency and trustworthiness. Administrators have the responsibility for ensuring that staff members comprehend the business operations side of the organization and the interplay of the various parts that comprise the whole. Every single stakeholder can have an impact on whether our schools continue to receive the financial resources to endure.

Let us question the programs, practices, and principles that we hold sacrosanct and discern whether they have lost their relevance and power. If so, we must discard them without sentimentality, for we have a responsibility to our stakeholders and our institution. In the effort to steward our resources wisely, we need to streamline operations, plan strategically, and take a hard look at how to improve our value in every way.

Let us not fear conflict, but rather work through it, for struggle can yield an abundant harvest. Let us seek the self-differentiated leader, one who embraces the role of vision keeper and "high priest" who leads the symbolic dimension of the school. We might apply tenets of systems theory to our chronically anxious communities to counteract the various behaviors toxic to leadership, to substantive change, and to the realization of our schools' potential.

Let us embrace the thrilling adventure and set forth with courage on the exploration of this strange new world. Engage!

Appendix

235

I.   Position Descriptions

The utility of position descriptions is often overlooked in independent schools, yet they are essential tools in virtually every other sector. Having a clearly articulated set of duties, knowledge, skills, and abilities clarifies expectations for purposes of recruitment, training and development, performance management, and personnel decisions. They define lines of reporting and how one position relates to others. Crucially, they also serve to defend the organization's decision in case of termination. Detailed descriptions of specific positions appear below; descriptions of the functions of the teams appear in Chapter 6.

A statement indicating that "duties are not limited to those described and include others as assigned" should appear on all position descriptions as well as the following:

All school employees share the responsibility
- To embody, manifest, and advocate the mission of the school
- To articulate the vision for the school and its future
- To monitor school climate and culture
- To respond to communication from stakeholders within one full business day
- To attend the major events (performances, guest speakers, etc.) in the life of the school

Community Life Team

Coordinator of Service Learning/Activism/Community Engagement

Creates and implements curriculum comprised of action, reflection, and assessment, focused on addressing the systemic political and socio-economic issues of injustice, with the purpose of realizing authentic and lasting change for the better. Facilitates direct student participation in the political process through working with neighborhood and community leaders.

- In collaboration with others, integrates service learning with the curriculum
- In collaboration with other members of Community Life Team and the administration, develops, refines, communicates, implements, and assesses plan for school culture and invests students, teachers, and families
- Actively seeks opportunities for meaningful engagement with the community, whenever possible characterized by collaboration and mutual benefit and working beside, rather than "ministering unto"
- In collaboration with others may provide input regarding Advisory curriculum
- In collaboration with Arts faculty, creates opportunities for artivism, the nexus of art and activism
- Identifies and utilizes resources to extend students' education beyond the campus into the larger community
- Develops the School Forum: a venue in which community activists, artists, esteemed educators, businessmen, scientists and political leaders are brought together to enrich our "marketplace of ideas"
- In collaboration with Symposium Committee, develops the annual theme (Environmental Sustainability, Local History, Creation vs. Consumption, etc.) integrated throughout the

curriculum and culminating in an event in which experts and students share their work and research
- In collaboration with other members of Community Life Team and the administration, develops, refines, communicates, implements, and assesses plan for school culture and invests students, teachers, and families
- In collaboration with Community Life Team, develops, refines, and communicates weekly advisory curriculum
- *This position requires considerable time off-site, which may lead to a reduced course load*

Coordinator of Community Peace and Justice:

- In collaboration with others, develops programs to promote positive student behavior as well as intervention strategies and consequences for behavior, and restorative justice
- Assists with the day-to-day affairs of the school by ensuring that consistency and cooperation are present in the enforcement of discipline, the shaping of positive behavior, the promotion of honor, and the cultivation of leadership
  - Maintains student discipline and follow-through with correspondence and record-keeping relating to discipline
  - Communicates effectively and sensitively with students, parents, and others
  - Develops programs to promote positive student behavior as well as intervention strategies and consequences for behavior
  - When dealing with more serious disciplinary issues, acts as member of the Student Performance Review/Honor Council board and provides final recommendation to the head of school
  - In addition to emergency meetings on serious disciplinary issues, conducts quarterly class committee meetings involving all faculty at the mid-term of each quarter to identify students currently at risk
- Develops appropriate drug and alcohol interdiction policies
- Refers major rule infractions to the Student Performance Review Board
- Collaborates with Class Curators, Community Life Team members, teachers, families, and administrators to foster a healthy student culture
- In collaboration with Community Life Team, develops, refines, and communicates weekly advisory curriculum
- Course load to be determined

Class Curators:

- Class Curators are assigned to a class during the freshman year and stay with that class through graduation to curate the school experience for students. They get to know students on a deeper level and closely monitor their progress throughout their time at school. Class Curators work closely with other employees and students to create events and activities that are relevant to the respective class year
- Class Curators must be skilled collaborators to work as a unified group with each other, with the Grade Coordinators, with students, and with the administration to provide and communicate a uniform set of expectations that will help students mature and become responsible and productive members of the community

237

- Class Curators are the primary contact for students and parents who have questions or concerns about issues:
  - Intervene in times of academic or other difficulty and collaborate with Student Services team to strategize solutions
  - Keep the administration apprised of student progress and special issues
  - Maintain open and collegial communication with faculty about specific circumstances that affect a student's academic performance
  - In collaboration with Learning Support and/or other members of the Student Services Team, attends individual conferences with parents and students in the spring to review overall experience at School (academic performance, testing, social adjustment, and student activities in and out of school), schedules parent/teacher conferences when needed, maintains records and correspondence relating to parent conferences
  - Read, review, and follow up on quarterly grade comments as well as periodic monitoring as needed
  - Work together to coordinate Parents' Night and Parent-Teacher Conferences in both semesters
- Encourage class unity, organize, chaperone, and coordinate class trips and class projects, and be responsible for all class activities
- Coordinate the co-curricular and extra-curricular activity programs of the school; assists in the planning and the presentation of school assemblies and programs
- Foster leadership abilities of existing and potential student leaders
  - Organize the class officer elections, guide the class officers through decision-making processes for various events and activities, such as dances and fundraising activities
- Further responsibilities of the Class Curator:
  - In cooperation with Registrar, manages student attendance issues as well as all issues relating to the well being of the students
  - Collaborates in the coordination of new student orientation
  - Keeps the administration fully informed on student issues and all other relevant matters pertaining to school life
  - In collaboration with Director of Communications assists in maintaining a comprehensive calendar of school events
  - Supports the school and its leadership
  - In collaboration with Community Life Team, develops, refines, and communicates weekly advisory curriculum
- Due to the comparative workload, a Curator will have a reduced load of four classes when attending to 9th grade, and otherwise will teach a normal course load of five classes, as this administrative function will be considered service to the school

238

Student Services Team

Director of Learning Support :

     This position's main responsibility is to ensure that all students receive the support they need to become effective and enthusiastic learners. This position sets policy, develops initiatives and strategic goals for learning support, supervises the Learning Specialist and Center Coordinators, and shares responsibility for the Advisory program with the Counseling Office. This position works intensively with staff, students, and families to ensure that they understand students' learning strengths and challenges and the accommodations, interventions, and methods that will help the students to succeed.

- Responds by the end of the next business day to students' and families' concerns about students' learning challenges, serves as liaison with and refers students and families to classroom teachers, Learning Specialist, Counseling Office, and other staff as appropriate, and *follows up continually to ensure follow through and resolution*
- Maintains highly collaborative and respectful relationships with families and Learning Specialist and other staff; schedules meetings and reports evaluation findings with students, teachers and parents when indicated, helpful or necessary; makes appropriate referrals to Counseling Office and other staff, as appropriate
- To assess students referred for evaluation, interprets or administers a wide variety of neuropsychological instruments such as Wechsler, RAVLT, WRAT, etc., as well as in-class observations, review of the student's educational history, conferences with the students' teachers and coaches, evaluation and analysis of the student's academic performance and learning characteristics
- Prepares Individual Educational Programs (IEPs) for students with learning exceptionalities **of all kinds**
  - o Collaborates with classroom teacher(s) to ensure the implementation of the established academic goals of each student in the Educational Program
  - o Biweekly monitors and evaluates the effectiveness of the Individualized Educational Plan
  - o Serves as Case Manager of assigned students
  - o Assesses students recommended for retention, more challenging curriculum, and early graduation
- Educates students and their families in the identification of their strengths and challenges, and how best to work with them to maximize success
- Maintains appropriate confidentiality and records on all referred students and student/parent contacts in accordance with federal and state law and the procedures of the school
- Develops a database of and coordinates contact with service providers for out-of-school referrals
- Serves as a resource and consultant to administrators and other school personnel to meet the learning needs of students and trains staff in best practices for student success including:
  - o Multiple Modalities of instruction
  - o Differentiated instruction
  - o Multiple types of assessment

239

- o Guided Lecture Notes
- o Verbal and written directions
- o Accessible assignments with frequent benchmarks, due dates and checks for understanding
- o Incorporation of accommodations, interventions, and modifications
- o Selection of instructional materials and technology geared to meet the needs of a wide range of student abilities
- In collaboration with Counseling Office, serves as a resource and consultant to school personnel on the nature, causes, and solutions to the learning, behavioral, and developmental problems of children
- Maintains positive relationship with public schools and their support staff
- Commits to ongoing professional development, especially through virtual means, as this position's responsibilities necessitate availability on site as much as possible; keeps abreast of assessment techniques, advances in learning theory, improvements in instructional media, technology and materials, and statutory requirements; maintains professional competence and disseminates and implements initiatives accordingly

Learning Specialist:

This position supervises the day-to-day functions of the academic center that assists students and their families by training them in executive function and other skills for success, and by helping them understand challenging content or complete an assignment. The incumbent should be skilled with assistive technology (Kurzweil, Livescribe, dictation software, etc.), which will be offered in the academic center. This position is responsible for extensive training of tutors and scheduling tutors needed for students with diagnosed learning differences as well as those for occasional assistance. The incumbent also works with the study hall proctors to supervise students in academic distress and ensure that they remain on task and focused on the intended work.

- Monitors **all** students' academic progress by means of weekly LMS-generated at-risk reports, follows up on students of concern, and communicates with relevant parties; and, in collaboration with and as directed by the Director of Learning Support, may perform educational assessment of students referred for evaluation, including in-class observations of the student, review of the student's educational history, conferences with the student's teachers, and an evaluation and analysis of the student's academic performance and learning characteristics
- Maintains highly collaborative and respectful relationships with students, families, the Director of Learning Support and other Academy staff and makes appropriate referrals to Counseling Office and other staff, as appropriate
- Educates students regarding the identification of their strengths and challenges, and how best to work with them to maximize success
- Refers students and families to the Counseling Office and confers and collaborates when appropriate
- Trains, coordinates, monitors, and evaluates tutors and ensures that they are assisting students appropriately, ensures that records are maintained and parents and staff are

notified of students' attendance at tutoring sessions
- As directed by Director of Learning Support
  - May serve as Case Manager of assigned students
  - May assist in coordinating, developing, monitoring and evaluating the effectiveness of students' Individualized Educational Plan
  - May schedule meetings with staff, students and families
  - Maintains confidential records on all referred students and student/parent contacts in accordance with federal and state law and the procedures of the school
  - Provides thorough and timely reports and information as requested
  - Assists in the preparation and implementation of professional development programs for school personnel within areas of professional competence
- Helps identify within the school all types of exceptional students
- Serves as a resource to staff in dealing with classroom management and differentiation issues
- In collaboration with the Director of Learning Support develops policy for tutoring, coordinates its execution, supervises tutors, and provides documentation of hours to Human Resources
- Commits to ongoing professional development, especially through virtual means, as this position's responsibilities necessitate availability on site as much as possible; keeps abreast of assessment techniques, advances in learning theory, improvements in instructional media, technology and materials, and statutory requirements

School Psychologist:

- Assesses students referred for evaluation; administers, utilizes, and interprets a wide variety of neuropsychological instruments such as Wechsler, RAVLT, WRAT, etc., as well as in-class observations; reviews students' educational history; confers with teachers and coaches; evaluates and analyzes the students' academic performance and learning characteristics
- Identifies at-risk students, performs psycho-social evaluations of referred students, and monitors student progress
  - Refers students and families to Learning Support when appropriate
  - Confers and collaborates with Learning Support
- Educates students in the identification of their strengths and challenges, and how best to work with them to maximize success
- Collaborates extensively to coordinate advisory program,
  - Coaches and monitors advisors, assists with planning advisory activities and curriculum
- Maintains confidential records on all referred students and student/parent contacts in accordance with federal and state law and the procedures of the School Academy
- Maintains *appropriate* confidentiality, and ***makes appropriate referrals***
- Develops a database of and coordinates contact with all out-of-school social/referral agencies
- Schedules meetings with students, teachers and parents when indicated, helpful or necessary
- Reports non-confidential, relevant evaluation findings at meetings with teachers and parents, as appropriate
- Schedules and conducts therapy sessions with students as needed

241

- In collaboration with Guidance, develops student crisis protocol and assumes responsibility for its implementation
- Schedules special programs and gatherings, such as D.A.R.E., etc.
- Serves as a resource and/or consultant to school personnel on the nature, causes, and solutions to the learning, behavioral, and developmental problems of children
- Serves, upon request, as a resource and/or consultant to administrators and other school personnel on best practices for meeting the needs of students
- Assists in the preparation and implementation of professional development programs for school personnel within areas of professional competence
- Professional Development
  - Keeps abreast of assessment techniques, advances in learning theory, improvements in instructional media, technology and materials, and statutory requirements
  - Maintains professional competence through reading, course work, attendance at conferences, workshops, memberships in professional organizations and other relevant activities in accordance with school guidelines

Coordinator of Life Planning and Guidance:

Responsible for guiding the members of each year's graduating class through post-secondary planning.
- In collaboration with others, develops, evaluates, oversees and makes continual improvements to a comprehensive four-year program that guides students individually and in advisory groups to reflect on their values, strengths, and interests and formulate a post-secondary plan that will help them to find fulfillment in relationships and meaningful work and engagement with their community
- Meets with individual families annually beginning in the eighth grade to discuss planning and advise on course selection, extra-curricular activities, summer plans, and their consequences on vocational preparation and the college application process
- Meets with families and students individually to develop a college visit list and potential internship opportunities in junior and senior years
- Collaborates with writing instructors to guide students in application essay composition in the spring of junior year
- Orchestrates a College Application Boot Camp in the summer
- Creates and continually improves the school College Admissions Guide
- Writes or organizes the team that writes letters of recommendation included in application packets to colleges, universities, gap year programs, scholarship agencies, etc.
- Supervises students' application progress from finalizing their lists of colleges, gap year or other programs, and sending off applications
- Helps seniors to understand and decide among their financial aid packages in April
- Maintains and communicates current knowledge base of trends in higher education and developments in specific institutions through professional media such as *The Chronicle of Higher Education, Journal of College Admission,* etc., conferences, and visits

Markets the school effectively to secondary institutions and prospective students and parents.
- Visits college campuses frequently to establish relationships with college admissions offices and coordinates their visits to the school

- Composes the annual school profile in collaboration with the Communications/ Marketing staff
- Attends and, ideally, presents at regional and national conferences
- Organizes fall and spring college tours

Advises the faculty, administration, and trustees regarding the college admissions process and trends.

- Attends administrative meetings
- Prepares annual reports for the board of trustees on the college admission process
- Advises academic administrators regarding the curriculum vis-à-vis college admissions
- Advises the faculty in their writing of college recommendations
- Counsels advisors and coaches on how to help students through the college selection process
- Establishes and maintains a yearly budget

Demonstrates superb skills as an administrator and communicator with various stakeholders.

- Ensures confidentiality of records and families' circumstances
- Maintains a content-rich and appropriately structured webpage and other means to communicate several times monthly regarding post-secondary planning and trends
- Publicizes scholarship opportunities and enrichment and summer programs of interest
- Oversees the development and maintenance of the online database Workspace K-12 (formerly Naviance)

Desirable Qualities:

- Integrity, sensitivity to families' needs, desires, and aspirations, confidentiality, a strong work ethic, flexibility
- Outstanding communication (especially *listening*), negotiation, and organizational skills
- Enthusiasm for working with adolescents and their parents
- Ability to establish rapport with students, families, and stakeholders
- Abundant energy and a lifelong desire to learn

Subject Support Staff: Provide targeted support in Writing and Math. Assistance in Writing and Math is available during the day, especially lunch period and during tutorial, with possible extended hours on some weekdays and weekends by appointment.

Writing Center Coordinator: A full-time teacher with a reduced load who has expertise in *teaching* writing assists students on all grade levels to become better writers through one-on-one consultation in all stages of the writing process, from note-taking and pre-writing to revision strategies and proofreading techniques. Writing assistance is available during the day, especially lunch period and during tutorial with possible extended hours on some weekdays.

Math Center Coordinator: This may be staffed by a full-time teacher with a reduced load who has a credential and specific training in *teaching* mathematics[315] at least through the pre-

---

[315] In a longitudinal 10-year study of students statewide, researchers discovered that teacher credential, experience, and test scores contributed to student achievement in math more than other subjects. Clotfelter, Ladd and Vigdor. *How and Why Do Teacher Credentials Matter for*

243

calculus level or by current Math teachers on a scheduled basis for half their planning period. Students will also have access to engaging software for personalized learning and adaptive assessments, such as ALEKS or some analog, to develop a strong foundation of skills in computation, geometric and algebraic reasoning, and higher math.

Tutors:
Tutors should be positive, proactive, patient and persistent, and have a positive attitude toward students and learning. Tutors should be trained in executing their various roles:

- Pedagogical: To support the learning process itself by providing instructions, stimulating questions, examples, feedback, and motivation etc., to the learners
- Managerial: To help the student organize work, establish benchmarks and track deadlines; to track student progress and data etc.
- Social: To establish a friendly and comfortable environment that stimulates learning

Academic Services Team

Vice President for Education/Chief Academic Officer

Academic servant-leader of the school, responsible for developing, guiding, implementing, communicating, and assessing its philosophy, mission, vision, and curriculum, the wellbeing of students, and the school's day-to-day operation. Monitors and addresses school culture and climate. Serves as a consultant to teachers in matters of classroom management, teaching methods, and general school procedures, particularly in academics, including individualized and differentiated instruction, modifications and accommodations, layered curriculum and learning contracts, pre-, formative, and summative assessments, respectful interaction with students, parents, and colleagues, and the sustainment of a rigorous but not overwhelming learning environment.

- Develops, implements and evaluates a coherent college preparatory program, subject to continual modification
- Keeps abreast of educational research as well as trends in higher education, assesses their relevance, communicates to stakeholders as appropriate, and implements new initiatives as appropriate
- Oversees the academic advising and college counseling programs and student placement
- Monitors student academic progress and addresses student academic emergencies; etc.
- In collaboration with others, adjudicates issues of academic dishonesty
- Communicates with parents regarding academic concerns
- Attends major school events and demonstrates support for academic and co-curricular programs
- May represent the school at conferences such as NAIS, regional and school affinity

---

Student Achievement? National Center for Longitudinal Data in Education Research. March, 2007.

group associations, such as Independent Curriculum Group
- In collaboration with the VP for Technology/CIO, supervises Registrar in the maintenance of complete academic records on all students
- Oversees assessment of students and the reporting of standards and methods used by teachers in measuring student achievement
- In collaboration with Assistant VP for Education
    - Observes, supervises, and evaluates the faculty in the development and implementation of curriculum
- In collaboration with Assistant VP for Education and others, determines yearly staffing needs and teaching assignments
- Makes decisions regarding the hiring, retention, and the assignment of faculty
- Conducts regular meetings with faculty and Grade Level Coordinators, which deal both with routine school matters and with the stimulating exchange of ideas on issues of educational interest and concern
- Substitute teaches in accord with abilities; ideally teaches a section or more
- Oversees the preparation of a master school class schedule and assigns teachers and students to classes and other obligations
- Assists in the admission process for the testing, interviewing, and evaluating of applicants for enrollment
- Supports the school and its leadership

Assistant Vice President for Education/Dean of Faculty:

- Serves as a consultant to teachers in matters of classroom management, teaching methods, and general school procedures, particularly in academic matters including individualized and differentiated instruction, modifications and accommodations, layered curriculum and learning contracts, pre-, formative, and summative assessments, respectful interaction with students, parents, and colleagues, and a rigorous but not overwhelming learning environment
- Ensures compliance with legal requirements of government regulations and agencies
    - Maintains the educational standards established by the State and by those agencies that examine and accredit the school
    - Serves as the lead in the accreditation process
- Establishes programs for the orientation and mentoring of new teachers, for in-service training of all teachers, and for the evaluation of classroom teachers, to ensure that teachers are familiar with and adhere to school policies in all areas of the school operation
- Supervises and observes each faculty member to become familiar with the pedagogy of each teacher
- Coordinates Professional Development days and maintains a calendar of professional development opportunities in collaboration with Director of Student Research
- Develops and monitors comprehensive professional development plans for all faculty members
- Supervises Grade Level Coordinators
- Collaborates with VP for Education, Director of Communications, and Human Relations on recruitment of faculty

245

- o Reads resumés with acuity
- o Communicates with applicants
- o Coordinates travel, campus visits and itineraries
- o May interview applicants, as needed
- Develops means to ensure retention and foster collaboration, high levels of esprit de corps and morale
- May represent the school at conferences such as NAIS, regional and school affinity group associations, such as Independent Curriculum Group
- In collaboration with VP for Education/CAO, sets faculty meeting agenda and conducts regular meetings with faculty and others, dealing both with routine school matters and with the stimulating exchange of ideas on issues of educational/philosophical interest and concern
- In collaboration with VP for Education/CAO and others, determines yearly staffing needs and teaching assignments
- Coordinates substitute teachers and provides documentation of hours to Human Resources
- Teaches a reduced course load of two sections

Grade Level Coordinator:

- Each Grade Level Coordinator is assigned permanently to one grade, unlike the Class Curator, which progresses with a class. The function of the GLC is more academic, while the Class Curator function is more social, though there is overlap
- Each GLC works collaboratively with the Class Curator for that year, the grade level staff, and the administration in the development of plans and procedures that support instruction for the upcoming school year in scheduling, student placement, and ensuring opportunities for interdisciplinarity in the curriculum
- The GLC is the "point person" to ensure that grade level curricular goals and student outcomes are clearly communicated and that support is in place to implement the curriculum.
- Provides leadership regarding staff development and curriculum development needs.
- . The 9th Grade Coordinator will assist extensively with Orientation, while the 11th Grade Coordinator will assist the College Counseling Office with College Tours, and the 12th Grade Coordinator will help with the college application process and transitioning to the world beyond
- Apprises the VP for Education/CAO of concerns to allow the cooperative problem solving and proactive planning necessary to address staff needs/concerns
- Orients and provides support for new teaching staff
- Orients students to the curriculum, activities, and developmental concerns typical for the grade
- Coordinates activities, field trips, and distribution of materials, in collaboration with Class Curator when appropriate
- Collaborates with the grade level and the administrative staff, student services staff, and the Parent Association as appropriate
- Teaches a normal course load of five classes

Curriculum Coordination Team

Coordinator of Instructional Technology and Online Learning

Academic Integration
- Assists students and employees, with the integration of technology in the classroom; provides in-service to groups of employees as well as individualized assistance as requested
- Keeps abreast of developments in instructional technology, assesses their relevance to school context, acquires in collaboration with VP for IT, conducts trials, instructs stakeholders usage, and evaluates
- Assists with curriculum development as it relates to educational technology
- Provides technology training opportunities, including instruction regarding privacy and appropriate use, throughout the school year for students, parents, and employees
- Provides training and support to teachers, students, and parents in using Learning Management Systems and Student Information Systems
- Encourages and instructs teachers in the development of online pre-, formative and summative assessments
- Provides demonstration teaching to students in the appropriate use of technology in the classrooms and/or computer labs

Technical Support
- Solves or refers minor problems related to networks, servers, workstations and peripherals in classrooms, labs, and school offices
- Refers more serious problems related to networks, servers, workstations and peripherals in classrooms, labs, and school offices to the appropriate technology staff
- Keeps informed of the latest technologies, practices, and programs in the education field
- Assumes responsibility for professional growth and keeps materials, supplies, and skills up-to-date
- Examines and recommends computer hardware and software to teachers and administrators
- Assists in the implementation of the school-wide technology plan
- Cooperates with other staff members in promoting a positive organizational climate
- Responds to parents and students' concerns regarding access and login issues and computer problems
- Takes all necessary and reasonable precautions to protect students, equipment, materials, and facilities

Online Learning:
- Assists with student registration in online courses, serves as liaison with virtual/online providers in case of difficulty
- Proposes other online learning providers and provides documentation and recommendation to VP for Education regarding accreditation and
- In collaboration with VP for Education, develops policy for, coordinates, and publicizes online learning opportunities

247

Director of Student Research

- Inspires a love of learning through projects that ignite students' curiosity and passion
- Initiates contact and actively collaborates with teachers and students to anticipate and ascertain their information needs
- Enthusiastically seeks out for a promoting student research (i.e. science fairs, history day, and similar venues) on local through international levels and leads, coordinates, and chaperones school participation
- Teaches the research process, assists classes and individuals in research strategy, source gathering, organization, extrapolation, synthesis, and presentation of final product
- Helps students to identify potential mentors and collaborators in their subject area locally and globally

Information Literacy Instruction:

- Provides leadership to the faculty regarding information resource tools
- Trains students and teachers in the use of the databases
- Collaborates with teachers to develop and deliver lessons that integrate information skills with the curriculum
- Instructs students in pre-research techniques, resources, academic integrity, and respect for intellectual property
- Meets individually with students engaged in research projects to teach them the research process: selecting a topic, mind mapping, creating an outline, composing searches, gathering resources, synthesizing and citing

Academic Resources Development:

- Actively acquires and encourages the use of materials that complement and enrich textbooks, teaching materials and methodologies
- Keeps abreast of and communicates developments and pertinent articles and research in various disciplines and general pedagogy
- Supervises the development and maintenance of the central and classroom collections
- Evaluates usage of print and digital collections and adjusts holdings accordingly, i.e. purchases and discards resources, negotiates contracts, and acquires resources from community purveyors when feasible
- Locates online and software-based resources, including test preparation materials, and makes them accessible for students and teachers
- Develops a calendar of professional development opportunities for school staff in collaboration with Assistant VP for Education

Additional responsibilities:

- Ensures that the information commons is a positive, pleasant, and inviting space for both collaborative and quiet independent work
- Conducts competitive intelligence regarding innovative programs in peer institutions and presents results to appropriate parties
- Participates in continuing education opportunities
- Performs traditional library functions of reference, circulation, and technical services

Interdisciplinary Arts Coordinator

- In collaboration with classroom teachers, actively seeks out opportunities for the integration of dramatization, music, dance, and visual art to be utilized as learning vehicles, taking care to ensure that creativity supports rather than diminishes academic rigor and that the highest standards are upheld in the evaluation of artistic merit
- Communicates effectively with students, parents, and colleagues the perspective that artistic expression is integral to the human experience, rather than a mere avocation
- Encourages and models the efficacy of an arts-friendly classroom in
  - addressing numerous learning styles
  - balancing creative chaos with an atmosphere of orderly systematic learning
  - establishing alternative and creative assessments, grading and evaluation
  - effectively teaching math, science, history and social studies
  - teaching character and emotional intelligence
  - fostering productive collaborations and "out-of-the-box" problem-solving
  - boosting morale and motivation
- Nurtures relationships with arts organizations, area universities, and the community, including non-profit and commercial sectors
- Encourages student participation in the arts and art education, both in the school and in the community

Teachers:

Teachers foster a lifelong love of learning, spark curiosity, encourage students to make good choices, and serve as role models. They provide excellent classroom experiences that engage and inspire students, and ensure that all students have rigorous and inclusive access to the curriculum and instruction every day to meet their learning goals.

Teachers nurture strong bonds between and among employees and students, and are actively engaged in the life of the school. They are expected to support students by attending important events in their students' and/or advisees' lives, such as performances, occasional athletic events, and/or other events such as students' work showcased at the Scholastic Art Awards, or debate competitions. Advisors are required to meet at least once each term with their advisory group outside of school for a meal, a movie, or some other event.

Teachers routinely substitute for each other, team teach and collaborate, and seek out other means to contribute to the good of the school beyond the classroom, from directing a program or coaching a sport to escorting tours at Open Houses. When asked to serve in an additional capacity, it is expected that the teacher will gladly welcome the opportunity and perform to the best of his or her ability.

In Curriculum Coordination Teams, teachers meet at least twice a month to work collaboratively on such areas as creating and revising curriculum, reviewing student work, selecting and developing instructional resources, planning and coordinating portfolio and exhibition activities, meeting with specialists, and preparing common assessments.

Teaching and Learning:
- Create a caring, welcoming and safe learning environment for all students to grow and learn by collaboratively establishing standards centered on mutual respect and understanding of our core values
- Develop a course-specific syllabus for each course taught that reflects the educational philosophy of the school
- Present current student work on bulletin boards inside the classroom as well as outside halls
- Write the daily objective of the lesson, the agenda and homework (if any) on the board for each class
- Apply learning contracts to foster student autonomy, control, and responsibility for their learning
- Develop, analyze and/or use data effectively to inform instruction and curriculum
- Participate in Learning Support meetings, and utilize differentiated instruction to support all students according to their accommodations and learning styles
- Work reflectively to set goals, receive constructive feedback and try new strategies to improve student achievement
- Be available for collaboration or extra help for students for 45 minutes prior to the first class and for an hour after the last

Advisory Responsibilities: (Teachers will be offered training and curriculum for advisory)
- Serve as mentor, role model, and academic coach for students in advisory group
- Effectively "check in" with students at least weekly to monitor psycho-social state and refer student to Student Services when indicated
- Serve as liaison between student and school or parent and school to provide assistance or to direct student or parent to appropriate person in the school
- Review student progress weekly with students and collaborate with students and teachers and Student Services team as needed to determine effective course of remediation
- Assist students with generating or planning advisory activities

Administrative Responsibilities:
- Keep accurate records by taking attendance in every class including homeroom/advisory, by using the Student Information and Learning Management Systems, and by completing and reporting assessment and assignment reports
- Partner with families and parents via conferences, phone calls, or emails on a regular basis, and when a student's grade drops a letter grade, and when a student receives a grade of C- or below and documenting these communications
- Notify parents of potentially objectionable content in classroom resources and provide alternate assignments as needed
- Participate in Admissions Open Houses and other school events
- Collaborate with appropriate Student Services staff and administration to share important information regarding student health, behavioral, academic, and social-emotional issues
- Cover classes as necessary of colleagues who are absent for sick, professional, or personal days

- Keep accurate inventory of textbooks and other resources in classroom and those distributed to students
- Develop and implement field trips (minimum two weeks notice), community service, and other outside educational activities with adequate notice and preparation following the appropriate guidelines and approval process (Not required in all classes)
- Plan and support school events, such as town meetings, assemblies, celebrations, and graduation

Professionalism:
- Model professionalism in attire, speech, and behavior
- Maintain excellent attendance and punctuality to school
- Provide appropriate substitute plans in advance of planned absence
- Read and respond to email at least daily, and reply to parent communication before the close of the next business day
- Arrive on time and actively participate in all required meetings
- Share rooms and resources with colleagues, being mindful of professional manners

Professional Development:
- In keeping with Professional Development Plan guidelines, develop a comprehensive plan that may entail taking courses, workshops and other training to keep current in their field and/or develop leadership by participating in professional development days, facilitating workshops, conference events, and special school events etc.

Performance evaluation is essentially a collaborative process. Teachers should expect to be observed frequently and should observe colleagues. The above position description serves as a basis for evaluation along with the Performance Appraisal Portfolio.

II.   Performance Appraisal

Portfolio Elements

Great teaching creates absorbed learning and fuller understanding. In the effort to maintain standards of excellence, we commit to the frequent review of teachers' performance. In keeping with best-practices research, we will conduct 360° evaluations. This process entails the collection of self, peer, student, and administrative evaluations for each teacher.

Prior to [date], each teacher must prepare a file including the following elements:

1. Syllabus for each course

2. Completed projects – Descriptions, process, and products of any projects that your students have completed in the past term

3. Planned projects – Describe any projects that you have planned for the upcoming term

4. Evidence of student learning – Attach or provide examples of assignments and other student work completed, etc.

5. Evidence of Formative Assessment – Attach examples of formative assessment conducted prior to, during, and following instruction, learning contracts, narrative feedback, etc.

6. Evidence of collaboration with colleagues

7. Evidence of differentiated instruction

8. Evidence of communication with parents

9. Evidence of service to community, including extra-curricular involvement

Each teacher will also be asked to complete a peer evaluation for a colleague and administer and collect student evaluations.

The Chief Academic Officer will observe classes and student-teacher interactions.
Each teacher will additionally be evaluated on the basis of the following:
- Advising, in collaboration with the designated member of the Student Services Team
- Coaching, in collaboration with the Athletic Director
- Personal attention to students
- Esprit de corps
- Being in harmony with the mission and organizational culture

252

Teacher Self-evaluation

This evaluation is intended for teachers' personal use to frame goals and assess their progress toward them.

Rate your performance on the following items:

1=never, 2=not often, 3=sometimes, 4=usually, 5=almost always

_____1. I make class work interesting.
_____2. I ask questions in class to see if the students understand what has been taught.
_____3. I give assignments related to the subject we are studying.
_____4. My students and I discuss and summarize each lesson just studied.
_____5. I tell students how they can use what they already have learned to learn new things.
_____6. I maintain discipline in my classroom.
_____7. I return tests and assignments quickly.
_____8. I give students detailed feedback about their performance and how to improve.
_____9. I am very knowledgeable about the subject(s) I teach.
_____10. I use learning contracts to provide students with autonomy over and responsibility for their learning.
_____11. I understand and support the project-based, interdisciplinary mission and vision of the school.
_____12. I create alternate assignments to ensure that advanced students are challenged.
_____13. I generate and implement accommodations to help struggling students to succeed.
_____14. I guide students to create projects that encourage independent exploration of the topic of study and application of desired skills.
_____15. I am well organized.
_____16. I enjoy it when students ask questions.
_____17. I conduct assessment prior to, during, and following instruction.
_____18. I encourage students to look at problems in new ways and to find new ways to solve problems.
_____19. I am available to help students during class time and other times during the day.
_____20. I monitor student work as they are doing it to see if they understand the lesson.
_____21. I contact parents when students miss more than two homework assignments.
_____22. I contact parents when students earn any grade below 70%.
_____23. In advisory, I ensure that students are encouraged toward positive behavior.
_____25. I monitor advisees' grades and speak with advisee, parents, and teachers to find out more and improve the situation.

Mid-Course Feedback Form
(To be distributed at the mid point of a term for teachers' use).
1. In considering this course and your involvement in this course, what are you learning about yourself this semester?

2. What 3-4 things in this course (teaching methods and approaches, assignments, readings, experiences, etc.) are going well, are working best for your learning?

253

3. What 3-4 things in this course (teaching methods and approaches, assignments, readings, experiences, etc.) are not going so well, are working least well for your learning?

4. In terms of #2, what can I as the teacher do differently to help your learning?

5. In terms of #2, what can you, the student, do differently to help your learning?

Student Feedback Form

Directions: The statements below are designed to find out more about your class and teacher. This is not a test. Do not put your name on this paper. Please answer all the statements.
1=Never 2=Not often 3=Sometimes 4=Usually 5=Almost always

_____ 1.   My teacher makes class work interesting.

_____ 2.   My teacher asks questions to see if we understand what has been taught.

_____ 3.   My teacher gives assignments related to the subject we are studying.

_____ 4.   We discuss and summarize each lesson we have just studied.

_____ 5.   My teacher tells us how we can use what we have already learned to learn new things.

_____ 6.   My teacher maintains discipline in our classroom.

_____ 7.   My teacher returns tests and assignments quickly.

_____ 8.   My teacher gives me useful feedback about my performance.

_____ 9.   My teacher knows a lot about this subject.

_____ 10. My teacher uses learning contracts so I can choose how to meet the learning objective.

_____ 11. My teacher guides me to create projects that make me want to learn more.

_____ 12. My teacher makes me feel challenged.

_____ 13. My teacher creates different assignments for me when I need more challenge or if I am struggling.

_____ 14. My teacher guides me to create projects that encourage me to explore the topic and apply skills.

_____ 15. My teacher is well-organized.

_____ 16. My teacher likes it when we ask questions.

_____ 17. We work in different groups depending upon the activity in which we are involved.

_____ 18. My teacher encourages us to look at problems in new ways and find new ways to solve problems.

_____ 19. My teacher is available to help me during class time and other times during the school day.

_____ 20. My teacher finds out how much we know about a topic before we study it.

I work on homework for this class for about _____ minutes on a typical night.

III.   Summer Assignments

A.   **Introduction**
B.   **Summer Reading**
      1.   **Rationale**
      2.   **List of Recommended Reading**
      3.   **Instructions for Summer Reading Assignments:**
          a.   **Three Books**
          b.   **Dialectical Journal**
          c.   **Coordinating Assignments**
C.   **Contract**
D.   **Sample of Subject Preparation Summer Assignment**
E.   **Additional Summer Project Ideas**

A.   Introduction

Developed through research and experience, with students' wellbeing, success, and college admissions in mind, our curriculum challenges the prevailing educational paradigm of standardized testing with life-changing learning opportunities for young people. We are confident that parents, students and staff will find the academic program at our school to be challenging and inspirational. The Summer Assignments in each subject are an integral part of our program. All students are required to work for at least an hour each week on the ALEKS math program to strengthen their skills (tracked by the program). Students are encouraged to work for at least an additional hour each week during the summer on other subjects, read extensively, and track their progress weekly at the online portal.

There will be a staff member available one morning and one late afternoon every week and by appointment throughout the summer for assistance.

B.1.   Summer Reading: Rationale

We advocate summer reading to ensure that students continue to progress in their learning and develop as literate members of society. The summer break from classes provides a superb opportunity for students to improve their cultural literacy by engaging with important texts as well as books of their choice.

Our Summer Reading List and Coordinating Assignments integrate writing with reading and stimulate thinking skills through response to reading. Students need to practice to become proficient readers. In September, students will be held responsible for their participation in the Summer Reading Program by contributing their perspectives to classroom discussions and writing about their chosen texts.

255

Consider the following, from teacher Amy Rader [Washington High School, Washington Court House, Ohio]:

- Independent reading improves grades and standardized test scores in all subject areas and builds fluency and comprehension. Basically, the more you read the easier it gets to read more. You get better at accurately and effortlessly dealing with the word-identification demands of reading, which lessen difficulties in comprehension and boost overall reading achievement. We become better at what we practice.
- Independent reading builds vocabulary. One study showed that students learn an average of 45 words with each novel they read (see chart below).
- Independent reading increases engagement in texts and makes it more likely students will read outside of school and after graduation. It builds background knowledge. By reading widely, students are exposed to diverse topics and information.
- Independent reading improves speaking skills, listening comprehension and writing style, and complexity of sentence structure is increased as the amount of reading increases.

Expanding vocabulary through reading happens in incremental exposure. Some interesting statistics on the correlation between reading, standardized test results, and the impact on personal vocabulary:[316]

Student Percentile Rank	Minutes Read per Day	Est. Words Read per Year
98	90.7	4,733,000
90	40.4	2,357,000
70	21.7	1,168,000
50	12.9	601,000
20	3.1	134,000
10	1.6	51,000

B.2. Summer Reading: Lists of Recommended Reading

❖ 100 Best Nonfiction (as selected by the Modern Library board and 400,000 readers) http://www.modernlibrary.com/top-100/100-best-nonfiction/

❖ 100 Best Fiction (as selected by the Modern Library board and 400,000 readers) www.modernlibrary.com/top-100/100-best-novels/

❖ Top 100 works of world literature (as selected by a panel of 100 authors from 54 countries) on what they considered the "best and most central works in world literature. www.infoplease.com/ipea/A0934958.html

---

[316] Anderson, Richard C., Wilson, Paul T. & Linda G. Fielding. "Growth in reading and how children spend their time outside of school." *Reading Research Quarterly*. 23.3 (1988): 285-303.

❖ Radcliffe's Top 100 Best Novels
www.modernlibrary.com/top-100/radcliffes-rival-100-best-novels-list/

❖ Banned and Challenged Books
www.ala.org/bbooks/frequentlychallengedbooks/classics

You may use Amy Rader's guidelines for judging a "just right" book from these lists:

Too Easy:
- You can read the words fluently
- You know how to say all the words
- You have a lot of background information on the subject
- You totally understand the story
- Your reading rate may be quicker
- Your thinking comes easily as you read the words

Just Right:
- You can read most of the words
- You can understand most of what you are reading (there may be some tricky areas you have to slow down and reread or think about, but that's okay)
- You enjoy the book
- You may have some background information on the subject
- You can read the book with smooth fluency but there are some choppy places
- Your reading rate is just right--not too slow and not too fast
- You can figure out the tricky words and still get the meaning of the story

Too Challenging
- Many of the words are too hard to decode (more than five words per page)
- You don't know what the tricky words mean
- Your reading becomes choppy more than it is fluent
- You don't have any schema for the subject
- You lose focus as you are reading
- You are not enjoying the book because you have to do too much word work
- Your thinking is confused
- Your reading rate slows way down

B.3. Summer Reading: Instructions

1.   On the school website, find the grade level that you will enter in September. The books that students must read appear there along with the Coordinating Assignment. Evaluation of your work will be based on the rubric (see the General Assessment Rubric in Appendix Section VI) and you will have a chance to improve. Be sure to contact your teacher with any questions.

2.   Each student should *select an additional book* to read from the List of Recommended Reading above. The student should create a dialectical journal (see instructions in Appendix Section IV.A., Alternate Assessments) for that book with at least 20 entries and may select one

of the Coordinating Assignments (Appendix Section IV, Alternate Assessments) to complete.

3. Students are encouraged to read additional books over the summer and document their reading on the portal or in some other way, e.g. the website www.reading-rewards.com, Goodreads, or Amazon. They can also choose to complete a dialectical journal and/or other coordinating activities.

4. We shall hold all students accountable for the summer reading. Failure to complete the summer reading assignment will have consequences since this is an expectation that applies to the entire community.

We hope that you will value the importance of reading.

C. *Summer Reading: Project Contract*

Student Name (please print): _____

I have read and understand my responsibilities regarding the Summer Reading Project. I understand that this should be my own work. I have selected the following book(s) and am committed to completing this assignment. I recognize that any assistance from the Internet, movies, or secondary sources (such as Sparknotes or Cliff Notes) will be viewed as academic dishonesty.

I understand that if I have questions or if I am struggling, I should attend the extra help sessions and/or e-mail [name] and/or make an appointment for assistance.

1. Book Title:_____

Book Author:_____

2. Book Title:_____

Book Author:_____

3. Book Title:_____

Book Author:_____

Student Signature: _____
My name is my honor.

As the parent/guardian, I commit to supporting this assignment this summer and ensuring its completion.

Parent/Guardian Signature: _____

This form should be completed and returned to [name]

D. *Samples of Subject Preparation Summer Assignment from Dr. Teresa Thornton*

Example A: Environmental Science and Ecology Class
[This is a class for rising 9th graders; hence this is part of their introduction to the school]

Summer Field Trip

In order to promote lifelong learning and to better understand the locations where we spend our time, students who have signed up for Environmental Science or Ecology are expected to present their summer vacation (and stay-cation) projects on the ***first day of school!*** If you have any further questions you can contact Dr. Thornton

1. Ask your parents where you will be spending your summer vacation this year. No length of time in any one place is necessary. Every state in the USA has its own habitats, history, and unique stories; one does not need to go far to explore new habitats and ideas!
2. ***Perform research before you go*** as you will better be able to photograph the requirements of this project knowing an area's geology, hydrology, habitat, exports, culture, etc. Most of these concepts were covered in the middle grades, so everyone should be familiar with terms and ideas.

Project Directions:

1. Once you have found the area where you will be vacationing, find a topographic map. It is OK if it is just your neighborhood, you will have lots to learn about in your own backyard!
2. Include a topographic map of the area in your PowerPoint so everyone can be clear about your talk.
3. Find out the formational geology of the area:
    a. What formed the bedrock; geologic processes that create topography (i.e., orogenic features, wind and/or wave erosion, sea bottom, rifting, etc.)
    b. When was it formed? There are lots of videos on geologic formations at: http://education.usgs.gov/videos.html#geology
4. How does geology affect habitats (or a specific habitat) where you will be vacationing?
    a. Are there mountains? Wetlands? Sinkholes? Rainforests? Volcanoes? Beaches? Islands?
    b. What are the major tree and animal species? [You can include birds, insects, or whatever you find interesting.]
    c. Average rainfall, maximum and minimum temperatures, daylight, wind, etc (can be by season): http://www.wunderground.com/; http://www.noaa.gov/wx.html
5. What **exports** are native to this habitat (foods, energy sources, unique objects, etc.)?
6. Can you give a brief history of the area?
    a. How did the area get its name?

    b. Is there a native tongue?
    c. Are indigenous people present?
    d. Who inhabits the area today?
    e. You may also include your impressions and observations as well as frequently asked questions (FAQs) with answers about the site/area.
7. Can you give an overview of how geology affects the inhabitants?

Presentation: Make us interested in going there!

1. This presentation should be timed to not be more than 5-7 minutes in duration, so practice before you come in.
2. Your supporting documentation:
    a. PowerPoint with photos, a vacation poster (tourism), pamphlets, found objects such as rocks, etc.
    b. Include photos of yourself at the site/area with the native features you will research (pictures of the geology, trees, habitat, native peoples, etc.).
3. Format:
    a. Every slide must have at least one photo
    Verbiage on the slide must be brief   No more than *five **bullet*** points per slide (Use as a guide to what you want to say. Never put all of what you want to say in words on slides--too long)
4. If you have a visual aid that requires a link or is an action object make sure it works before you bring it in.

Example B: Honors Environmental Science Research (For rising 10th-12th graders)

Part I: Procedural Overview

DUE: Friday, June 22nd
Submit to Dr. Thornton ideas for research including potential partners. Have ISEF guidelines (https://student.societyforscience.org/forms) reviewed and ask appropriate questions so that it can be completed by the following Friday, June 30th. Also have a start on two to three journal articles that are considered seminal papers in your field of interest/study.

DUE: Friday, June 30th
Submit a proposal of two to three paragraphs that comprise Sections A and B in the ISEF Guidelines for Students. Use your seminal papers, any other resources, and put citations and references in APA 6th Ed. Format. A bibliography in the same format should be included.

DUE: Friday, July 7th
Submit introduction with literature review (See II: "How to Write an Introduction" for details).

DUE: Friday July 20th
All Revisions from **Introduction** and **Methods**, Section C of ISEF Guidelines for Students, and any of the other sections necessary (depending on research type). The idea is to have a working

methods and material section so that research can begin. Remember to include a control as well as independent and dependent variables.

Keep a logbook. Often, when an experiment is performed, observations of every event are kept in a specific book. Each page is signed and dated by the researcher, as these are legal documents. They entail what the scientist did and include errors as they occur. These books give insight to the process and help analyze results. Furthermore, science and ISEF judges request to see these books when the research results look "too good to be true".

Explicit details can be seen below at III: "How to Write Methods and Materials." Additionally, there are several ISEF forms that may need to be filled out depending on the type of research you desire to perform. *BE AWARE OF WHAT FORMS YOUR RESEARCH NEEDS.*

DUE: Friday, September 7th
Second revision of introduction, revision of methods and materials, and ALL DATA COLLECTED TO DATE is due. At this point collected data will be analyzed and it will be determined if more data needs to be collected.

Part II: How to Write an Introduction
Part III: How to Write Materials
For Parts II and III, see relevant portions of Kastens, Kim, Stephanie Pfirman, Martin Stute, Bill Hahn, Dallas Abbott, and Chris Scholz. "How to Write Your Thesis." *How to Write a Thesis.* n.d. Web. 5 May 2012: www.ldeo.columbia.edu/~martins/sen_sem/thesis_org.html

E.   *Additional Summer Project Ideas:*

❖   *This I Believe:*
[Originally appeared in May 2012 on website of Atlantic County Vocational School District, Mays Landing, NJ. No longer available on that site]

Participate in a worldwide reading and writing project! "This I Believe is an international organization engaging people in writing and sharing essays describing the core values that guide their daily lives." http://thisibelieve.org/ The essays are short and most are very well written. Additionally, many have an audio component so you can read along as the authors read their works. There are dozens of themes and thousands of essays to choose from, so every student should be able to find topics that are of interest to her or him.

As you read the entries, keep a **reading journal** that chronicles quotes, vocabulary words, and key ideas that you explore through this project. Be sure to use this journal writing as source material for your final report to be turned in when school begins in the fall. (You will not turn this work in, but it is important!)

Review the list of themes on this web site: http://thisibelieve.org/themes/

261

Choose at least five themes to work with. Read several of the essays in each theme before choosing four essays from each theme to summarize (for a total of twenty summaries). Remember to take notes as you explore the site!

- State the author's name and the title of the essay.
- Document the URL or web address of each essay.
- Include at least **one carefully chosen quote** from the essay that you found interesting. (Each quote should have a few sentences of analysis detailing its significance to your reading of the essay)
- Write roughly a single paragraph (5-8 sentences).
- As you read and summarize the 20 online essays, you should also find and define ten vocabulary words that are new to you.
- When you have completed the summaries of the 20 online essays, **consider what YOU believe**. What will your own essay focus upon? What aspect of your experience will you explore in a short (500 word) essay?
  YOUR ESSAY CAN BE ON ANY SCHOOL APPROPRIATE TOPIC.

❖ *The New York Times* Summer Reading Contest
  Every Friday from mid-June through mid-August, teens are invited to post an entry regarding what interested them most in The Times that week. Winners are selected every Tuesday and posted on The Times blog.

❖ An excellent list of things to occupy the summer:
  www.wiselikeus.com/collegewise/2010/05/50-summer-activities-for-high-school-students.html
  Some highlights:
  o Pick a cause in your community that you care about. Find groups who care about it, too.
  o Start a business with your friends.
  o Offer to intern for free someplace where the work seems interesting, like the city councilman's office, or an advertising agency, or the local animal shelter, state park, etc.

IV.   Alternative Assessments

There are many ways that students can demonstrate mastery of a learning objective beyond tests and quizzes. The list below describes a variety of creative options.

A. Dialectical Journal   B. Writing Options   C. Multimedia Options

A.   *Dialectical Journal:* [Accessed May 2012, http://arnold.gpisd.org; link no longer live]

The dialectical journal process is an important way to understand a piece of literature. By writing about literature, you construct your own meaning of the work in order to truly understand it. When you do this yourself, then the text belongs to you; you have made it yours. The passages are there for everyone to read; however, the connections and interpretations are uniquely yours. Be willing to take risks, try your ideas, and be honest.
Instructions

Since the journal is a conversation between you and the text, you'll need to record parts of the text and your thoughts about the text. On the left side of your journal page, record phrases, sentences or short passages that interest you. On the right side of the page, write your thoughts about the quoted text. Use literary terms in your reflections and elaborate as you express your thoughts!

This is an individual assignment, so no collaboration with other students. Any assistance from the Internet, movies, or secondary sources such as Sparknotes or Cliff Notes will be viewed as cheating.

If you have questions or are struggling, e-mail _____

Procedure:
1)   Label the top of each column: left TEXT and right RESPONSE
2)   In the TEXT column cite passages verbatim from the novel, including quotation marks and page numbers
3)   Choose two passages from each chapter. Consider writing passages down when:
   • You note details that seem important to you
   • You have an epiphany
   • You learn something significant about a character
   • You recognize a pattern (overlapping images, repetitions of idea, details)
   • You agree or disagree with something a character says or does
   • You find an interesting or potentially significant quotation
   • You notice something important or relevant about the writer's style
   • You notice effective use of literary devices
4)   In the RESPONSE column reflect upon the passages
   • Raise questions about the beliefs and values implied in the text
   • Give your personal reactions to the passage, the characters, the situation
   • Discuss the words, ideas, or actions of the author or character
   • Tell what it reminds you of from your own experiences

- Compare the text to other characters or novels
- Write about what it makes you think or feel
- Argue with or speak to the characters or author
- Make connections to any themes that are revealed to you
- Make connections among passages or sections of the work
- Make predictions about characters' futures
- DO NOT MERELY SUMMARIZE THE PLOT

6) Each RESPONSE must be at least 60 words (include word count at the end of each response)
7) Write down your thoughts, questions, insights, and ideas while you read or immediately after reading a chapter so the information is fresh
8) As you take notes, you should regularly reread the previous pages of notes and comments
9) First person is acceptable in the RESPONSE column.
10) Remember that quotations do not have to be dialogue!

Some sentence leads could include:

Why did ... Who is ... This setting reminds me of ... This doesn't make sense because ...
This idea/event seems to be important because ... The language makes me feel the author is ...
When the author does ... , it creates a ... tone that ..This character reminds me of ... because ...
If I were (character), at this point, I would ... What would happen if ... Now, I understand ...
The details create / show ... The ... is compared to a ... and it really makes me see how ...
The ... symbolizes ... and it ... (the effect) With the ... , the author creates an image of ... that

Sample Journal:

TEXT	RESPONSE
"The completeness of this transformation appalled me. It was unlike anything I had imagined. I became two men, the observing one and the one who panicked, who felt negroid even into the depths of his entrails" (Griffin 11)	In many movies and books, people wake up and realize how old they truly are. I think that the people this happens to feel the same as Mr. Griffin does because he feels that he still a white man; but when he looks in the mirror, he notices that his skin color disagrees with his thoughts. Similarly, some people feel they are still young, but they are trapped in a body of a person who looks too old, too different to be them. (85 words)
"Behind him walked his opposite, a huge man ... and he walked heavily, dragging his feet a little, the way a bear drags his paws." *(1)	What a great image the metaphor creates! The man is lumbering along like a bear. It makes me think he's bulky and slow. Bears can be fierce and protective too. I wonder in what other ways the man will be like a bear. *(2)

| The flower garden was strained with rotting brown magnolia petals and iron weeds grew rank amid the purple phlox ... the last graveyard flowers were blooming. (The Scarlet Ibis, 12) | The description makes me see and smell decay and death. It seems ironic that anything would be blooming in this place. The effect is a heavy, dark tone that creates a sense of foreboding.... (more needed, sample only) |

*(1) Points will be deducted on the TEXT side for failure to document accurately and completely according to the model provided
*(2) Points will be deducted on the RESPONSE side for superficial and / or incomplete responses.
Source: *Black Like Me, Of Mice and Men* & *The Scarlet Ibis.* Adapted from
www.lynchclay.k12.oh.us
Assessment Rubric:

Outstanding = Meaningful passages, plot, and quotation selections. Thoughtful interpretation and commentary about the text; avoids clichés. Includes comments about literary devices such as theme, narrative voice (point of view), imagery, conflict, etc. and how each contributes to the meaning of the text. Makes insightful personal connections and asks thought-provoking questions. Coverage of text is complete and thorough. Journal is neat, organized and professional-looking; student has followed directions in creation of journal.

Strong   = Less detailed, but good plot and quote selections. Some intelligent commentary; addresses some thematic connections. Includes some literary devices, but less on how they contribute to the meaning. Some personal connections; asks pertinent questions. Adequately addresses all parts of reading assignment. Journal is neat and readable; student has followed directions in the organization of journal.

Emerging = Few good details from the text. Most of the commentary is vague, unsupported, or plot summary / paraphrase. Some listing of literary elements; virtually no discussion of meaning. Limited personal connection; asks few or obvious questions. Addresses most of the reading assignment, but is not very long or thorough. Journal is relatively neat, but may be difficult to read. Student has not followed all directions for organization: no columns; no pages numbers; etc.

Needs Improvement = Sparse details from the text. All notes are plot summary or paraphrase. Few literary elements, virtually no discussion on meaning. Limited personal connections, few good questions. Limited coverage of the text; too brief. Did not follow directions in organizing journal; difficult to follow or read. No pages numbers.

Redo = Did not complete or plagiarized

B.   *Writing Options:*

o   A **prologue or epilogue** to the book. Describe events that could have taken place before or after the plot of the book. Include at least four events that are connected to the existing plot of the book. The connection should be explained if unclear.

o   An **original skit or screenplay** based on the book or an important portion of the book. Include a minimum of 80 lines of dialogue. Characterization and dialogue must be authentic and relevant to the plot. You will pair or group with other students and work together on presenting the scene during the first week of school. Visuals, costumes and props are required.

o   A **graphic novel** (a comic book for grown-ups). Use your artistic talents to create an original piece of work based on your book. Use all the techniques of graphic novels; for instance, dialogue bubbles above characters, different fonts, etc. Storyboard: Complete a series of five drawings that show five of the major events in the plot of the book you read. Divide a white sheet of paper (11 x 17 or smaller) into five boxes. As you read your novel, periodically draw scenes in the squares to create a storyboard that will summarize the events of the novel. Write captions for each drawing so that the illustrations can be understood by someone who did not read the book. On the back justify in one paragraph (5-7 sentences) why you chose to create your storyboard in the way you did. Make sure to use evidence and quotes from the text to help support your answers.

o   A **series of correspondence** (letters, e-mails, IM's, phone conversations) between and among characters in the book. What information would this correspondence contain that could shed more light on the characters? (Make it look real!)

o   A **series of poems** (and even pictures, if you're a good artist or photographer) that relate to the book's characters, themes, mood, setting, etc.

o   A **family tree of key characters** with biographies and character descriptions based on your observations and evidence from the book.

C.   *Multi-Media Options:*

o   A **website**. Design the homepage of a website for the main character of your book. Include details specific to the book. The design should reflect the theme of the book.

o   A **newspaper**. Create a newspaper for your book. Create sections typical of a real newspaper. Summarize the plot in one article. Write a feature story on one of the more interesting characters. Include an editorial and a collection of ads that would be pertinent to the story. Be sure to include pictures. Use a computer program or cut and paste by hand.

o   A **scrapbook or memory box**: Choose one of the major characters in your book and, as that person, put together a scrapbook or memory box of special memories and mementoes. Letters, photographs, postcards and souvenirs are all good items for the memory box and can be easily created! Think about whom your character is close to and what he/she does and values. Remember, this should represent your chosen character. Create, collect, or find at least six souvenirs that the main character would have put into the scrapbook or collect in a memory box. These objects should reflect events in the story or important aspects of your character. Include an explanation next to each object describing its significance. Be true to your character.

- o A **photo album.** Take photographs or create illustrations and make a photo album that depicts the experiences of a character in the book that you have chosen. Include a minimum of 15 original photographs. Photos must include captions that indicate relevance to book.

- o A **TV or radio report.** Find at least three news articles from the past year that cover the same topic/s as the book that you have read. Include a brief summary of each article. Those brief summaries must be compiled into at least a two page paper and a recorded presentation which discusses your summary and analysis of the topic and how it connects to the book.

- o A **retrospective.** Imagine that you are a person who is living in 2115 and has found the book that you, the 2015 student, have actually just read. Create a written essay and presentation in which you give your view of what you think this particular book tells you about what life must have been like for teenagers living in America during the summer of 2015. What issues, characters, plots, themes, symbols, settings, and conflicts are archetypal and therefore have meaning for Americans living in any time period? How do these story elements presented in the particular book relate to people living in 2015 and likely in 2115 as well? This creative writing assignment must be at least two full pages in length and be turned into a presentation that includes visuals.

- o A **sculpture.** Create a sculpture of a character from the book. Use any combination of objects or an armature with papier-mâché. A written explanation of why you chose to depict the character the way that you did and how this character fits with the book should accompany the sculpture.

- o A **soundtrack.** Burn a CD of the songs that reflect the book in terms of characters, chapters, themes, setting, mood, tone, etc. Create a CD jacket with a list of the songs. Include the lyrics to the songs and several sentences telling why you made each musical selection. PLEASE REMEMBER THAT YOUR AUDIENCE IS MADE UP OF TEACHERS, SO DO NOT INCLUDE SONGS THAT CONTAIN OFFENSIVE LANGUAGE.

- o An imagined **interview with the author/subject** (if it's an autobiography or biography) or with the characters of a book. Interview should be written and recorded.

Used with permission from Dorchester County Public Schools, Cambridge, Maryland.
http://www.ndhs.dcpsmd.net/files/English%209%20Honors%20Summer%20Reading%20Assign
ments%20-%20Aldridge-1.pdf

V. Cornerstone Project

Capstone and cornerstone projects are becoming more common in schools both public and private and on levels both secondary and tertiary. These projects typically demand that students demonstrate competency or mastery of specific learning objectives, particularly research, or broader academic achievement. While **capstone** projects typically occupy seniors, **cornerstone** projects work differently. Students may start and finish a separate cornerstone project in each grade, but it is more typical and desirable to begin work on a **cornerstone** project in 9th or 10th grade and make some major professional presentation of the completed work in junior year, with additional data collection and perhaps an internship in the senior year with final exhibition. Thus, the cornerstone timeframe entails protracted and deeper engagement and facilitates the presentation of the project as part of a college application. It is important to note, however, that students are not required to continue the project in subsequent years and may pursue new interests in each successive year.

Introduction
Every student will complete a project that demonstrates your engagement with what you are learning and your mastery of key skills.

Requirements
1. You will design a project with a real-world application that answers specific questions and responds to a specific problem.
2. You will present your project to an audience consisting of teachers, administrators, parents, and community participants at the Cornerstone Fair.
3. You will compose a Cornerstone Portfolio to document your process and progress that includes the following elements:
   - An annotated bibliography of at least 15 sources which you used to create your project
   - All of your completed steps
   - All of your fully completed journal entries
   - A reflection of 3-4 pages that identifies the motivation for your topic, the challenges you faced, the successes and failures you had, what you would do differently, and ultimately, what you learned in the process

Typical Cornerstone Timeline, (Year 1)		
Problem Solving Step	Due Date	Sub-goals
	November 1	Cornerstone assignment assembly
Define the problem	November 10	Selection of topic
	November 18	Cornerstone proposal
Identify and implement a strategy	December 1	Exploratory research Establish central questions and problems LAST day to finalize groups
	December 15	Selection of presentation method(s) Last day to switch group and/or change topic
Evaluate progress toward the goal	January 30	Researching and creating (stage 1)
	February 20	Researching and creating (stage 2)
Solution and reflection	March 30	Finalize the presentation
	April 15	Make the presentation
	April 30	Write the self-assessment reflection and submit the Cornerstone portfolio

The Cornerstone Project is adapted with permission from Weymouth High School Capstone Project, Weymouth Public Schools, MA.

Cornerstone Evaluation Rubric

Your Cornerstone Project demonstrates mastery of our expectations for our students. You need to accrue 70 or more points during the project. Scores in each of the categories are determined by the specific skill rubrics.

Target Skill	Advanced	Proficient	Needs Improvement	Needs significant improvement
Strategic Reading	16-14	1310	9-6	5-0
Research	16-14	13-10	9-6	5-0
Problem Solving	16-14	13-10	9-6	5-0
Collaboration	16-14	13-10	9-6	5-0
Technology	13-11	10-8	7-5	4-0
Written Communication	17-15	14-11	10-7	6-0
Oral Communication	17-15	14-11	10-7	6-0

If using grades, the following is the table for the Cornerstone Project Grade

	Advanced A to A-	Proficient B+ to B-	Needs Improvement C+ to C	Needs significant improvement C-	No credit
Score	111-97	96-75	74-60	59-36	35-0

Terms   [See Appendix VI for detailed rubrics]

Strategic Reading: Score is determined primarily by the content and quality of annotated bibliography.

Research: Score is determined primarily by the quality of bibliography and use of research to create the project

Problem solving: Score is determined primarily by the real world application of the project, the journal of progress, and the demonstration of process through the portfolio

Collaboration: Score is determined primarily by the weekly contact with advisor, journals, and ability to work in a group, if applicable

Technology: Score is determined primarily by the use of technology during the process and in the presentation

Written communication: Score is determined primarily by the reflection paper, journals, and written portions of presentation

Oral communication: Score is determined primarily by the judges' and advisors' scoring during the oral portion of presentation

Step 1:

Cornerstone Assembly

To support your successful completion of this project, you will be matched with a faculty member who will serve as your Cornerstone Advisor. This person will meet with you regularly and help guide your learning experience. At the Cornerstone Assembly, you will have the chance to meet your Advisor and review the Cornerstone Handbook. The Assembly marks a very important beginning to your Cornerstone Project. At the Assembly, you will also learn how to access the project online, submit your assignments, and contact your Advisor.

Step 2:

Selection of Topic

In selecting a topic, consider whether this is something that is manageable and will sustain your interest.
Be sure that you will be able to do the research necessary in the time available.
This should stretch you and encompass a new area of learning and growth and demonstrate your mastery of the seven skills noted.
You will need to have audio/visual evidence of your project or the process you used to create your project.
You will give a presentation of your work at the Cornerstone Fair.
Your project needs a real world application.
Consider carefully the people who will compose your group.

Step 3:

Cornerstone Proposal

Student Name_____

Project Advisor_____

As you complete your proposal, you will want to break the project into steps in order to make the process much easier for you. Setting up a timeline will help you begin and assist you in continuing to make progress throughout the time allotted for the project. Figuring out how much this project is going to cost may keep you from running into problems later in the project. If you put some time and effort into planning at the beginning, you will find the process of completing your project much easier to handle.

Project Title _____

My goal(s) for this project (Make sure these have a real world application):

My strategy to accomplish the project:

My real world application:

For my Cornerstone Presentation, I plan to use the following visuals, technology, and materials:

I acknowledge that I will focus my project on the use of the Target Skills: Strategic Writing, Research, Problem-solving, Collaboration, and Technology.

Student Signature_____   Date_____

Parent/Guardian Signature_____   Date_____

For Advisor:
Project (circle one):   Approved   Rejected

If Rejected, Reason:

Advisor Signature_____Date_____

Cornerstone Project
Parent/Guardian Acknowledgement

To the parents/guardians of _____ :

The Cornerstone Project will provide enormous benefits for your child now and in the future. Successful completion of the Cornerstone Project is a valuable tool in demonstrating their mastery of critical 21st Century Skills that they will need in college and beyond.

Please read and sign the following acknowledgement:
As a parent and guardian of a student, I am aware that my son/daughter is required to successfully complete a Cornerstone Project. Failure to complete the project will be noted on the transcript sent to colleges.

I fully understand that the student selects the project independently of staff and administration, but is subject to approval. I understand that if the project is a product, it must be physically present at school for the Cornerstone Project Presentation. If the project is a service or activity, it must be documented by photos or video. The project selection is student-centered. I assume all responsibility for all risks and costs that might be incurred by the project chosen.

Finally, I know that if my son/daughter decides to use work that is not completely original in any component of his/her project, he/she will have to complete an entirely new project by _____ in order to earn a passing grade.

Parent/Guardian email address:_____

Parent/Guardian Signature_____Date_____

Student Signature_____Date_____

272

Step 4:

Exploratory Research

What is Your Central Question?

Introduction:
The first step in developing your Cornerstone topic is to identify a central question. Since your Cornerstone Project requires that you answer a central question, you should try to select a question that interests you and that you feel passionate about. Your central question will be the focus of your research. You should start with a general question that requires more than just a yes/no answer. You will be required to do preliminary research based on your central question. During this step, you must submit your question along with a list of sources to your advisors before your project can be officially approved. Your central question does not need to be extremely complex, but it does need to be researchable and capable of demonstrating your mastery of the designated seven skills.

Central Question Examples:
Can data analysis be used to calculate the effects of pollution on the weather in South Florida?

Can lessons that involve hands-on learning more effectively help young children learn?

My Central Question is:

Central Question checklist:
- ☐ Can be expressed as a project that demonstrates mastery of the seven target skills
- ☐ Has a real-world application
- ☐ You have read 10 sources about your Central Question
- ☐ You have composed an annotated bibliography with at least 10 sources in an appropriate format (MLA or APA)
- ☐ The Central Question submission includes a preliminary description of how the student(s) plan to address the Question in the Cornerstone Project.
  Describe how your Cornerstone will address the Central Question here:

- ☐ The Central Question submission includes a discussion of who will benefit most from this project (i.e. community, professionals, fields of study).
  Describe your discussion of impact here:

- ☐ The Central Question submission identifies any background knowledge and preconceived beliefs and what you will do to ensure that your research results will not be affected by any bias in your analysis, interpretation of results, and implementation of the Cornerstone outcome.
  Describe your background knowledge and preconceived knowledge here:

- ☐ The Central Question includes an explanation of why you feel it is important.
  Discuss why your Central Question is significant here:

273

Annotated Bibliography

Below is a template for an annotated bibliography entry from Purdue Online Writing Lab, a great online source for writers. You must hand in <u>ten</u> of these with Step 4 and another <u>five</u> with Step 6.

Holland, Suzanne. *The Human Embryonic Stem Cell Debate: Science, Ethics, and Public Policy*. Boston: MIT Press, 2001. Print.

After a brief summary, it would be appropriate to assess this source and offer some criticisms of it. Does it seem like a reliable and current source? Why? Is the research biased or objective? Are the facts well documented? Who is the author? Is she qualified in this subject? Is this source scholarly, popular, some of both?

The length of your annotation will depend on the assignment or on the purpose of your annotated bibliography. After summarizing and assessing, you can now reflect on this source. How does it fit into your research? Is this a helpful resource? Too scholarly? Not scholarly enough? Too general/specific? Since "stem cell research" is a very broad topic, has this source helped you to narrow your topic?

Step 5:

Journal of Progress

The Cornerstone Project is an exciting and dynamic assignment that calls upon you to use the seven target skills in a real world project of your choice. To help you stay on task, be accountable for your scheduled timeline, and effectively reflect on your experiences, you will keep a Journal of Progress during the time you work on the project. The Journal of Progress will be a quick and efficient way to show your advisor exactly where you are in the process, and, moreover, will serve as an invaluable resource when you write your final reflection at the end of the year.

Each journal entry should be dated and titled based upon the part of the process in which you are currently working.

Entries should be made bi-weekly to keep the most accurate records possible for you and your Advisor.

The first entry each week should address what you anticipate for the week, including
> What you plan to accomplish by the end of the week
> Your needs, including time, space, materials, and personal contacts
> Any obstacles you anticipate

The second entry each week should include the following
> A summary of your progress for that week
> An exploration of what core skills you employed during your work

The Journal of Progress will be used in steps 4-8 of the Cornerstone Timeline.

Starting with Step 4 and ending with Step 8, you must send your advisor your journal entries once a month on the date that the step is due. You will compile all of these entries into your Cornerstone portfolio. This will be displayed when you present at the Cornerstone Fair and will be submitted to your advisor along with your reflection paper at the end of the project.

Find a sample journal progress entry on the next page. Plan to follow this format.

Journal of Progress

Current step:
Name:
Date:
Did I check in with my advisor this week? (Yes or No and include the date)

Start of Week: Date
    This is where you should talk about what you plan to accomplish by the end of the week. What are your needs, including time, space, materials, and personal contacts. What obstacles do you anticipate and how can you overcome these obstacles? How can your advisor help you this week?

End of Week: Date
    This is where you include a summary of your progress for the week and a discussion of how you employed each of the target skills this week.
    · Strategic reading-
    · Research-
    · Problem solving-
    · Collaboration-
    · Technology-
    · Written communication-
    · Oral communication-

Step 6:

Selection of Presentation Method

Describe how you will share your Cornerstone Project with a real world audience beyond the attendees at the fair.

Describe how you will present your Cornerstone to your Advisor and the attendees of the Cornerstone Fair.

Please sketch out how your table will look at the Cornerstone Fair.

Describe how your presentation plan will allow you to showcase your mastery of each of the 21st century target skills

Target Skill	Description of how the presentation of your project will help you to demonstrate mastery of this skill. Refer to the rubrics in the Appendix to help you with this.
Strategic Reading	Suggestion: Strategic reading of your research and annotated bibliographies
Research	Suggestion: Research done to answer the central working question
Problem Solving	Suggestion: Following logical steps to address a relevant, real-world project in a feasible way
Collaboration	Suggestion: Working effectively with a group and/or your advisor
Technology	Suggestion: Website, Prezi, etc.
Written Communication	Suggestion: Self-assessment reflection and your written communication at the Cornerstone Fair
Oral Communication	Suggestion: Presentation of the project at the Cornerstone Fair

Step 7:

Researching and Creating—Stage I

January:

Submit a bibliography in the recommended format (APA or MLA) of at least 15-20 sources to your Advisor

Submit your annotated bibliography with 5-10 entries to your Advisor

Continue weekly journal entries

Show progress in your use of the seven skills

Update your checklist of the skills achieved so far (use your journal to help you)

Target Skill	Description of how you are progressing with the target skill. Refer to the rubrics in the Appendix to help you with this.
Strategic Reading	
Research	
Problem Solving	
Collaboration	
Technology	
Written Communication	
Oral Communication	

Meeting with Advisor
Discuss the research and creation process
Establish a plan to address skills not yet demonstrated

Step 8:

Researching and Creating—Stage II

February:

Continue journal entries

Begin creation process of presentation product and submit an updated description of product

Write your updated description here:

Describe what you have done or plan to do to share your Cornerstone with a real world audience beyond the attendees at the Fair.

Review and revise your use of the seven skills:

Target Skill	Explicitly discuss how your project demonstrates your proficiency in each of the Target Skills. Refer to the rubrics in the Appendix for help.
Strategic Reading	
Research	
Problem Solving	
Collaboration	
Technology	
Written Communication	
Oral Communication	

Meeting with Advisor
Discuss project creation progress

Step 9:

Finalizing the Presentation

As the presentation date approaches, be sure that you have documented all experiments, experiences, and meetings with experts. Finalizing your Cornerstone Portfolio will help you to make sure that you have followed through on all aspects of your project. Once you conclude the research phase, you must put your project into a presentation format. You are encouraged to utilize a presentation method and format that best demonstrates your skills and talents, and that highlights your Cornerstone Project. Project presentation may vary. While many students will opt for a multimedia presentation format, others may prefer a spoken presentation. If your project includes some form of performing arts, you may even choose to perform some portion of your presentation. Your Advisor could help you to discover the best presentation method.

The presentation must include the following:
- Poster –or Tri-fold board –or website showing
  o Project Title
  o Central Question
  o Answer to Central Question
  o Cited research that helps support your answer to the central question
  o Visual documentation of process
  o If applicable, visual aids or manipulative of the product created
  o How you used technology to create your Cornerstone project
- Cornerstone Portfolio in a binder, PDF, or PDF on a USB with your name, project title, and central question on the cover
  o Steps 2-8
  o 20 Journal entries
  o Annotated bibliography with 15-20 sources
  o MLA or APA bibliography with 15-20 sources

Step 10:

Making the Presentation

Attend the fair
You should plan to explain your project to the Cornerstone Fair attendees as they circulate and approach your station. You should be prepared to answer questions that may be asked by any of the individuals assessing the projects.

You must arrive at least 60 minutes prior to your presentation. Copies of your presentation in electronic format must have been sent to your Cornerstone Advisory. You must make sure that all electronic equipment is set up and working before the presentations start.

Be professional:
Appearance: Dress appropriately for your presentation
Ladies: A dress that is knee-length and covers the shoulders, or a skirt and blouse with sensible shoes
Gentlemen: A button-front shirt, a tie, and dress pants and shoes

Present your Project
Whatever your method of presentation, you should begin by introducing yourself and your Cornerstone Project. Your goal is to provide attendees and/or judges with a clear and concrete sense of what you did and what you gained from the experience.

Organization: Speak in a coherent line of thinking and a logical order for the project. The visual aid should be organized and arranged to show that logical order. Provide a synopsis of the "story" from beginning to end.

Clarity: Speak confidently and in a manner that is easy to hear and understand. For the presentation, YOU are the expert. You are the one who has invested the energy and countless hours into the project. The attendees are there to listen. They are truly interested in what you have accomplished and the lessons you have learned.

Delivery: Be enthusiastic. Explain why you selected this project and engage the attendees in your experience. Your display(s) should also be engaging and capture the attention of the attendees.

Content: Reflect on the experience and show evidence of what you learned. Show evidence of all seven skills. Show the progression you achieved throughout the project. Be prepared for questions that may require you to expand on your responses. Demonstrate that you have done some analysis of your experience. Show a depth of understanding of the topic. Your presentation or display should also include components of your self-evaluation (reflection paper).

Work Product: Be sure to bring, display, and incorporate the resulting work product into your discussion and presentation. This will be extremely interesting to the reviewers and will provide evidence of real life and practical results from your effort.

Real World Application: Be read to discuss and demonstrate how your Cornerstone Project benefits someone or something in the real world.

Presentation Skills/Speaking Skills: You are the expert with significant time and energy in the project. Speak clearly and at an appropriate pace. Make eye contact with your attendees. Stand straight and show your confidence and enthusiasm for what you have achieved. This is an enormous accomplishment and you have the right to be proud of yourself.

Step 11:

Writing the Self-Assessment Reflection

Congratulations on successfully completing and presenting your Cornerstone Project! The last requirement of the Cornerstone Project is to reflect on the process by writing a three to four page reflection on your process and product addressing the following questions. You must place this reflection paper at the back of your Cornerstone Portfolio binder [or PDF] and submit the binder to your Advisor for your Cornerstone Project to be graded. As you begin to draft your final reflection, consider how you might respond to the following questions.

The Cornerstone Project is a unique and demanding challenge. In completing it, what did you learn about your subject? Your skills? Yourself? How is this project relevant to you, to the school, or to the community?

What skills do you feel you have mastered?
Which do you still need to work on?
What impact did your Cornerstone Project have?
Thinking about the whole process and your finished product, what are you most proud of?
What was a difficulty you encountered and how did you solve the problem?
What is one thing about your approach to your project that you wish you could change? Why?
What is one thing about your finished project that you wish you could change? Why?
How accurately did you answer the Central Question? Did your question change during the course of your project? Why?
How effectively did the presentation method you chose work for presenting your project in a clear and engaging manner? Why was it effective? Would you change your presentation method now if you could? Why?
What source from your research helped the most? Least?
What advice would you give to students who will be completing their Cornerstone Project next year?

VI.   Assessment Rubrics

Rubrics are an essential means of rendering explicit objectives, expectations and the criteria that will be applied for assessment. While there are many sites that offer educators templates and samples of rubrics, I highly recommend the particularly exceptional slate of 16 rubrics (with more to come) created under the aegis of the Association of American Colleges and Universities and available at the website (aacu.org). While they are intended to apply in the university setting, they are equally applicable to the secondary level. They currently cover the following topics: Inquiry and analysis, Critical thinking, Creative thinking, Written communication, Oral communication, Reading, Quantitative literacy, Information literacy, Teamwork, Problem solving, Civic engagement—local and global, Intercultural knowledge and competence, Ethical reasoning, Foundations and skills for lifelong learning, Global learning, and Integrative learning.

In this section, I have included from that and other sites some of my favorites that I have used and promoted extensively over the years for the following:

- Annotated Bibliography
- Collaboration
- General Assessment
- Oral Communication
- Problem-Based Learning
- Research Skills
- Use of Technology
- Written Communication

Assessment Rubric for Annotated Bibliography

CATEGORY	Advanced	Proficient	Needs Improvement	Needs significant improvement
Quantity of sources **3 pts.**	Document cites the number of sources outlined in the assignment.	Document is one source under the required number of sources.	Document is two to three sources under the required number of sources.	Document is four to five sources under the required number of sources.
Quality/ Reliability of Sources **4 pts.**	All sources cited can be considered reliable and/or trustworthy.	Most sources cited can be considered reliable and/or trustworthy.	Some sources can be considered reliable and/or trustworthy.	Few sources cited can be considered reliable and/or trustworthy.
Variety of Sources **3 pts.**	Excellent variety of sources; cites more than four types of sources.	Good variety of sources; cites four types of sources.	Adequate variety of sources; cites three types of sources.	Poor variety of sources; cites two types of sources.
Writing fluency of annotations **4 pts.**	All annotations are thoughtful, complete, and well written.	Most annotations are thoughtful, complete, and well written.	Some annotations are well written but some are lacking in completeness, thought, and /or writing quality.	Most annotations are lacking in completeness, thought, and/or writing quality.
Citation and Document-ation **2 pts.**	Citations are formatted correctly in the document.	There are a few formatting errors in the document's citations.	There are some formatting errors in the document's citations.	There are many and/or frequent formatting errors in the document's citations.

Adapted. Reprinted with permission from Owen Williamson, Lecturer, University of Texas at El Paso
utminers.utep.edu/omwilliamson/engl1311/ABrubric.doc

283

Assessment Rubric for Collaboration

Evaluation Sheet: Group Project

BRIEFLY answer the following and submit your completed evaluation sheet.
Note: *These evaluations are strictly confidential and will be seen by _____ 's eyes only, so do be honest in your responses.*

NAME:_____

	Name	Name	Name	Name
General attitude toward project 2 pts				
Choose one: Leader, team player, lone wolf, slacker, control freak				
Amount of effort 3 pts				
Quality of work submitted 3 pts				
Number and quality of ideas 2 pts				

ANSWER the following questions:

Describe how your group divided the labor (i.e. project manager, research & development, design & production) and specify the tasks assigned to group members.

List the agreed upon deadlines for tasks/responsibilities (this is the project manager's duty). Did you meet deadlines?

Describe your own contribution to the project. (What tasks did you take on? Did you inspire, procrastinate? etc.)

284

Did group members live up to their end of the bargain and follow through with assigned tasks? Explain.

In both the design and presentation of your project, did you draw upon one another's strengths and compensate for one another's weaknesses? Explain.

Did you read and follow the parameters/goals of the assignment?

Did you run into any problems along the way? If so, how were they resolved?

What would you do differently?

Did you meet outside of class? (If so, how often and how long?)

How and how well did your group communicate?

What grade would you honestly give yourself for the project? Justify your response.

General Assessment Rubric

Criteria		4 Outstanding	3 Strong	2 Emerging	1 Needs Improvement
Content	Assignment meets requirements specific to chosen topic (weighted twice)	All requirements are met	Most requirements are met	Some requirements are met	Few requirements are met
Usage and Mechanics	Grammar, Spelling, Punctuation are correct	Few to no errors	Few errors do not distract from readability of assignment	Frequent errors somewhat distract from readability of assignment	Frequent errors severely distract from readability of assignment
Close Reading	Understanding of the book	Project portrays complete understanding of the book	Project portrays strong understanding of the book	Project portrays weak understanding of the book	Project portrays little to no understanding of the book
Effort	Neatness, effort, etc.	All aspects of the project show time and care were taken in preparation	Most aspects of the project show time and care were taken in preparation	Some aspects of the project show time and care were taken in preparation	Few aspects of the project show time and care were taken in preparation

Reprinted with permission from Henrico County Public Schools. It is easily adapted to a variety of assignments.

Assessment Rubric for Oral Communication

CATEGORY	Advanced	Proficient	Needs Improvement	Needs significant improvement
Eye Contact	The speaker is looking at the audience almost all of the time. The speaker makes direct eye contact with most of the members of the audience at some point in the talk.	The speaker is looking up for most of the talk. The direct eye contact with members of the audience is sporadic.	The speaker looks at the audience part of the time. When looking up, there is little direct eye contact with members of the audience.	Most of the time, the speaker is not looking at the audience.
Voice	Every spoken word can be heard and understood clearly with no difficulty by each person in the audience. The speaker speaks in standard English, using correct vocabulary for the subject area and language appropriate for the audience.	A very brief portion of the talk may be unclear or inaudible to some members of the audience, OR the audience has to make an effort to hear and understand. The speaker speaks in standard English using correct vocabulary for the subject area.	Several parts of the talk are unclear or inaudible to some members of the audience, OR one portion is unclear or inaudible to most of the audience. The speaker occasionally speaks in nonstandard English and uses some terms incorrectly.	Several portions of the talk are unclear or inaudible to most of the audience. The speaker frequently speaks in nonstandard English and uses terms incorrectly.
Preparation	Preparation is highly evident. The speaker makes smooth transitions between parts of the talk. No delays occur when referring to the brochure.	Preparation is evident. Most transitions between parts of the talk are smooth. A small pause or two may occur during the talk when referring to the brochure.	Preparation may or may not be evident. Unnecessary delays or pauses exist in the talk or when referring to the brochure.	Preparation is not evident. The talk seems to be unorganized. Unnecessary pauses or awkward delays may occur when referring to the brochure.
Pace	Talk moves at natural rate and rhythm. No inappropriate pauses or silences occur.	Talk is slightly hurried or slow. Occasional gaps of "dead air" occur that do not detract very much from the meaning.	Talk is somewhat hurried or sluggish throughout, OR several noticeable pauses occur in an otherwise well-paced talk.	Talk is noticeably rushed or protracted, OR several lengthy pauses occur during the talk.

Accessed in 2012 from Intel. Original link no longer functional: ftp://download.intel.com/education

287

Assessment Rubric for Problem-Based Learning Assignments

Category	Advanced	Proficient	Needs Improvement	Needs significant improvement
Problem identification 2 pts	Demonstrates the ability to identify problems.	Demonstrates the ability to identify problems with some assistance.	Demonstrates the ability to identify problems with a great deal of assistance.	Not able to identify any problems.
Organization & structure 4 pts	All arguments were clearly tied to an idea and organized in a tight, logical fashion.	Most arguments were clearly tied to an idea and organized in a tight, logical fashion.	All arguments were clearly tied to an idea but the organization was sometimes not clear or logical.	Arguments were not clearly tied to an idea.
Understanding of the topic 4 pts	Demonstrates an in-depth, high-level understanding of the topic and issues.	Demonstrates an understanding of the topic and issues.	Demonstrates a low-level of understanding of the topic and issues.	Fails to demonstrate an understanding of the topic and issues.
Argument & counter-argument 4 pts	All information presented in the argument and counter-argument was clear, accurate and thorough.	Most information presented in the argument and counter-argument was clear, accurate and thorough with no more than one weak point.	Most information presented in the argument and counter-argument was clear and accurate, but was not thorough or several points were weak.	Information had several inaccuracies or was usually not clear or was not relevant.
Learning outcome 4 pts	Demonstrates an understanding of information that is relevant, fosters higher-level thinking, and clearly relates to the skills and content in the curriculum.	Demonstrates an understanding of information that is semi-relevant, fosters higher-level thinking, and begins to relate to the skills and content in the curriculum.	Demonstrates an understanding of information that touches on relevant information, displays lower-level thinking, and begins to relate to the skills and content in the curriculum.	Demonstrates an understanding of information that is not relevant, discourages higher-level thinking, and fails to relate to the skills and content in the curriculum.

Accessed 2013 http://teach.its.uiowa.edu/files/cft.uiowa.edu/files/PBL%20Rubric.pdf

Assessment Rubric for Research

Category	Advanced	Proficient	Needs Improvement	Needs significant improvement
Identifies and determines extent of information needed 3 pts	Identifies focused, clear, and complete research question; many key concepts; and clear idea of extent and depth of information needed.	Identifies a clear and complete research question, a sufficient number of key concepts; and acceptable idea of extent and depth of information needed.	Identifies an unfocused, unclear, or partial research question; some key concepts; and incomplete idea of extent and depth of information needed.	Fails to identify a research question, key concepts, or idea of extent and depth of information needed.
Accesses needed information using effective and efficient search strategies 4 pts	Retrieves a variety of relevant sources of information that directly fulfill the information need using a broad variety of appropriate search tools and methods.	Retrieves a sufficient number of relevant sources of information that fulfill the information need using a variety of appropriate search tools and methods.	Retrieves sources that generally lack relevance, quality, and balance. Uses few or inefficient search methods and tools to gather information. Tends to use a minimum of resources (2-3) repeatedly.	Fails to retrieve relevant sources of information to fulfill the information need. Ignores appropriate search tools and methods. Relies heavily on 1-2 resources.
Critically evaluates information & its sources 3 pts	Researches and evaluates the accuracy, relevance, appropriateness, comprehensiveness, and bias of electronic information sources from a wide variety of sources.	Usually evaluates accuracy, relevance, appropriateness, comprehensiveness, and bias of electronic information sources	Seldom evaluates accuracy, relevance, appropriateness, comprehensiveness, and bias of electronic information sources	Fails to evaluate information from a limited number of questionable sources.
Effectively uses information to accomplish a specific purpose 4 pts	Demonstrates understanding of breadth and depth of research. Synthesizes and integrates information from a variety of sources. Draws meaningful conclusions. Clearly communicates ideas.	Uses appropriate information to accomplish purpose. Draws relevant conclusions. Synthesizes information from a sufficient number of sources. Effectively communicates ideas.	Uses incomplete information and only partially accomplishes intended purpose. Draws incomplete conclusions. Inconsistently communicates ideas.	Does not use relevant information. Fails to accomplish intended purpose. Does not draw conclusions. Fails to effectively communicate ideas.
Ethically & legally accesses and uses information 2 pts	Consistently, thoughtfully, and accurately builds on and incorporates the ideas of others into assignment, correctly cites sources.	Accurately builds on and incorporates the ideas of others into assignment. Correctly cites sources.	Inconsistently incorporates the ideas of others into work. Incomplete citations.	Does not properly incorporate the ideas of others into assignment. Does not cite sources or copies sources without crediting authors.

Reprinted with Permission from AAC&U Standards. https://www.aacu.org/value-rubrics

Assessment Rubric for Use of Technology

Category	Advanced	Proficient	Needs Improvement	Needs significant improvement
Selects appropriate technological tool to produce the assignment **4 pts**	The tool selected enhances the fluid and clear communication and illustration of ideas. Designs and develops advanced products with little or no assistance.	The tool selected assists the fluid and clear communication and illustration of ideas. Uses technology to design, develop, publish, and present a product with minimum assistance.	The tool selected detracts from clear and fluid communication. Needs much assistance to create a product using technology.	Even with much assistance, fails to create an acceptable product using technology
Uses selected means effectively for communication with group and Advisor **4 pts**	Communicates professionally, clearly, and often with group members and/or Advisor. Responds in a timely way.	Communicates clearly and somewhat regularly with others.	Communicates occasionally with group members. Delayed responses to others' posts.	Rarely communicates with others.
Use of Graphics **3 pts**	All graphics are attractive (size and colors) and support the topic of the presentation.	A few graphics are not attractive but all support the topic of the presentation.	All graphics are attractive but a few do not support the topic of the presentation.	Several graphics are unattractive and detract from the content of the presentation.
Text – Font Choice & Formatting **2 pts**	Font formats (color, bold, italic) have been carefully planned to enhance readability and content.	Font formats have been carefully planned to enhance readability.	Font formatting has been carefully planned to complement the content. It may be a little hard to read.	Font formatting makes it very difficult to read the material.

Assessment Rubric for Written Communication

Category	Advanced	Proficient	Needs Improvement	Needs significant improvement
Thesis and Introduction	Thesis statement addresses the central question in a way that evidences sophisticated and nuanced understanding of issues. Introduction fully engages the reader and leaves reader with no doubt as to the purpose and structure of project	Thesis clearly answers central question, author's position is clear. Reader clearly understands the general framework of the project. Key terms are defined, necessary background information is given	Thesis adequately addresses central question. Terms unclear, some background information missing, overview unclear	Thesis is unclear. Introduction unclear, though some attempt is made to lay foundation for essay
Organization	The essay is so well-organized that the relationship of each part of the project to the others is crystal clear and the reader completely understands the flow of ideas	Each paragraph is well-organized, the relationship of the paragraphs to one another is clear, the project follows a logical progression of ideas	Project demonstrates logical progression of ideas.	Some effort to organize project.
Support	Logical support is flawless, quotes are appropriate and engaging, examples fully illustrate the point, statistical evidence is compelling, analogies clarify position, the combinations of support prove thesis beyond a reasonable doubt	Multiple types of support are used for thesis and topic sentences, each type of support effectively proves the point	Adequate support for thesis and topic sentences, more than one type of support is used	Some support for thesis and topic sentences
Audience	Essay reflects a full understanding of audience and the style of writing appropriate for that audience	The essay reflects an understanding of who the audience is and is written in a way appropriate for that audience	Essay is written in a way that reflects some sensitivity to the audience	Little sense of who the audience of the essay is
Grammar & Spelling	No errors. Word choice and grammatical construction are excellent and enhance project.	No spelling or grammatical errors	Few errors of spelling and grammar	Many errors of spelling and grammar
Conclusion	Project is not only summarized in highly effective manner, the conclusion goes beyond summary to wrap up the essay in a sophisticated way that helps reader appreciate the nuances of the conclusion and the implications	Project is effectively summarized	Project is summarized in conclusion	Some attempt to summarize the presentation

291

VII.   Parent Survey Questionnaire

Whole-school parent surveys are just one of many ways to elicit feedback regarding parents' level of satisfaction with different aspects of their experience with the school. Feedback should be requested frequently, at least twice a year, in order to proactively anticipate challenges before they become more serious and immediately consider and implement responses to any problems.

1.   What is your relationship with [school]?
    Parent of 9th grader
    Parent of 10th grader
    Parent of 11th grader
    Parent of 12th grader
    Parent of students in multiple grades
2.   Overall, how satisfied are you with your experience **this semester** at [school]?
    Very satisfied   Somewhat satisfied
    Neither satisfied nor dissatisfied
    Somewhat dissatisfied   Very dissatisfied
3.   Please tell us why you feel that way.
4.   Please indicate your degree of agreement with the following statements
    Strongly Agree   Slightly Agree   Neither Agree Nor Disagree
    Slightly Disagree   Strongly Disagree

    My child is receiving a quality education.
    My child is safe at the school.
    My child has the opportunity to be a leader at the school.
    My child has access to learning support when he or she needs it.
    My child is encouraged to explore.
    My child has opportunities at the school that she or he would not have at another school.
    (Please specify the opportunities).

5.   In terms of academics, I wish the school would improve/ develop/ create:
6.   In terms of arts, I wish the school would improve/ develop/ create:
7.   In terms of the community, I wish the school would improve/ develop/ create:
8.   In terms of athletics, I wish the school would improve/ develop/ create:
9.   In terms of extra-curricular activities, I wish the school would improve/ develop/ create:

For questions 10-13, please use the following scale:
    Strongly Agree   Slightly Agree   Neither Agree Nor Disagree
    Slightly Disagree   Strongly Disagree

10.   Please indicate your degree of agreement with the following statements:
    School employees treat me with courtesy and respect
    Questions about my child/children are answered fully
    School employees respond to me in a timely manner
    Teachers inspire my child to learn

11. Technology
   There is adequate computer technology instruction in the school
   The overall level of technology services is adequate
   There needs to be more technology at the school (Please specify)

12. Values/Character Building
   The school is committed to building character and integrity
   The school reinforces my family's values
   I do not expect the school to cultivate character
   The school does little to instill values and character

13. Communication
   I receive too much communication from the school
   I receive about the right amount of communication from the school
   I would like to have more communication from the school

14. Please tell us how to improve school communication with you.

15. What does the school do well?

16. What does the school need to do better?

17. If you could change one thing at the school immediately, what would you change?

18. Please contact me immediately to discuss the following (please provide your name and contact information):

VIII.   Student Research

Below is a representative sample of students' projects initiated and conceived in 9th and 10th grades and carried through to senior year, with the guidance of Dr. Teresa Thornton. To achieve such astonishing results, adults need to expand their understanding of what students are capable of and students need inspiration, effective mentorship, assistance in identifying potential partners, perseverance, and freedom from a curriculum that focuses their attention on preparing for standardized tests, rather than projects of their own invention.

Contaminants in Drinking Water as a Result of Private Well Homeowner Behavior by I.B.

In Florida, approximately one million people rely on private groundwater wells for drinking water (USGS, 2005). Like many states there is little to no regulation on the health of private well water. This lack of attention to private wells was believed to be one cause for a 2010 cancer cluster In Loxahatchee, FL. Although speculation regarding the exact source of the cancer continues to cause debate, during remediation studies it surfaced that homeowners were unknowingly creating a cancerous substance (trihalomethanes) through improper maintenance of their private water filtration systems. This ignorance of personal responsibility was confirmed in 2012 and 2013 when hundreds of high school students from three different Palm Beach County schools participated in a program called GET WET! (Groundwater Education Through Water Evaluation & Testing). They worked with local governmental representatives, ENGOs, and universities to chemically test groundwaters and to increase awareness of the need for water systems monitoring. One student decided to evaluate homeowner behavior in the Loxahatchee and Jupiter Farms area through a survey sent out to private homeowners. Behaviors regarding their knowledge, usage, and maintenance of private wells, septic systems, and filtration systems were addressed. Included in the survey were questions pertaining to what might motivate homeowners to test their water systems. Results show that homeowners are not aware that the groundwaters may be stressed due to natural and manmade contaminants. Results also indicate homeowners do not understand how to properly maintain their systems, are uncertain of the chemicals they should test for, and are not quite sure whom to contact regarding this matter. Furthermore, the results for homeowner motivation to test their systems also shows a lack of groundwater understanding.

Student has presented her research at five different national and international water conferences, at two of those she was requested to speak. This honor is usually reserved for graduate students and professionals. She plans to submit her research to the Journal of American Water Resources by Spring 2015.

Using Native Algae Coelastrum (Col.) 108-5 to Manage Industrial Effluents and Filter Wastewater by J.S.

Blue-green algae are known to contain carboxylic groups in their cell walls. These carboxylic groups allow blue-green algae to capture and remove heavy metals from water. While this concept has been demonstrated with other algas, this has never been attempted with Coelastrum strain 108-5. In order to test this concept 10.0ml of 10ppm lead was added to 10.0ml of algae inoculated water to bring the concentration of lead in the test tube to 5ppm. After forty-five minutes, the final concentration of lead was tested using the Lamotte lead reagent system, and a Lamotte Smart 3 Colorimeter. This testing determined that between forty-five minutes to one hundred and twenty minutes Coelastrum strain 108-5 was able to remove an average of 76% of the lead in solution. Some of the highest readings demonstrated a reduction of 96% of lead in solution within the appropriate time frame. This technology can be applied as a means of at point pollution containment. What this means is that Coelastrum 108-5 can be used as an effective means by which to remove lead from polluted water supplies.

Student has presented his research at three different national and international water conferences, at one of those he was requested to speak. This honor is usually reserved for graduate students and professionals. Student plans to parlay his many contacts and goals into an entrepreneurial opportunity.

Assessing the Strength of African American Stereotypes in High School Students Using The Personalized IAT by C.B.

Racism in high school teens is believed to have ended. With the increased representation of black culture in American media and the inauguration of Barack Obama in 2008, it is suggested that influences have eliminated racial bias. Social psychology studies suggest otherwise. In 1996, Greenwald et al. developed a task-switching computer program to elucidate unconscious bias in humans. Through the use of this tool, research since the inception of the Implicit Association Test has suggested that racial bias, stereotypes, and prejudices have become largely unconscious, thus the apparent absence in racism in America. The purpose of this paper was to investigate the strength of African-American stereotypes in a sample of high school students (n = 114). Using a version of the IAT, the personalized implicit association test (P-IAT), the authors found that roughly 70% of subjects (n=61) held a moderate to strong preference for African American scholars versus African American entertainers (p<0.0001). The authors reported that while the p-value suggests a near flawless application, the numbers might be indicative of test confusion, environment, and cultural knowledge. Additionally, these results may help educators of high school age students to better formulate lessons that directly apply to the students' experience and idealization of relevant historical figures in African American culture.

Student has presented his research at a national conference and expects to present this Spring 2015 at an international conference focused on social sciences. This honor is usually reserved for graduate students and professionals.

A Re-evaluation of DDT and DDE Residues in the Loxahatchee National Wildlife Refuge Post-Farm Waste Water Flooding by K.S.

Dichlorodiphenyldichloroethylene (DDE) is an organochlorine pesticide that was banned in 1972 due to the suggested correlation between the pesticide and breast cancer, diabetes, obesity, asthma, and other health risks. Before its ban, it was commonly used on the farms within the Boynton Beach Farms Basin of Southeast Florida. Until 2007, these farms were located on canals that directly flushed into the Arthur R. Marshall Loxahatchee Wildlife Refuge (ARMLNWR). Between 2001 and 2004, a study by Frakes, Arrington, Bargar, Bogg, Tutton, & Sowers (2010) was conducted to determine the pesticide levels in the Refuge; most levels were innocuous, but levels of DDE were still significantly higher than its probable effects concentration (PEC) of 31.0 (ug/kg).

According to previous research, DDE should degrade within the year in tropical and subtropical areas, yet this is not the case within the ARMLNWR. This study will focus on three sites within the refuge that contained the largest DDE concentrations to determine if there remains o,p'DDE and p,p'DDE at levels that may cause potential health risks. Assistance in sample collection is through cooperation with the U.S. Fish and Wildlife Service and the National Park Service. Biochemical testing will be conducted in the biotechnology laboratory at Palm Beach State College, with permission and assistance from Alexandra Gorgevska, Ph.D., Department Chair of both the Biotechnology Program and the Department of Natural Sciences.

The Iranian Sexual Revolution of 1979: A Survivors Perspective by A.D.

This research primarily focuses on effects of Iranian women before and after what is now referred to as the Sexual Revolution of 1979. This revolution transitioned Iran from a secular state under Mohammad Reza Pahlavi Shah to an Islamic Republic. During the revolution, women lost many freedoms and were forced into a more conservative lifestyle. Working with international universities with Middle Eastern Women's Studies departments, a population sample will be secured that includes women who lived through the revolution and their opinions regarding the revolution. Results will also be compared to women in the Western Society, the United States. Throughout the preliminary research, specialists have been contacted and have become mentors including the women's center at the FIS (Foundation for Iranian Studies), Dr. Elaheh Rostami-Povey from the University of London, and Professor Houra Yavari from Columbia University, NY.

IX. Sample Honor Pledge Ceremony

Honor codes have a greater likelihood of achieving the goal of inculcating integrity and honesty as a cultural norm when stakeholders demonstrate a shared understanding and acceptance of the policies. This is a process that takes time to develop deep roots in a community. Ceremonies like these that require stakeholders to reflect and publicly profess their adherence to the policies are only a first but significant step. Policies must be reiterated continually and enforced assiduously.

Materials:
Small table with cloth
Oil lamp
Copies of the Order of Ceremony for all present
Pens
White taper candle for each student
Recorded or live music

Semi-formal Dress:
Ladies: A dress that is knee-length and covers the shoulders, or a skirt and blouse with sensible shoes
Gentlemen: A button-front shirt, a tie, and dress pants and shoes
Faculty: White and/or black semi-formal attire, covered shoulders, with closed toe shoes

Introit:
As music plays, student ambassadors and staff will distribute Order of Ceremony as people enter. They will direct students to sit according to their graduating class. The first chair on the left of the front row of each class is occupied by the Class Advisors.

Administrator 1:

[Words of welcome]. [School] commits to being a community characterized by civility, respect, and trust, a school that fosters the virtues of discipline, perseverance, and responsibility. We strive to be a place where moral socialization takes place. We encourage our students to know and to abide by rules of proper conduct. We take very seriously policies and guidelines regarding cheating and academic integrity and we promote mutual respect between teachers and students. Thank you for joining us for this important annual ceremony.

Please rise for the Invocation.

Administrator 2:

Invocation:
> During this and every school year,
> May the [school] community continue to be blessed,
> May each of us grow as we become the unique person we are meant to be,

May we treat one another with kindness and compassion and be a positive influence on those we meet,
May our learning help us to better understand ourselves, understand others and understand the world around us.
May we feel blessed for having work to do.
May we act with integrity and truth in all things, and give the very best of ourselves in all we do,
May all be blessed who study here, who work here, who contribute to this community.
Let us be grateful to our founder for creating this school.
Let us be grateful for blessings yet to come.
So may it be.

Employees, remain standing. Everyone else, please be seated.

Administrator:
[EMPLOYEES]

[School] employees please find in your Order of Ceremony the [School] Honor Pledge. Take a moment to read it. [pause]
Let us take this pledge together:
> **As a member of the [School] community, I commit to act responsibly and with honor and integrity on and off campus.**

Thank you. We appreciate your commitment to our community and to shaping our youth in a positive way. Please be seated. [pause]

[PARENTS]

By enrolling a child in this school, parents are expressing a belief in the values, educational principles and expectations of the school. Parents are expected to support the school's rules and the academic standards of the curriculum, and asked to treat the school's adult community as professionals who are working for the best interests of our students.

Parents have an Honor Pledge to take as well to ensure the wellbeing of our community, which you have already signed.
Parents, please rise and find in your Order of Ceremony the Parents' Pledge:

Let us take this pledge together:
We pledge to uphold and comply with [School]'s Honor Code.
We pledge to support the academic standards of the curriculum and treat the staff as professionals who are working for the best interests of the students.
We will encourage our children to do their best work and their own work.
We will not offer or approve or provide unauthorized assistance with assignments.
We will not endorse the sharing of homework without permission.
We will not allow the discussion of a test that some have taken and others have not.

We will teach our children to treat others the way that they would be treated. We pledge to ensure that all social events in my home for teenagers will be chaperoned by a parent and free of alcohol and other drugs.

Thank you. We appreciate your partnership and commitment to ensuring that our students are safe and positively guided.

Anne Frank wrote, "Parents can only give good advice or put them on the right paths, but the final forming of a person's character lies in their own hands."

Parents, you have set your students on the path to a life of honor and integrity, and they walk it with your support, but the decisions they make are their own.

Please be seated.

Students, please rise. You take responsibility for the decisions that you make in life. As the twig is bent, so grows the tree. The daily choices that you make shape your character.

> Watch your thoughts, for they become words.
> Watch your words, for they become actions.
> Watch your actions, for they become habits.
> Watch your habits, for they become character.
> Watch your character, for it becomes your destiny.

Student Government President
Find in your Order of Ceremony the Honor Pledge. Take a moment to read it. [pause] Let us take this pledge together:

As a member of the [School] community, I commit to act responsibly and with honor and integrity on and off campus.

Student Leader of Senior Class:
Students, please respond to the following with "I promise."

Do you promise to submit only work that is your own, achieved through personal merit and without unauthorized aid from friends, from family, from the Internet or any other source?

Student Leader of Junior Class:
Do you promise to do your work to the best of your skill and knowledge?

Do you promise to treat others as you would have others treat you, with kindness and compassion, with dignity and respect?

Student Leader of Sophomore Class:
Do you promise to promote the welfare and common good of the [School] community?

299

Student Leader of Freshman Class:

All students will affirm our commitment to our Honor Pledge by signing our names in the Pledge Book at the beginning of each year and by signing the following words on each and every assignment, "My name is my honor."

Student Leader of Senior Class:

Seniors, remain standing. Other classes, be seated

We ask that the parents of seniors also rise to demonstrate their support.

Class Advisors and Class Officers will lead the students to sign the Honor Book [The Class Advisors will lead the students to sign the Honor Book].

[After the class has signed]: Seniors and parents please be seated.
[Repeat with successive classes]

After freshman class has signed the Honor Book,
Student Government

All students, please rise.

[Class Advisors will light their candles from the oil lamp at the [School] Honor Book and light the end of each row. The students pass the light to the person beside them until all are lit.]

This candle symbolizes the right conduct of a [School] student
As you light your candle and that of your neighbor, we ask that you consider the
importance of supporting one another in acting with integrity.
Keep guard over your actions as they reflect not only upon you but also upon [school].
You are called upon to keep this light alive within your heart and carry it forward,
kindling the flame within others.

Administrator

[Inspiring Closing Remarks....]

Thank you all for joining us for celebration of our lasting tradition that marks this school as a community that values honor and integrity. This concludes our Honor Ceremony. You may extinguish your candle and take it with you to remember your commitment. Let us look forward to a wonderful year.

Exeunt: Music

Acknowledgements

This book, and so much else in my life, would not have been possible without the encouragement and unflagging support of my husband, Frank Don.

I am also grateful for the opportunities provided by RCP and WIK.

I deeply appreciate the willingness of the stakeholders of scores of independent schools to share with me their innovative practices, both successful and in process of evolution, as well as their triumphs and challenges.

The cover image was created by Jim Van Dijk and appears courtesy of Frank Don.

About the Author

Carolyn Kost is a consultant and partner with East West College Educational Consulting and College Counseling LLP. She was the founding Vice President for Education/Chief Academic Officer for an independent secondary school and was an administrator in an independent boarding and day school. She has over two decades of experience in high schools and colleges, teaching subjects as varied as Spanish, World History, Information Literacy, Religious Studies, and Leadership Studies. She has also been a public school board member and worked in non-profit libraries for over a decade.

Carolyn Kost holds a B.A. in Religious Studies and Spanish (Fairfield University), Certificates in Secondary Education (Southern CT State), Non-Profit Management (San José State), and College Counseling (UCLA), a Master's degree in the Management of Information Organizations (San José State), a Master's in the Social Scientific Study of Religion (Drew), and has satisfied all requirements for the Ph.D. except the dissertation.

To see ways that schools spark students' curiosity and nurture their talents and interests, see the **Engaged Education** page that Carolyn curates at www.scoop.it/t/engaged-education

Previous title co-authored by Carolyn Kost and Frank Don:

On To College: What high school students and their families need to know about college selection, application, and admissions. CreateSpace. August 2014.

A college education is likely to be one of the most important and expensive investments made in a lifetime, yet most students lack the knowledge they need to choose and apply to the programs that will best suit their needs and interests. With many years of insider experience in college counseling and teaching, authors Kost and Don reveal for the first time proven strategies to be a savvy applicant, cut costs, and evaluate the hidden quality of a program—the single most important and neglected aspect of the process.

Make your application essay a winner by using the authors' proven strategies. Learn the secrets of fortifying your application without padding your resume. Use the tips and comprehensive timeline to stay focused, organized--and in front of college admissions officers. Follow the templates to effectively request letters of recommendation and compile an activities list and resume that will highlight your accomplishments. Understand the upcoming changes to the SAT and PSAT and why they are to your advantage. Get information about athletics directly from Division 1 coaches to be sure you have what they are looking for and be aware of the reasons to consider other ways of participating in sports. Find invaluable hints for artists of all kinds about auditions and portfolios and how to decide between specialized art schools and a more comprehensive university. Be inspired to consider attending universities in other countries from Canada to Australia to save money and time (3-year programs are more common) and acquire international experience.

Truly a stand out among the college guides, *On To College* will be your go-to resource every step of the way.

Forthcoming by Carolyn Kost and Diego Durán-Medina:
Building a Better World: Global and Service Learning.

Made in the USA
San Bernardino, CA
27 April 2015